Learning from the Japanese City

Learning from the Japanese City

West meets East in Urban Design

Barrie Shelton

E & FN SPON · ALERE FLAMMAM · Taylor & Francis Group

London and New York

First published 1999 by E & FN Spon
11 New Fetter Lane, London EC4P 4EE

Simultaneously published in the USA and Canada
by Routledge
29 West 35th Street, New York, NY 10001

E & FN Spon is an imprint of the Taylor & Francis Group

This book was commissioned and edited
by Alexandrine Press, Oxford

Typeset in Sabon
by Keystroke, Jacaranda Lodge, Wolverhampton
Printed and bound in Great Britain by
TJ International Limited, Padstow, Cornwall

British Library Cataloguing in Publication Data
A catalogue record for this book is available from the British Library

Library of Congress Cataloguing in Publication Data
A catalogue record for this book has been requested

ISBN 0–419–22350–9

Contents

Preface

Western attitudes to Japanese city form have rarely been very positive. Further, for those with the sketchiest knowledge of Japan's design history, the schizophrenic and excessive nature of much modern Japanese architecture and urban fabric seems unfathomably at odds with the refined and restrained design traditions. Writing a few years ago, Pierre Vago (former editor of *Architecture d'aujourd'hui*) was not untypical when, under the telling title of 'Taking Fright in the Far East', he wrote of his 'disappointment' and 'disquiet' with the country's recent architecture and urban character, and its 'brutal rupture (with) tradition' (Vago, 1992, p. 81). At the same time, it was clear from his tone that he was neither ungenerous towards the Japanese nor uninformed of their urban and architectural developments: he could nevertheless not contemplate a visit without great trepidation.

In recent years, it has been more common for commentators, while often remaining critical of appearances, also to speak in awe of the energy, vitality, efficiency and technological sophistication of Japan's cities. These are, however, qualities that can hardly be viewed from afar but must be 'sensed' in the full scope of the word.

I empathize with Vago for I too must admit to once having an extreme reluctance to visit Japan and it took a very dear friend to entice me to go there. When I did eventually set foot in a string of Japan's cities, I was baffled, irritated and even intimidated by what I saw. Yet at the same time, I found myself energized, animated and indeed inspired by them. The effect was liberating and my intuition was quick to suggest that further exploration of their chaotic vitality might be extremely rewarding.

At that time (1989), my association with urban planning had spanned over two decades and my grounding in the history and theory of Western urban design was particularly strong. Over the previous few years, I had prepared a handful of entries which had all met with some level of success in urban design competitions. Further, these were founded on compositions and processes that sought to bring order to their subject sites in, more or less, well-tried Western ways (well-defined public spaces, coherent groupings of buildings, etc). To start to appreciate Japanese city form in its own right, I realized that my knowledge and experience may have been more handicap (with preconceived and inflexible notions of good city form) than advantage (i.e. as a sound basis for critical judgement). Increasingly, the many notions of urban form that I held dear in my own cultural domain seemed irrelevant in Japan.

Indeed, it was the differences between what I had come to value in the urban West and what I experienced in the far Far East that triggered a fascination with Japan's cities that continues to endure. During that visit almost a decade ago, I started to ask myself certain questions which remain at the heart of this book:

Why do Japanese cities look the way they do?

What relevance, if any, do they have to the wider world of contemporary urban design?

And, how sharp is the divide between what we experience today and the country's urban traditions?

Since that date, I have returned to Japan on numerous occasions and each time made it my business to investigate on foot as many corners of the cities visited as possible: alleys, shrine and temple precincts, highways, railway stations (and their 'magnetic' fields), roof-tops, observation decks, arcades, underground streets, bars, gardens etc. I have gained entry to a great range of dwellings including old merchant and warrior houses. In all, I have tried to witness the city from the most seedy to the most sophisticated of quarters; and I have been careful to include the common with designer-label places. Paralleling these 'field excursions' has been an almost compulsive poring over city maps (old and new), museum models, old photographs, postcards, etc. And in addition, there have been sessions with urban scholars and designers, and the inevitable piles of books and other papers consulted at home and away.

Nevertheless, I am only too aware of at least two considerable limitations in my quest to explore urban Japan. The first is that my travels are far from comprehensive. 'My' Japan extends only from the Kumamoto and Nagasaki areas of Kyushu north-westerly to Tokyo region and generally falls within what might loosely be called generous commuting distances of the Shinkansen (or bullet train) spine. This does however include the nation's historical heartland, the Yamato Region. Also, I have only a poor knowledge of the language thus Japanese sources are essentially through translated publications and the help of Japanese friends. Where I deal with the language in any detail, emphasis is upon visual characteristics of the written and printed text. Where meanings are concerned I am mostly in the hands of others.

The book has been accumulating in my mind throughout this time, although in material form only over the last three or four years. The result is often speculative and generated not only from observation, reading and discussion of architecture and city places but also from forays into other aspects of culture that prompt urban insight. There are, for example, detours into the nature of Japanese writing and mapping as well as even broader meanderings into the Shinto and Buddhist religions, and indeed their coexistence. In other words, the book is broad in sweep in order to comment on its particular urban focus.

As background, Chapter 1 reflects on changing Western attitudes to Japan's city forms. Chapter 2 explores contrasting Japanese and Western ways in thinking about space, showing some consistencies over a range of visual phenomena and scales from writing on a sheet of paper to settlement on a landscape. The third and largest chapter presents a miscellaneous array of Japanese urban characteristics and building types (past and present) that offer insights into today's cities: these range from the bridge and its environs as an urban node through historic samurai and merchant houses to contemporary building types. The next (Chapter 4) extracts aspects of religion and culture which bear upon attitudes to urban form and space. The fifth and final chapter gathers threads from throughout the book to show consistencies between many Japanese urban design traditions and much contemporary thought.

Without wishing to steal too much ground from subsequent chapters, I shall at least hint of three conceptual threads that run through them in response to those earlier-posed questions. The first is that behind Japan's urban forms are ways of thinking and seeing which are quite different from those of the West; and these are rooted deeply in the wider culture. Here, for example, it is suggested that one fundamental difference between Japanese and Western thinking about space is that the former has more affinity with area (hence the importance of the *tatami* mat and the floor in building and the *machi* as an areal unit of organization in the city) while the latter has more to do with line (with an emphasis on linear phenomena like walls in building and the sequential ordering of buildings along city streets).

The second is that the deep roots, being cultural, are mostly also old roots, although modern appearances may often belie this. Indeed, some physical manifestations may seem superficially at odds with the past yet are underlain by attitudes and values that have considerable age. For instance, Japan has put greater emphasis in city place-making on content (information, activity and animation) while Westerners have been more preoccupied by form (object, physical pattern and aesthetic composition). Consistent with this emphasis is the profusion of signs, lights and animation which cover whole buildings and even districts in today's urban Japan. Irritating Western sensibilities, such sights tend to be attributed somewhat simplistically to the big bad world of twentieth-century commercialism. This overlooks the fact that the sign-suffocated building has a long tradition in Japan and that steel, neon and electronic animation have simply supplemented or displaced the wind-generated flappings, inflations and gyrations of cotton and bamboo. Thus, while so many aspects of today's cities appear so very different from those of earlier times, there are also some surprising continuities – but of essence or principle rather than form or material.

A third thread is that many characteristics of Japanese cities, though rooted in national culture and history, have much affinity with contemporary ideas in science and philosophy which are mostly Western-generated – ironically, more affinity than the characteristics of Western cities themselves. These ideas embrace fracture, transformation, the autonomy of parts, non-linear qualities, etc and it is here that the apparently chaotic but flexibly ordered Japanese city emerges as a potential source of learning and inspiration in today's uncertain and pluralistic world – for both people with professional design and broader cultural interests alike.

Hobart, Australia
December, 1998

Prefatory Notes

1. I have assumed that most readers will be familiar, directly or otherwise, with more significant Western sights and objects to which I refer. Also, Japan is the main focus of attention. Thus, in many of my city contrasts, I make only fleeting reference to the Western examples and show relatively few illustrations. A name is deemed sufficient for an Eiffel Tower or a Bellini painting whereas a picture is shown of Tokyo Tower or an Hiroshige print, Where points of Western reference are pictured, it is usually of more obscure places – for instance, from my native Nottinghamshire or adopted Australia.

2. Events are frequently placed in time by reference to periods in Japanese history which bear, more or less, standard names. To assist the reader, dates are given in Appendix A.

Acknowledgements

Work of any magnitude cannot be completed without a great deal of assistance and this book is no exception. I am grateful to many people and organizations – too numerous to list individually without over-taxing both my memory and the reader's patience. The following, however, deserve, particular thanks.

First, is my wife, Emiko Okayama, without whom I may never have experienced the subject and without whose support I may never have persevered with the project. Certainly, there were Japanese sources (texts and people) from which I could only benefit thanks to her very special knowledge of her native language far beyond translation and interpretation. I must also thank her for her calligraphic contribution. A further family contribution was from our young son, Herbert Maki, whose ability to interchange between the habits of two cultures was a great inspiration.

I am most grateful to the Japan Foundation for their support over a period of four vital months (as a Japan Foundation Fellow) during which time my hunting and gathering in various Japanese cities, universities, museums, bookshops etc, and my writing and thinking were at their most intense. During that time, I had a base at the Department of Architecture, Nagasaki Institute of Applied Science where Professor Kazuma Hayashi and his colleagues kindly introduced me to useful resources and relevant places. Thanks also to Professors Toshihide Katayose and Masami Hibino (formerly of the same institution, now of Kwansei and Toyo Universities respectively) for their parts in introducing me to aspects of Nagasaki and general encouragement.

Personal thanks must be extended to the Okayama family who were gracious in allowing me to create considerable household disruption while occupying one of their rooms as a very messy office-cum-library, always generous in placing a variety of helpful equipment and facilities at my disposal, and remarkably tolerant in accepting the kind of withdrawn behaviour that is so often necessary during short intense periods of observing, collecting, thinking and writing. While the list is in fact longer, Akio, Sugie, Umeko and Katsue deserve special attention.

I am especially indebted to Professor Hidenobu Jinnai, of the Department of Architecture at Tokyo's Hosei University, without whom I could not have experienced so many pertinent nooks and crannies of his beloved Tokyo nor sensed so profoundly the capital's history. Though my one meeting with Professor Yoshinobu Ashihara occurred back in 1989 it was crucial in encouraging my interest in the topic and may well have made the difference between my later starting this project or not. I have certainly found the writings of both of these authors greatly helpful. Three people I have never met but whose extensive writings I have read (and, in the case of Maki, buildings I have seen) and found particularly informative, insightful and inspiring are: architectural critic, Botond Bognar; architect and theorist, Fumihiko Maki; and writer/journalist, Peter Popham.

For reasons which will soon be all-too-obvious, searching for places in Japanese cities can be an elusive and time-consuming business, even for the Japanese. For me, much help was forthcoming from many people to make this process both more pleasurable and more rewarding. A few, in particular, sensed my needs and led me to pertinent places in their own cities and regions. The late Hironori Okubo and his wife, Teiko, were enormously generous in introducing me to some very special Fukuoka places (and people). Several, staff from the Assumption Junior College, Osaka (Naoko Nakajima, Yoshie Fusejima and Chad Wynn) explained hidden corners of Osaka and the wider Kansai region. Others in Japan who deserve mention include: Mayuko Sano of *Kokusai Koryu* for advice and assistance in obtaining materials and interest in the subject: the several Nagasaki and Fukuoka city officers (particularly Kengo Gosho of Nagasaki and Ryuji Inoue of Fukuoka) who helped me 'see' their cities more clearly by assisting with site visits and information: Katsuhiro Kobayashi of Tokyo Metropolitan University for extending my horizons of the capital's buildings: and Michiyuki Hirashima of Fukuoka Yomiuri Technical College who enhanced my understanding of Japan's traditional town houses.

From the University of Tasmania, the help and interest of several colleagues have been particularly appreciated: Richard Blythe, Julian Direen, Terry Lobban, Petrina Moore, Jill Roberts, Rory Spence, Leigh Woolley and Jianfeh Zhu gave collectively valuable photographic, computing, graphic, administrative and 'intellectual' assistance. The University itself supported a short period of study leave during which time I developed my initial publishing proposal while the final stages of production were assisted by my appointment as an Honorary Research Associate (after I left my full-time position).

I am greatly indebted to Ann Rudkin of Alexandrine Press, Oxford, who on behalf of the publishers did a splendid job in keeping me on track and more or less on time with good sense and good spirit – to make the potentially tedious later stages into a pleasant and positive process. And a very special 'thank you' to Miki Okamoto, of Monbusho Gakugeiin, who came generously to my rescue with some last-minute essentials (information and illustrations).

Last but by no means least, my thanks to: Kevin Nute of Hokkaido's Muroran Institute of Technology, who turned his sharp and sceptical mind usefully to my project as we tramped the streets and sands of Tokyo and Tasmania respectively; Professors Stephen Hamnett of the University of South Australia and Thong Nguyen of the University of Tasmania who expressed confidence in me and my project when circumstances required external support; and Jacqui Pickard, Librarian, without whose help and encouragement my reading might have been narrower and persistence weaker.

Please note. Substantial efforts have been made to contact copyright holders and identify sources of material reproduced in this book. Further, the author and publishers wish to thank many individuals and organizations for allowing items to re-appear here. These are acknowledged either above (in the Acknowledgements) and/or in the body of the work. However, if any errors or oversights have occurred, we would wish to correct these at later printing. Please contact the author, c/o E & F N Spon.

About the cover. The background is adapted from a 'Future Vision of Kyoto' competition entry prepared by three students (Julian Direen, Robert Lo and Andy Ng) in the author's 1997 urban design studio at the University of Tasmania.

The traditional street scene is taken from a print, 'Seihaku-sai (festival), Nanao-shi, Ishikawa-ken', by the Osaka-based artist, Mitsuru Fukui, whose permission to use it here is gratefully acknowledged.

To Justine and Macki

Chapter 1

Western Interest in the Japanese City

Europeans first stepped onto Japanese soil in 1543. Just ninety-six years later (in 1639), they were almost totally barred from the country. For the two-and-a-half centuries that followed (until 1854), contact between Europe and Japan was primarily through a handful of Dutchmen who were generally confined to a small man-made island in the harbour of Nagasaki.

During that first and relatively brief period (especially brief when you consider that the return sailing time between Europe and Japan was then in the order of two or more years), a trickle of Europeans (mostly Spaniards, Portuguese, Italians, Englishmen and Dutchmen) ventured to trade and often preach and teach at the edge of their known world. They discovered a populous country with extensive settlement and substantial cities and towns. Japan's population in the late sixteenth century of about eighteen millions was large compared, for instance, to England's four-and-a-half millions and Spain's eight millions. Settlement through lowland Japan was extensive and surprised visitors: in the 100 leagues plus distance between Miyako (modern-day Kyoto) and Suruga (Shizuoka), the Mexican-born Spaniard, Rodrigo de Vivero y Velasco noted that 'you would not even find a quarter of a league unpopulated' (Cooper, 1965, p. 282). Comparisons were readily made between the apparent dimensions of European and Japanese cities. Englishman, John Saris found Suruga to be 'full as bigge as London with all the Suburbs' and Osaka to be 'as great as London within the walls'

(Cooper, 1965, pp. 287 and 288). Likewise, de Vivero y Velasco wrote (with some justification) of Miyako 'that there is no larger place in the known world' (Cooper, 1965, p. 280)

Further, the cities and buildings of the time aroused a measure of fascination and even admiration amongst the visitors. The great castles, and particularly Osaka's, were viewed with awe. The capital was admired for its extensive grid of streets and the spaciousness of particular streets. Large Buddhist temples and more particularly their idols captured attention. It should, however, be noted that the capital and the temples were in essence more Chinese than Japanese and effectively cultural imports. Kyoto was modelled originally on the Chinese capital of Changan and was unusual in Japan, then and now. Castles were conceived and made in Japan although their scale was very much prompted by the arrival of European firearms. Superficially at least, they bore some resemblance to European fortifications, exceeding some in scale while, at the same time, adding a touch of the exotic.

However, the more extensive and more typically indigenous aspects of cities also drew responses. A common cause for comment was the sharp division within the cities between the areas of the warrior classes (where there were houses in gardens) and of the merchants and artisans (where buildings were aligned along streets) with the further division of the city into gated sections – according to trades in the latter areas. The separateness of the houses (many houses that may have appeared to be in rows still stood independently) and their largely single-storey nature were both noted characteristics. The vulnerability of the timber buildings to fire and their portability left strong impressions upon the minds of visitors, many of whom witnessed first-hand the destruction of whole city quarters and the moving of buildings. While European cities of the time were not immune to Acts of God and fire, they must have seemed, by comparison, remarkably solid and enduring. Further, given the appalling hygienic conditions in many contemporary European cities, it is not surprising that the cleanliness of Japan's cities was also a common point of comparison – the cleanliness referring both to streets and buildings (and people). In some cities, Osaka included, the number and quality of bridges also brought favourable remarks. One of the more perceptive comparative comments (as will later be gleaned) came again from de Vivero y Velasco who noted that 'our Spanish (or did he mean Spanish-Mexican where his observation may have been even more relevant) houses look better from without (but) the interior of these (Japanese) houses is far more beautiful' (Cooper, 1965, p. 294).

During that first century of contact, European commentary on Japanese cities appears to have been mostly descriptive but basically positive. Other aspects of culture such as manners, dress, customs, festivals, the arts, language and even buildings (especially noble houses) were perhaps the subject of more enthusiastic curiosity and investigation. Nevertheless, a variety of city features was both noticed and noted with favour but, at the same time, seen as very different, as were most things in Japan. Another perceptive visitor comment was from the Italian Jesuit, Alessandro Valignano, who wrote: '. . . Japan is a world the reverse of Europe; everything is so different and opposite that they are like us in practically nothing.' Yet he added that '. . . this would not be surprising if they were like so many barbarians, but what astonishes me is that they behave as very prudent and cultured people . . .' (Cooper, 1965, p. 229). Both the culture and the city seem to have been observed in a manner that accepted difference within a framework of tolerance. The cities may not have been proffered as great examples of urban civilization, but they appear not to have been belittled and included many elements that commanded respect. The impression is that they were seen as different but, in some sense, equal.

During the years of national isolation, Japan's merchant class expanded enormously and with them, the country's towns and cities. By the eighteenth century, Edo (now Tokyo) had emerged as the world's largest city easily outstripping the largest that Europe could offer, London and Paris. Thus, when Japan re-opened its doors in the 1850s, there were more, larger and denser cities than ever before for Westerners to view. There were also many more people from the West to see them including, for the first time, Americans for whom the journey was a relatively short single ocean hop. But with few exceptions, the new stream of Western visitors from both sides of the Atlantic (and other places) showed little generosity in their attitudes to Japan's cities and their built forms. To the 'Enlightened' Western eye of the latter half of the nineteenth century, the cities appeared drab, featureless and insubstantial.

Reflecting upon the changes in Western attitudes towards Edo-Tokyo (Edo was renamed Tokyo in 1868) between the pre- and post-isolation years, the Director of the German Institute for Japan Studies, Josef Kriener, is of the opinion that the early Europeans to visit Edo found a city 'which they perceived as comparable to European cities in some manner' and therefore comprehensible in some ways. He believes that this altered only after the Enlightenment in Europe and further suggests that this was more tied to changes in European self-consciousness than to changes in Japan (Kriener, 1995, p. 166).

Certainly, throughout the late nineteenth century and well into the twentieth century, Westerners, almost without exception, could not see beyond the flimsiness of the individual buildings and the collective monotony of the cities. There were, reported Douglas Sladen in 1903, 'plenty of Japanese houses which, when secured at night, would hardly stand up to a drunken man leaning against them' (Sladen, 1903, p. 2). Some twenty years before that, the indefatigable Isabella Bird had described Tokyo as 'a city of "magnificent distances" without magnificence'

meaning that it was an amorphous amalgam of grey featureless patches in a seemingly endless urban landscape. (Bird quoted in Yapp, 1983, p. 612) For the earlier quoted Sladen, the urban jewel in the nation's cultural crown, Kyoto, was 'as good (and I presume therefore as grim) as Glasgow for excursions' (Sladen, 1903, 388). For Western visitors of those times, the sighting of a Japanese city was invariably an anti-climax. W. E. Griffis was not untypical when he said of Fukui after first glimpsing the place: 'There were no spires, golden-vaned; no massive pediments, facades, or grand buildings such as strike the eye on beholding a city in the Western world (Griffis, 1876, p. 423). Temporariness and featurelessness dominated European and even American images of Japanese cities and, to a large measure, remain at the heart of Western scepticism of Japanese buildings and towns.

Even Lafcadio Hearn, who adopted Japan as his own and waxed eloquently about almost every aspect of the country's life (he even saw merit in concubinage), could not find much to say that was positive about the general fabric of Japanese cities. His commentaries upon his beloved Matsue were at best fondly descriptive (Hearn, 1976, pp. 139–171) while Kumamoto was 'devilishly ugly' (quoted by Francis King in Hearn, 1984, p. 13). Another Japanophile, who did much to record and disseminate abroad aspects of traditional Japanese culture as well as defend it in Japan itself in the face of the Western cultural onslaught, was the American, Edward S. Morse.

While Professor of Zoology at Tokyo University (from 1877 to 1880) he prepared the first authoritative work on the domestic architecture of Japan in which he meticulously and lovingly catalogued and described the types and details of Japanese dwellings and their surroundings. Yet even Morse admitted that the first sighting of a Japanese house was 'certainly disappointing' being 'insubstantial in appearance' and possessing a 'meagreness of colour'. Further, these same buildings (houses and commercial buildings alike) produced collectively a 'gray sea of domiciles' of 'sombre effect' and 'general monotony'. He concluded: 'Having got . . . a bird's-eye view of one city, we have seen them all, – the minor variations consisting, for the most part, in the inequalities of the sites upon which they rest' (Morse, 1972, pp. 1–6).

In general, Westerners were not inclined to learn from or even see merit in what they saw but behaved rather as design missionaries intent on wishing and, in the case of professionals, imposing a new architecture and urban order on a place that seemed to them so much more primitive. Many Western-style buildings were indeed built all over Japan by Western and Japanese architects alike. To be fair, 'imposition' is a slightly misleading term to describe entirely the proliferation of Western architectural forms during Japan's Meiji era (1867 to 1912) for the Japanese were themselves intent on 'catching up' with the West in all things connected remotely with finance, transport, manufacturing, technology, communi-

cations and culture. And in order to Westernize, they imported an impressive array of up-and-coming young talent from Europe (primarily Great Britain, Germany and France) and America to teach in their universities and to work with the Government. The fields of architecture and planning were no exceptions.

As a result, the country's own architecture had to wait some eighty years, following the country's re-opening, before there were collective Western voices to speak with profound admiration for its qualities and character. The eventual protagonists were a handful of progressive architects whom we now regard amongst the pioneers of Modern architecture. These people (including Frank Lloyd Wright, Bruno Taut and Walter Gropius) spoke positively because they discovered in traditional Japanese buildings, some of the design principles and qualities which they themselves were trying to adhere to or otherwise inject into their own work. Cities, on the other hand, have had to wait far longer and are only now beginning to be appreciated.

The one element of the Japanese urban scene which did receive immediate and unanimous praise from Westerners, specialist designers and general travellers alike, was the garden. A contemporary of Morse at Tokyo University was a young Englishman, Joseph Conder, appointed as the first Instructor of Architecture in the Engineering Department. While he imposed Western architectural styles in Japan through a prolific output of government, religious and establishment buildings, he did in part for the Japanese garden what Morse had done for the house: that is, he brought it to wider attention through publication. Conder, in 1893, wrote a similar volume on the history, types, composition and details of Japanese gardens (*Landscape Gardening in Japan*) but without the kinds of reservation that Morse had shown for architecture.

This immediate interest in the Japanese garden stemmed probably from the fact that it offered certain qualities that had been emerging in Western park and garden design since the eighteenth century in the Picturesque or Romantic garden landscape. The English Picturesque creation, which had spread quickly into Europe and the European colonial world, was intended to provide 'solitude; beauty; the uninterrupted, essentially passive spectator experience of nature' and the opportunity to wander 'without apparent destination in search of the several emotional treats' (Jackson, 1991, pp. 130 and 131) from tranquillity to terror that nature could inspire – much like the gardens of Japan. Thus, Japanese gardens were an exotic phenomenon which embraced qualities already valued in the West but with greater compactness – the creation of seemingly expansive space in often pocket-sized places. Further, this occurred at a time when inspiration was sought for the design of a proliferating number of small urban spaces (public parks and private gardens) and when ideas and objects derived from global expansion enjoyed a

peculiar kind of status 'at home'. In other words, Japanese gardens were fortuitously able to inform and expand upon developing themes in Western landscape design.

A few other areas of the visual arts had gained some measure of Western interest. Before the awakening to the Japanese garden, the Japanese crafts of ceramics, lacquerware and, to a lesser extent, metalwork had together won an early respect from some Western designers and exerted a strong influence upon them. There followed a Western interest in that genre of Japanese print known as Ukiyo-e (pictures of the floating world). The crafts were powerfully influential upon the European Art Nouveau movement as were the Ukiyo-e upon such notables as Monet, Manet, Whistler, Gaugin and Van Gogh. Further, the 1890s witnessed the enthusiastic acceptance of forms and design principles from the Japanese garden, through the influence of such works as Conder's and the appearance of various Japanese gardens in public places, particularly in the United States.

Thus, the landscape garden may be regarded as the third strand of influence upon Western visual art (after crafts and prints) but, more importantly from the standpoint of this work, as the first wave of influence upon the built environment.

While Morse's *Japanese Homes and their Surroundings* appeared in 1886 and examples of Japanese buildings appeared at international expositions in Philadelphia (1876), Chicago

(1893) and San Franscisco (1894), their influence was minor. Frank Lloyd Wright, the Green Brothers, and McKim, Mead and White in Chicago, California and on the Eastern seaboard respectively are known to have been influenced by what they saw (Nute, 1993 p. 18). Nevertheless, the West did not open its mind in any significant way to the design principles of the common traditional buildings of Japan until the advent of Modernism. It took the writings of Wright (1943) and Bruno Taut (1936 and 1937) to recognize and explain the characteristics and qualities at the heart of traditional Japanese building design as ones which might be studied to advantage and, in principle, emulated in the West. In other words, some of the early makers of the Modern Movement found in the traditional Japanese building a working model which offered new insights and informed their own explorations of form and space and so bolstered their own evangelical cause.

Before Wright ever stepped foot in Japan (he says at twenty-three years of age) he was intrigued by the 'elimination of the insignificant' as 'a process of simplification' in the Japanese print. When he later travelled there and set up an office, he found the ordinary traditional home to offer the very same 'supreme . . . elimination of the insignificant' and 'the perfect example of the (same) modern standardizing' that he himself had been working at: the latter was evident in the *tatami* or standard floor mat as a basic module for all dimensions (Wright, 1943, pp. 194 and

196). He was, among other things, impressed by the insulated roofs, the underfloor ventilation, the notion of screens as walls and the continuous space between garden and house. He advocated the Japanese home as an essential source of inspiration for the West, for to Wright 'the question of modern architecture seemed more involved with Japanese architecture in native principle than with any other architecture' (Wright, 1943, p. 200).

Bruno Taut was invited to Japan in 1933. After a substantial stay, his *Houses and People of Japan* was published in 1937. Taut was both wider ranging and more specific than Wright in his observations, looking at both the Japanese way of life and specific buildings, including Katsura Imperial Villa which impressed him greatly. Of the Villa, he wrote: 'the entire arrangement . . . followed always elastically in all its dimensions of purpose which each one of the parts as well as the whole had to accomplish, the aim being that of common or normal utility, or the necessity of dignified representation, or that of lofty, philosophical spirituality' (Taut, 1937, p. 291). It was, for Taut, 'the absolute proof of (his) theory, which (he) regarded as a valid base for modern architecture' (Taut, 1937, p. 291) Indeed, Taut saw Japanese buildings very much through the ideals and intentions of Modernism.

However, while both Wright and Taut may have seen in Japanese architecture primarily what they wanted to see, they do represent a turning point in Western attitude towards traditional buildings in Japan. The latter's Modernist characteristics and qualities became a focus of attention. The things that particularly stirred the Modernist hearts were the modular frame construction, elevated floor, free space both within the building and between inside and outside, honest exposure of the construction, minimal decoration and the otherwise spartan aesthetic. Traditional Japanese architecture was transformed from something that was ignored or derided to something that had special (even cult) status amongst a significant professional community in the West.

Ironically, while the West was discovering some of the qualities of traditional Japanese building through Modernism, the Japanese were discovering Western Modernism in part as a continuation of their 'modernization' and imitation of the West. This latter process was mostly through literature and travel but also through a handful of young Japanese working in the ateliers of the European pioneers (Bunzo Yamaguchi and Chikatada Kurata with Gropius, and Takamasa Yoshizaka, Junzo Sakakura and Kunio Maekawa with Le Corbusier). By the mid-1960s Gunter Nitschke was able to report that Modern Architecture in Japan had returned 'step by step to its roots'. Modern Japanese architecture had, he declared, 'started by adopting wholesale the Western way of using form and space' but had 'eventually found itself at a stage that had already been reached a thousand years ago' in Japan (Nitschke, 1966, p 117).

This process of change is one that should not be overlooked when considering the fate of the Japanese city in the minds of later Western observers and critics. For, as with the architecture of Japan, the Western view of Japanese city form started in the negative. But unlike architecture, it deteriorated to reach its depths in the Modern age: that is, in the 1950s and 1960s. There had been no-one to shed light on city form in the late nineteenth century as Conder had done on the garden or even to the extent of Morse on buildings. Further, there was no urban design equivalent of Wright or Taut in the 1930s and 1940s for the Japanese city displayed no apparent principles that might have served the Western city planning cause. By the 1950s and 1960s, Tokyo was synonymous with chaos and confusion. It was, according to the Australian writer Hal Porter, 'makeshift and confused, a freak weed sprung from a crack in history, and drenched by a fertilizer that makes it monstrous but not mighty, immense but immoral, overgrown and undercivilized'. And this, he said, was in spite of 'two unparalleled opportunities – it was incarcerated flat by the 1923 earthquake and the World War II bombings – to disentangle and straighten out its Gordian knot of streets' (Porter, 1968, p. 19).

Even the travel-experienced eye of Jan Morris failed to see Kyoto (which the Americans had spared of wartime attacks) as much more than a 'plain place, shabby and shanty-like' in spite of its 'nearly two thousand Buddhist temples,

Shinto shrines and palaces of importance'. These special places were, to her eyes, 'scattered across the city like gems in mud' (Morris, 1986, p. 220). When she returned to her 1957 essay after nearly thirty years for the purpose of re-publication, she admitted that she 'did not terribly like Kyoto' and may have 'totally failed to understand it' for 'in Japan, of all countries, it is dangerous to be ignorant' (Morris, 1986, p. 218).

Such views are those of so many Westerners who visit to this day. To most Western visitors, Japanese cities remain cluttered, garish, unfathomable and, seemingly, without trace of urban planning. At best, there may be a delight in the vibrancy and intensity of city life but an unease and distaste with the form, without the grace of Morris who acknowledges that the wearing of cultural spectacles may have severely skewed her view. To most Western eyes, Japanese cities lack civic spaces, sidewalks, squares, parks, vistas, etc; in other words, they lack those physical components that have come to be viewed as hall marks of a civilized Western city. The reaction reflects an underlying attitude in the West that Japanese cities are somehow inferior – that in spite of their densities and liveliness, they are somehow less than 'urban'.

Further, and sadly, these are notions that many Japanese architects and planners have themselves taken on board. For instance, the eminent Isozaki is of the opinion that his country 'has yet to evolve a convincing urban archetype' and that Japanese cities are little more than the 'meander-

ings of overgrown village lanes' (reported by Sudjic, 1989, p 16).

Japanese cities may have different (in some instances almost opposite) patterns and forms to those of the West, but to suggest that these are somehow less valid or that there is no convincing archetype or that the rural origins of some urban patterns devalues them is, I think, misleading. Like many views of cultural artefacts the world over, such misgivings seem to be somewhat Eurocentric in their viewpoint.

There are however ripples, perhaps even waves, in the thinking about Japanese city form which promises to turn the West's rather suspicious and negative stance into something more positive and respectful. Discussion and presentation of Japanese cities by Japanese designers and urban scholars has been changing from one of embarrassment and apology to one of confidence and promotion. It is a slow process of discovery, acceptance and eventually perhaps even embrace of patterns and forms previously dismissed as unworthy of serious investigation. There may, as yet, be no strong movement or theory that sees formal merit in the Japanese city but the process may well turn out to resemble that which earlier affected architecture. However, the city is a more complex creature than a building and change is, of necessity, likely to be more subtle, less certain, less dogmatic and perhaps more rewarding.

Drawing upon the pioneering 1960s work of Teiji Itoh, Arata Isozaki and colleagues (Toshi Design Kenkyutai, 1968), one of the first

1.1 *Hard Shells and Soft Yolks. Although usually higher density, the Japanese city is generally less centralized than its Western counterpart with a series of 'hard shells' and 'soft yolks' over a wide area (right), while that of the Western city tends to rise to a more restricted and visually dominant centre (left).*

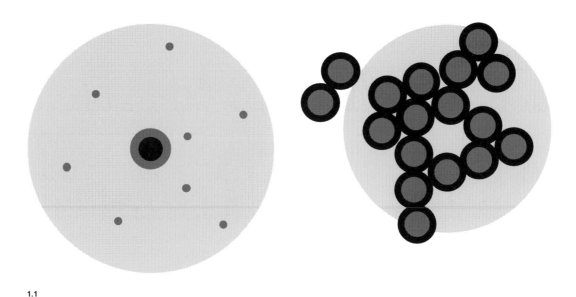

1.1

Western writers to attempt to understand the Japanese city on its own terms was Gunther Nitschke (1966). He admonished those Europeans who had earlier seen only the superficialities of traditional Japanese architecture while in pursuit of their Modernist ends, namely transparency, flexibility and lightness. Specifically he tried to get closer to the Japanese idea of space, including city space and made a number of important observations. He recognized that the Japanese sense of space is not something created by compositional elements. In other words, a city in Japan was not something 'enclosed' by buildings and walls. Its shape was forever 'vague'. A space or 'place' was an area defined by 'certain human activities'; consequently, it would move with the activity that gave it definition. He stressed this point by way of reference to the grand European parade or gathering where spatial setting (Paris's Champs-Elysees, Rome's St Peter's Square or London's Mall) is more important than the activity in the process of place-making; whereas in Japan, it is the procession or other event independent of spatial setting that makes a place (Nitschke, 1966, p. 126). Consequently, a Westerner must put aside his precious notions of enclosure and physical definition to appreciate Japanese space. Nitschke also noted that communal facilities in Japanese cities tend not to be centralized as in the West but scattered. These are all points upon which many writers have since elaborated and to which I shall return.

1.2 *Hard Shells and Soft Yolks. In the Japanese city, lower buildings and relatively quiet streets commonly lie between high buildings on busy thoroughfares over a wide area (bottom). In the Western city, however, the built skyline has tended to peak around a dominant centre (top).*

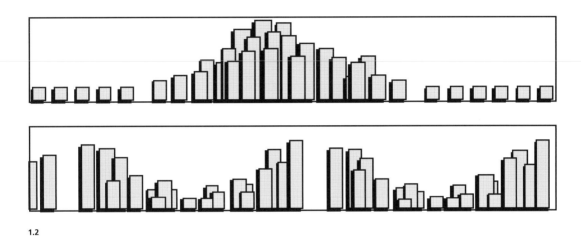

1.2

Nitschke still had in mind traditional Japan. More recently, some observers have tried to see merit in Japan's much maligned modern cities. One observation (consistent with that of a 'scattered' centre) is that city form constantly thickens and thins, and rises and falls over a wide area. Within this pattern, Westerners are surprised by the cheek-by-jowl proximity of the big concrete-and-neon networks of roads to the labyrinths of little lanes enmeshed within the big networks.

On this point, the Tokyo-based English writer, Peter Popham has likened the urban fabric of Tokyo to a series of nesting circles, each with a high hard concrete commercial 'shell' containing a pliable retail and service 'white' and a positively soft residential 'yolk' (Popham, 1985, p 48). Unlike in Western cities, he notes that the quieter streets and places of relative tranquillity are not necessarily that way because they are peripheral but because they exist within a series of hard protective shells. Popham is one who has looked at Japanese cities with the kind of critical but compassionate eye that is rewarded with insight.

Botond Bognar is another author who has recognized the outsiders' difficulties in overcoming their perplexing first impressions of Japan's cities and made a more scholarly probe of the country's cultural, architectural and urban traditions. As backcloth to his excellent and informative survey of *Contemporary Japanese Architecture*, Bognar expands upon the kinds of observations made by Nitschke and Popham – the traditional absence of well-defined centres, the absence of towers and squares, the dependence of 'spatiality . . . on the current happening', and so on. He concludes that the spatial structure of Western cities 'is primarily centrifugal in character' whereas that of Japan 'moves, centripetally

11

1.3 *Tsukudajima from the Air. The Tokyo district of Tsukudajima is an example of a pocket of low (often timber) dwellings and small businesses flanked by big (concrete and metal) towers. Once an island, it is now a 'soft yolk' surrounded by a 'hard shell'. (Courtesy: Tokyo Metropolitan Government)*

1.4 *View from a Tsukudajima Street. This Tsukudajima street looks out to the tall 'hard shell' buildings about its edge.*

1.3

1.4

from outside in'. Further, he sees a consistency with architecture for he likens the city to the traditional house which is laid out horizontally and has no central space (Bognar, 1985, p 67).

Writing some twenty years later than Nitschke, Bognar places rather more emphasis upon the experience of the city and on the present, constantly making connections between traditional and contemporary form. He refers (by way of Kazuhiro Ishii) to the structural clarity of the Western city in contrast to Japanese irregularity and adds his own insights. 'The Japanese city', writes Bognar, 'is created, perceived and understood as an additive texture of its parts or places and thus is denoted by the external distribution of signs and symbols rather than by the physical entity of its objects and enclosures' (Bognar, 1985, p. 67). Consequently, activity, signs and

symbols are collectively Japan's urban place-makers rather than buildings, monuments and spaces. Bognar concludes that the Westerner has 'A predominant reliance on visual perception (which) . . . tends to objectify and to instil feelings of mastery over the environment, since the eye sets everything at a distance and maintains order. In the Japanese environment only fragments signified by scattered signs and symbols are encountered. These fail to provide an objective

1.5 *Neighbourhood near Higashi Nakano Station. This shows a more peripheral part of Tokyo in the late 1970s. Close to the Higashi Nakano station, it is a dense but low-rise neighbourhood of houses and narrow pole-dominated streets in close proximity to a higher and harder surrounding shell.*

The contrast between the low centre and higher periphery may not be as extreme as in Tsukudajima but it is still very evident and one of a kind that is repeated in many city neighbourhoods across Japan. (Courtesy: Tokyo Metropolitan Government)

1.5

perspective of a definite overall spatial pattern' (Bognar, 1985, p 67).

This is the root of the failure of even the perceptive Jan Morris (and most visitors before or since) to respond to and make sense of even the relatively ordered Kyoto – although Morris, as earlier acknowledged, had the wit and experience to realize that her interpretive machinery may have been culturally too defective to allow for reasonable understanding.

While some Westerners have shown less antipathy to Japanese cities in recent years, many leading Japanese designers and scholars have themselves studied them more seriously than ever before and speculated on their formal traditions and character. Indeed, it is this writing that has informed much Western writing: practitioner-theorists such as Ashihara and Maki and scholars such as Jinnai have written extensively on the Japanese city (past and present) and on the design implications (future) of their conclusions.

Hidenobu Jinnai, in his extensive studies of

1.6 *Enclosed Square and Open Bridge. In Japan's cities, the central places were usually the bridges: these, together with their surrounds, would offer a sweeping sense of openness (right). By contrast, the solidly enclosed space of the square or piazza made the equivalent place in the European city (left).*

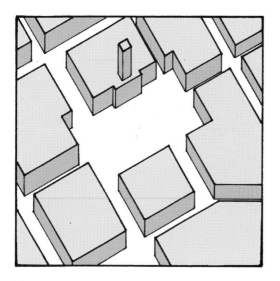 

1.6

Tokyo, has revealed just how much of the pattern of the present-day city (roads, activities, lot sizes, etc.) bears powerfully the imprint of previous forms. He shows how 'the structure of old Edo survives in the substructure of modern Tokyo' (Jinnai, 1987b, p. 24). For instance, new luxury hotels, almost all of Tokyo's college campuses and many of the city's parks all occupy former *daimyo* (i.e. lords') estates in the more elevated parts of the city and are served by old route networks. While, unlike in many Western cities, old buildings have been obliterated, links with the past are nevertheless strong, especially in the 'organization of space'.

More important, from the standpoint of this book, are his particular insights into the character of Japanese city space. For example, he contrasts the main central places of traditional Japanese and European cities: in Japan 'it was the bridges and their environs, which offered sweeping vistas and an exhilarating sense of openness' and were the equivalents of European squares with their contrasting heavy masonry enclosure (Jinnai, 1987b, p. 24). Thus, Edobashi (bridge) as an open functional node was to Tokyo as the Piazza San Marco was to Venice as a closed formal space.

Yoshinobu Ashihara is one of Japan's leading architects and a member of the country's elite Japanese Academy. He has likewise contrasted European city form with that of Japan. He has not only shown them to be different but actually proffered the superiority of the chaotic Japanese forms over their more ordered European counterparts. Ashihara concedes that Japanese cities do appear to be very messy but also observes that they work remarkably well, contending that behind the visual chaos (which so many writers have been quick to condemn or cheaply glamorize) there is a 'hidden order' which is rooted in Japanese geography, history and culture (Ashihara, 1989).

One after another, Ashihara pits the characteristics of Western and Japanese life, buildings and cities, past and present, against each other. He contrasts the traditional Japanese architectural focus upon the floor against the West's upon the wall, ambiguity between outside and inside against clarity, the irregular and omni-directional nature of the Japanese building against Western symmetry and frontality, elevated floor against ground-level floor and elevated furniture, temporary versus more permanent buildings, and so on. The differences are endless and mutually reinforcing and these are to some degree, extended to city scale. He examines Tokyo and Paris to conclude that while Paris may exhibit great physical beauty, it has a rigid inflexible order, compared to Tokyo which may look ugly and chaotic but shows remarkable dynamism and adaptability. Paris, he writes, is a 'city divided with foresight into parts "cut" from the whole' while Tokyo follows the sense of 'the whole enveloping all of its various parts' (Ashihara, 1989, p. 43) – an observation which is consistent with that of Bognar when he contrasts the centri-fugal spatial structure of Western cities with the centripetal structure of those of Japan.

Here, Ashihara is inspired by Mandelbrot's Fractal Geometry of nature and the 'notion of a flexible orderly structure embracing randomness in what is apparently chaos' suggesting a hidden order with amoebic adaptability (Ashihara, 1989, p. 64). Thus the Japanese city is quick to sever, discard, replace and re-form its parts according to the new needs of a rapidly changing world and without the Western concern for the wider visual context or pattern. Hence, the quality which so infuriates the Western observer seems also to be the Japanese city's strength.

But of all of the Japanese writers (certainly of those who are accessible in English), it is the distinguished architect, Fumihiko Maki who extends these contrasts in the most poetic manner and, by implication at least, brings them closest to contemporary scientific and philosophical thinking. He again notes the absence of a 'clear relationship of center and periphery' in the Japanese city. He also suggests that there is no clear relationship between figure and ground (i.e. between built form and exterior space) in contrast to Western clarity. Further, he observes how 'everything from signs (and) vending machines . . . to infrastructures' participate equally with buildings in the imagery of urban Japan. Together, these characteristics result in an amorphous and more collage-like surface in Japan 'that favours fluctuations, fluidity and lightness' (Maki, 1988, p. 8). This presents each building with a higher degree of autonomy than in the West where city form is visually more coherent, with relationships of centre to periphery, figure to ground, building to sign, etc. showing themselves with greater hierarchy and clarity.

Indeed, Maki refers to two kinds of order: in one, the relationship of the parts to the whole is systematic and is termed 'clock' while in the second, the relationships are in an unstable equilibrium and are termed 'cloud'. In the context of this analogy, he says that 'the contemporary city is approaching the condition of a cloud' (Maki, 1988, p. 10). At this point he uses only the adjective 'contemporary' without distinguishing between Japan and the West. Nevertheless, the logic of his argument would suggest that it is the contemporary Japanese city that is the most cloud-like of all and that this cloudy condition has a more flexible order than its Western counterpart.

Maki's adaptable cloud-like condition clearly parallels Ashihara's flexible hidden order. Both men, as practising architects, are seeking to understand the condition of the contemporary city against its historical roots as a context for their design interventions in the present and future. The city-clock analogy of Maki conjures up images of a little urban universe of Newtonian regularity while the city-cloud analogy connotes more the unstable world of Chaos where the behaviour of a system (in this case, the city) is so complex that it might as well be random even though it may satisfy deterministic laws. The

implication is that the structure of the Japanese city is rather more flexible than its Western counterpart and is better able to accommodate dynamic change in the whole system as well as greater autonomy of the parts (i.e. individual developments) which is necessary in today's (and tomorrow's) urban world. As such, Westerners should pay greater attention to the cities of Japan than they do.

Consistent with such conclusions, there are some Western commentators who are convinced that they are seeing something of the future now in the most technological, commercialized and information-based of the world's urban places, namely those of Japan. John Thackera, for instance, sees the Japanese capital as a city of a 'new geography' – the modern decentralized metropolis in which the inhabitant is never physically orientated, for travel is between experiences rather than places with no sense of city plan. It is also the city of new building types – buildings-as-news, superbly detailed short-life buildings with 'sufficient design or fashion charisma' to raise the public profile and real estate values of their immediate environs (Thackera, 1989, pp. 66–67).

Such comments show insight but they also bear an element of superficiality. For in Japan, as earlier inferred, the 'new' centre-less or multi-nodal geography is, in fact, an old urban phenomenon. And even fine detailing of consciously temporary architecture is a long-established Japanese design tradition, having its roots in the regular recon-

1.7 *View from Nagasaki Ekimae (that is, from the front of the railway station).*

1.8 *An Osaka Street.*
These are typical Japanese city sights which Westerners find so vexatious.

1.7

1.8

struction of fire-prone city quarters and the rebuilding of shrines. Thus, some of the wonders (to Western eyes) of today's Japanese urban world are not merely a consequence of modern technology and contemporary commerce, as many writers would have us believe, but rather of a marriage of technology and tradition. For the Japanese, it may be a happy coincidence that, for the second time this century, the built-form traditions of their 'old world' culture should facilitate the expression of 'new' twentieth-century technology and 'new' ideas about city form and space.

The realization of this relationship between tradition and the 'new' is something that gives substance and intellectual depth to some Japanese writing about their own built forms, that is lacking in much Western, especially European commentary. The latter tends to emphasize the vulgar, the chaotic and the illegible in the Japanese city, although it is now more common to glamorize than to condemn these characteristics than was once the case. For instance, I cannot help but liken the tone of articles such as Thackera's 'Seeing is Disbelieving' on Tokyo to the in-praise-of-the-unpraiseworthy scripts-to-shock which appeared on Los Angeles and Las Vegas *circa* 1970. In the case of Las Vegas, a seminal work did of course follow the words of wonderment in (mainly European) pop journalism. It was Robert Venturi, Denise Scott-Brown and Steve Izenour who eventually took a study team to that American oasis of commerce and crime to dissect and record systematically its billboard-and-parking-lot environment, resulting in 1972 in the subsequently celebrated *Learning from Las Vegas*.

The book showed how the hitherto unreadable chaos of the commercial strip had its own powerful if pragmatic order from which design principles could be extracted for application elsewhere.

This is not to compare Tokyo with Las Vegas. In complexity, Las Vegas is to Tokyo as an amoeba is to man. Rather, it is to reflect upon a pattern of Eurocentric design prejudice, followed by a more sympathetic if somewhat sensational and journalistic awakening, followed in turn by a more serious and home-grown exploration of an hitherto bewildering form.

As an urban design system of awesome complexity, progress in understanding the patterns and forms of the Japanese city will always be difficult. It will expand through both the systematic exploration and intuitive insights of a great many observers, scholars and designers. There can be no single work that reveals proportionally as much on Japanese city form as did

exploration of Venturi *et al.* of the American commercial strip. And as a dynamic system, change will anyway outpace discovery as the cities sprout new patterns and forms that invite forever more exploration and examination.

Within these inevitable limitations, this book is, nevertheless, an attempt to shed at least some greater light on the structure, form and character (i.e. 'design') of the Japanese city and on how the Japanese themselves perhaps ponder and perceive their cities in the context of their wider culture. This is partly achieved by way of what might be termed a comparative method – in this case, comparisons with the West. Thus, it also reveals insights into Western culture and city form for understanding an alien way is one sure means of sharpening one's vision of that which is familiar, and therefore, of appreciating more profoundly its qualities as well as discovering its limitations.

Chapter 2

Areas and Lines : From Written to City Texts

Writing and page layout are both acts of spatial arrangement. They involve the placement of letters or characters and other graphic elements over a paper or equivalent surface. In this way, there is something in common with architectural and urban design for these too arrange things (walls, floors, buildings, squares, streets, trees etc) in space. It is pertinent therefore to have as my point of departure the young child who is learning to write. For just as the way we think is closely tied to our language, so the way we conceive and arrange space is related to the graphic qualities and visual expression of our language. Indeed, Rod Mengham concludes in his provocative but persuasive investigation of the historical development and role of *Language*: 'The planning of a language leads . . . ultimately to the planning of human sensibilities' (Mengham, 1993, p. 169). Likewise, our spatial sensibilities may be linked to the nature of our writing systems.

Written and Printed Texts

'. . . in likening a cityscape to a book, I notice an analogy between the brocade-like appearance of the mixture of Chinese characters, Hiragana, Katakana and sometimes even Roman alphabetic characters in written Japanese, and the heterogeneous aspect of the city.

On the other hand, I get an impression of flush surfaces when I look at a newspaper written in English.'

Akihiko Chiba, 1984 (in Nakamura et al., Process Architecture 49, p.62)

As a small English schoolboy, I was given paper ruled only with horizontal lines. My wife, on the other hand, as a Japanese schoolgirl, was given paper ruled with horizontal and vertical lines (i.e. in squares) for the same task.

For my wife, placement of the characters in the squares was all important. The young Japanese mind has to imagine each character's centre of gravity and place it at the centre of the square. By contrast, I was instructed to follow the horizontal lines: for the English child, there are top and bottom ones between which the letters must line up. Sometimes there are even extra lines for the tops and tails of lower-case letters. Further, because letters have to be read in groups to carry any meaning at all (which is not the case with Japanese characters), it is the composite linear spacing or formation which is paramount.

It is axiomatic that the square is an areal figure, while the line (pardon the tautology) is linear. Thus, from the outset, the young Japanese's focus in writing is upon area while that of the Western child is upon line.

Not surprisingly, these differences are reinforced by the contrasting nature of Japanese characters and Western letters. The basic building block of Western writing is the letter (a, b, c, etc.). This is a totally abstract unit which, of itself, carries no meaning whatsoever and, as already mentioned, has to be strung together with other letters to make any sense at all.

By contrast, each of the Japanese characters (known as *Kanji*) can stand alone. Further, *kanji*

2.1 *Squared and Lined Paper. When learning to write, a Japanese child is faced with a sheet of squares (top) and is asked to think of each character's geometry, imagine its centre of gravity and place this at the centre of a square. The Western child has a sheet of lines (bottom) and must think of 'strings' of letters and linear spacing.*

2.2 *Example Kanji Character. Independent and iconic, 'okii' is the character for 'big'. It is a human stick figure with outstretched arms. The smaller figure indicates an earlier form. (Calligraphy: Emiko Okayama)*

2.2

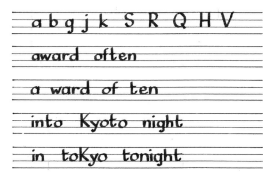

2.1

'big': this is a human stick figure with outstretched arms to express large size. Another is the character for 'high' whose origin lies in the gatehouses to walled Chinese cities: these were particularly prominent urban features due to their height and their pictorial representation came to denote 'high' as well as related meanings such as 'expensive' (Lindqvist, 1991, p. 238).

Clearly, to achieve similar meanings with the Western alphabet, letters have to be lined up in abstract linear patterns. Linear spacing is crucial and there is absolutely no iconic connection between word and object. Consequently Western letters do not and cannot achieve the graphic power and independence of meaning of Japanese characters. This independence goes hand-in-glove with the square as an autonomous conceptual base for written expression while the dependence of Western letters upon each other demands continuity of line.

Now, let us consider for a moment the

are invariably stylized pictorial representations of objects or ideas (and mostly taken from Chinese script). Directly or otherwise, they bear some iconic connection to the objects or ideas which they convey and, as such, carry meaning. Thus, each character is a powerfully independent sign. A simple example is the character for

2.3 *Gatehouse, Sujhou, China. It rises high above the surrounding wall to form one of the most prominent reference points in the city.*

2.4 *Example Kanji Character. 'Takai' is the character for 'high'. Of Chinese origin, it is a stylized picture of a gatehouse. The smaller figure indicates an earlier form. (Calligraphy: Emiko Okayama)*

2.3

2.4

directions that these characters and letters take to make a text upon the page. Western letters are extremely limited in the way that they may be placed if they are to be understood readily. It is in horizontal lines which run from the left-hand side to the right-hand side of each page. If, for instance (as I well know from the hands of less literate design students), only upper case letters are used for a substantial length of text, reading is significantly impaired. To abandon the rules for upper and lower case is to alter the rhythm, image and punctuation of the text and render the task of reading cumbersome. There is a feeling of awkwardness akin to performing a delicate task with the wrong or oversized tools. Arrange the letters in a vertical format and only two or three short words can be grasped easily. Western writing systems are essentially unidirectional – that is, in a horizontal format and from left to right upon the page.

This is in marked contrast to those of Japan

where the autonomy of the character and its areal compositional base are keys to a certain flexibility of direction. While it is true that for centuries Japanese characters were written mostly in lines from the top to the bottom of the page and that these lines progressed from right to left, it is also true that horizontal formats have been widely used over the last century or more. During the Meiji, Taisho and early Showa periods (essentially prior to World War II), horizontal formats read from right to left while later ones followed Western practice in moving from left to right. In other words, Japanese writing is multidirectional. Many signs remain on buildings from the earlier periods and, of course, many texts remain in libraries from the earlier 'right-to-left' era. Today, it is common for Japanese newspapers and magazines to display texts in both vertical and horizontal formats on the same page, resulting in images that are patchworks of conflicting directions. In the same way, city signs

2.5 *A Mixed Text Advertisement. Part of a newspaper advertisement showing a typical mix of vertical and horizontal text: it also mixes kanji and Japanese phonetic characters (hiragana and katakana) as well as Western letters. (Source: An extract from a Kusu Music advertisement, Nagasaki Shimbun, December, 1988)*

2.6 *Signs in a Shinjuku Street. As in the newspaper, the street texts display a mix of characters and directions.*

2.6

2.5

coexist in both horizontal and vertical formats. Thus the Japanese reader is constantly changing direction.

The fundamental contrast of area to line is also embodied in the chief instruments of writing in the two cultures – traditionally the quill and the brush. As Roland Barthes has astutely observed, the quill was uniquely prepared to 'scratch away at the paper in one direction' while 'the brush has a freedom of movement' in any. The quill is eminently suited to travel in lines across the page with wider up and down strokes and narrower ones in the horizontal. By contrast,

the brush can 'glide, jump and twist' (Barthes, quoted in Jeans, 1992, p. 182) upon the paper in whatever direction is desired and with equal ease. In other words, the quill (and subsequently its successor, the metal stylus) and the brush (and more recently the felt-tipped pen, which was incidentally a Japanese invention) are respectively instruments of linear and areal intent.

The final confirmation of the areal quality of one versus the linear quality of the other is the ways in which the respective instruments are held in the hand. The brush is held in the vertical with the hand in suspension above the page, ideal for those glides, jumps and twists towards any point of the compass. The stylus, on the other hand, is controlled at an angle and predestined to travel only from west to east with the wrist resting firmly upon the surface of the desk.

Another important difference between the two systems of writing is simply the number of Western letters when set against Japanese characters.

2.7 *A Composite Kanji . 'Toge', meaning the half way point on a mountain ascent, was developed by the Japanese by combining earlier (Chinese) characters. It brings together the characters for 'yama' or 'mountain' (left), 'ue' or 'up' (upper right) and 'shita' or 'down' (lower right). (Calligraphy: Emiko Okayama)*

2.7

There are a mere twenty-six letters in the English language (fifty-two if we allow for upper and lower case) and all meaningful expression stems from combining these into various linear patterns of countless permutations to make words. No letter can be taken away and none need be added. It is a complete and finite system.

Again, the contrast in Japanese is sharp. *Kanji* may no longer be expanding in its number of characters but it once grew to over fifty thousand. In this process of growth, old characters sometimes took on new meanings. Often, new characters emerged which were combinations of two or more old ones: a simple example of this is the character, *'toge'*: its meaning is the half-way point on the climb of a hill and combines the characters for 'mountain', 'up' and 'down' into a composite form within the square.

Theoretically it is necessary for such a system to keep expanding the numbers of characters in order to represent new concepts and objects. In fact, what happened was that the 'Japanese characters', once taken from China, grew mostly by incorporating two systems of phonetic symbols (*Katakana* and *Hiragana*) into the previously iconic system. *Hiragana* is used for the phonetic writing of Japanese words while *Katakana* is used mostly for writing foreign words (although European words are also often incorporated by using the alphabet). Thus, *kanji* is intrinsically expandable and incomplete. The fact that it continues to operate by incorporating different systems reflects its inherent flexibility and ability

to coexist with other systems. In other words, it is inclusive rather than exclusive and potentially infinite.

So far, I have restricted myself to characteristics of the written text which display direct parallels with those of the city itself although, as yet, the connections are at best inferred. There is another point I wish to make which, if laboured may seem too much like digression but if kept short is pertinent and concerns the structure of the language. In English and most modern European languages, one progresses in a sentence from the subject via the verb to the object – which again is a very linear and logical sequence. In Japanese, this is not so. The key element which most determines the meaning of the sentence (i.e. the verb) follows subject and object. Thus an Englishman or Frenchman is committed to a particular line of expression at an earlier stage. The Japanese has more flexibility and the listener is kept repeatedly in some greater measure of suspense awaiting indication of past, present, future, command, request, question or whatever. In English, and other European languages (Hungarian and Finnish are, I am told, the exceptions) it is necessary to plan the sentence further in advance. Thus the language is in this way part of the Western rationalist tradition.

Thus, to summarize, Japanese texts consist of strongly independent and powerfully graphic characters, each of which carries meaning. They may be multi-directional in layout and made up of a series of units which are potentially infinite.

24

2.8 *Character and/or Picture? With kanji, the distinction between character and picture can easily blur, as indicated by this newspaper advertisement in which the character is 'hashiru' meaning 'to run'. (Source: Extract from a Shinwa Shoken advertisement, in Nihon Keizai Shimbun, 17 February, 1994)*

2.8

These qualities support a visual organization which is areal and flexible in nature and fundamentally different from its linear and inflexible counterparts in the West where independent, abstract, unidirectional and finite qualities reign.

Further, because characters are pictographic, the line between text and true picture can easily blur. Characters and pictures are more freely mixed than in the West, with some sort of equality between the two. A typical Japanese household receives a massive daily dose of graphics (in newspapers, magazines and their accompanying advertisements) which incorporate *kanji*, *katakana*, *hiragana*, letters of the alphabet, and pictures which are both realistic and stylized (i.e. half way between the far-from-literal *kanji* and pictorial realism). These multiple symbols

appear in vertical and horizontal formats, and at various intermediate angles. They twist, dance and intertwine on the page to give often distinctly cloud-like appearances. In other words, they drift quickly into unstable and complex images with collage and superimposition a staple part of the Japanese visual diet.

Children's texts are no exception and I have to confess that my son's English (e.g. *Sesame Street*, *Toybox*) and Japanese (the *Tanoshii Yochien* series) magazines have assisted me greatly in reflecting upon the nature of Japanese city space. Take, for instance, the cover of a *Tanoshii Yochien*. It is brimming with countless images of the many characters, puzzles, toys, animals and other things which appear (and sometimes do not appear) between its covers. Drawings, photographs, several colour backgrounds and geometries, vertical and horizontal writing in four systems and numerous typefaces are scattered but packed over the page. The many images, whether large or small, of heroes (Ultraman, Sailor Moon) or the inconsequential, seem to compete with each other on equal terms across the entire surface of the page. All things partly obscure each other including the text. It is an intricate collage with no obvious centre and no clear edge.

How differently English language magazines appear, even where their expressed intentions are much the same – literacy, numeracy and creativity. There is invariably a hero (Thomas the Tank Engine in the example shown) at a

2.9 *A Cover from a Japanese Children's Magazine. This cover is a collage of large and small things which enjoy some kind of visual equality over the whole surface of the page. (Source: Tanoshii Yochien, Issue 10, 1995)*

2.9

dominant centre with other elements in a peripheral role of hierarchical support. There is a geometry to the composition: writing is strictly horizontal and its placement is effectively on two 'pillars' and within a 'pediment', through which the beaming star (Thomas) takes centre stage. Neither hero nor text are obscured. There is clarity of all parts. This suggests a very different order to that of its Japanese counterpart. It is altogether simpler and clearer. I might add that

2.10 *A Cover from an English-language Children's Magazine. This cover shows an altogether simpler and more hierarchical order. (Source: Thomas the Tank Engine and Friends, Issue 5, 1995)*

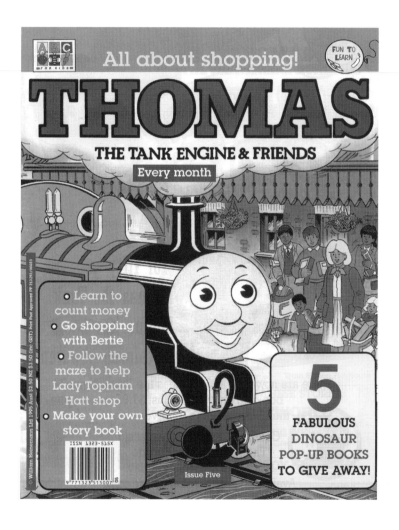

2.10

my son takes in quickly and coldly the English arrangements while lingering long and lovingly over the intricacies of the Japanese pages.

I bring these magazines to your attention for, whenever I see them side-by-side, I am led always to think of cities from the two cultural realms: of Melbourne against Osaka, of Paris against Tokyo, or indeed of Nagasaki (where my wife grew up) against Nottingham (where I spent my childhood). When I imagine most Western cities,

2.11 *Uninterrupted Space. In a Japanese building, partitions were inserted between columns to interrupt 'free space' and movement. In this seventeenth century house, the screens are removed to exhibit uninterrupted space. ('Shisendo' in Kyoto was the home of the poet, Jozan Ishikawa.) (Photograph: Rory Spence)*

I think first of their streets and other spaces and the patterns of relationship between these: of major to minor streets, of monumental buildings to spaces, and of dominant centres to peripheral places. When I think of Japanese cities, I think of scattered points with no clear relationship between each other and often no clear form within themselves. These are themes to which I shall return again and again, and from many different angles.

Finally, if language both reflects and determines the way we think then I have a tale which makes an appropriate ending to this short background beginning. It is the story of a Japanese speech-making competition for foreigners. The judging criteria concerned more than knowledge of the language and included aspects of presentation considered to be more broadly cultural. One candidate, having prepared his speech using Western sequential logic and written it on cards, had the wit to shuffle his cards and speak according to the random order of the shuffled cards. He was duly pronounced the winner!

Buildings

'A Japanese house is generally all on one floor; in fact one might say it is all one floor.'

'A Japanese room sometimes contains other furniture (than a chest of cupboards), but, as a rule, the Japanese is satisfied with the floor, to which he pays extravagant adulation.'

Douglas Sladen, 1903 (Queer Things About Japan, pp. 2 and 4)

I am a visitor to a traditional Japanese house. Having established my credentials I am asked '*agatte kudasai*' (that is, to please step up). Accordingly I step up from the common earth onto the platform floor which is the precious and private or family domain. To step up, even if I have already passed through the door (which is likely) is to enter. Inside the door and under the roof but still on the ground is substantially though not entirely to remain outside. Thus it is the floor which is the key and final defining element that separates inside from out and not the wall.

Indeed the principle of 'wall' in Japanese buildings has long been a negative – in effect, a series of widely and regularly spaced timber posts with nothing between. In this way there exists 'free space' between inside and outside, with the boundary between the two permanently delineated by a change in floor level and of surface. Further, within the building, there is again substantial free space. If the desire is to interrupt this space for whatever reason (privacy, weather, security, etc), then it is by way of light and removable sliding screens and/or suspended blinds. Hence, Ueda's reference to the wall in Japan as 'at most a space partition and an interruption of the line of sight' (Ueda, 1990, p. 37) This point is emphasized by the fact that the tenants of timber framed (post and beam) row houses commonly supplied their own screens to place between the columns much as an Englishman supplied furniture for a terrace house or apartment.

2.12 *Interrupting Space. Here (in Shimabara, Nagasaki) both paper and timber screens (shoji and amado) are to be seen interrupting the space between inside and out. In the foreground, the tatami receive most of the incoming light beneath a shadowy roof – these points are discussed later in the chapter.*

2.13 *Solid Walls and Hinged Doors. In the Western house, these have generally provided the all important dividing line between inside and outside. (The cottages, c.1840, are in Hobart, Australia.)*

2.11

2.12

2.13

Thus, for the relatively few Westerners who set foot into common Japanese buildings prior to World War II, the experience could not have seemed more at odds with the notions of building that they carried with them from their home countries. In England, there is an old saying that 'the Englishman's home is his castle' where the wall is the all important element in what amounts to the family fortress. It is generally the wall in the West that has provided the line of demarcation between inside and out. The wall is a solid, secure and *positive* element which is only

29

2.14 *Removing Shoes. Outside-tainted shoes are removed before 'stepping up' onto the area of the floor and thus entering the house.*

2.14

interrupted for the purposes of vision, light or movement – and then effectively by 'cutting out' holes in the form of windows and doors from the usually masonry walls. In this way, Japanese and Western concepts of 'wall' are complete opposites: in the former, something flimsy is hung within the void while in the latter, a hole or void is cut from a substantial solid. Ueda's experience of London's solid-walled suburbia (the fact that a neighbouring pianist could not be heard) surprised him: consequently, he wrote of 'the tenacity of the Western attitude toward the wall' (Ueda, 1990, p. 36).

Further, the importance of the floor in Japan is underlined by its treatment – with god-like respect. No earth-soiled shoe ascends from outside to contaminate the floor which, for centuries, has been the surface for sitting, sleeping and other 'clean' activities normally raised in the

West from floor to chair, table or bed height. On entering a Japanese house, shoes are removed and left in that in-between but undercover 'entry' space at ground level before stepping up and 'in'. In this context, the floor is an elevated platform but spatially continuous, potentially visible and accessible from the outside yet independent and uncontaminated by it.

In the West, however, it is the wall that has received greatest attention and respect. A significant rise from ground to floor levels was by no means essential and there has certainly been no requirement to part with one's shoes before enjoying an interior. If there are steps to a raised floor level, it is more to do with grandeur, ostentation, authority or drainage than anything else and then the steps are built up solidly from the ground – man-made perhaps but solid extensions of the earth itself. To exclude the outside, a door was hung (conceptually, a hinged piece of wall) in the hole through the very solid wall to provide the threshold between out and inside. In addition the wall was invariably patterned or decorated, and sometimes meticulously proportioned, with windows and particularly doors given special decorative treatment. Indeed, for much of Western history, walls have been built out of one thing and given a decorative overlay of something else. The Romans built with brick and concrete but surfaced these with decoration borrowed from the Greeks and sculpted from fine stone. The Renaissance and Baroque eras did likewise, with stucco increasingly to the fore as a surface material, and the Victorians, of course, hid their structural materials behind stage-set surfaces lifted from the whole of Western history as well as from miscellaneous exotic settings. Even Gothic, honest though it was in showing its structural material as wall surface, was still highly decorated.

Perhaps there is no stronger indication of the importance of the wall in the West than in the work of the Renaissance architect, Alberti. He earned himself a place in the history books on the basis of his writing and surprisingly few architectural works – just six to be precise of which four were concerned primarily with exterior remodelling (Fleming *et al.*, 1972, pp. 10–11) and these seem to have gained the lion's share of subsequent attention. Thus it is the Palazzo Rucellai and Church of Sta. Maria Novella street facades alone which gained for these buildings a place in almost every general history of Western architecture. Both works result from the wishes of a powerful Florentine (Giovanni Rucellai) to give a fashionable 'face' to his city and the wider world. This contrasts markedly with the dominant Japanese building tradition where a building design was the floor plan from which the carpenter/master builder proceeded to work: elevation and section were, more or less, superfluous.

Now let us consider the structure of the building within which that floor is set. In Japan, it is a simple timber post and beam construction with columns spaced upon a grid (albeit with jointing justly famous for its sophistication): within this,

'wall' panels and openings are of a standard size. In other words, it is modular, a quality which so appealed to the early Modernists. Add to this the minimal decoration and there is a certain neutrality about the structure that can offer an experience in which all sides look much alike. The result is a structure which, ground space permitting, can advance in any direction by the simple addition of the same.

Compare this with principles of composition which have long been prominent in Western architecture. Visual order has been imposed by way of axial planning, (plan, volumetric and elevational) symmetry, and even the manipulation of compositional elements (columns, porticoes, pediments, etc.) to exaggerate these qualities or alternatively 'perfect' them against the distorted perceptions of the human eye. Such notions have cumulatively become part of the Western architect's palette over a period of at least three millennia. Thus in buildings from the Parthenon (fifth century BC) through Palladio's Villa Capra (sixteenth century) to Terry Farrell's 'Villa Quattro' (1986), nothing may be added or taken away without destroying the overall concept. While I realize that relatively few buildings may quite possess the 360° perfection of these examples, it reflects nevertheless a strong tendency in Western design to control and design overall form. Much more common has been symmetry on a 'primary' and more decorated elevation to give a strong sense of frontality which has generally been lacking in Japanese design. Thus there has been

2.15 *360 Degree Western Perfection. Palladio's Villa Capra (1567) and Terry Farrell's competition entry, Villa Quattro, of 1986. (Source: Farrell, 1986)*

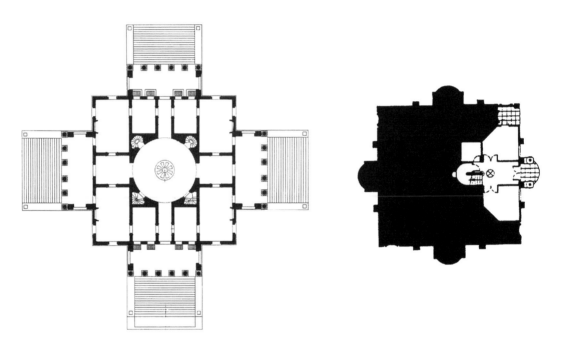

2.15

a strong tendency in Western design towards either finite solutions or ones in which growth is achieved easily in only a single or limited direction.

On another matter of flexibility, the traditional Japanese building exhibits a further quality that warrants comparison with the West, namely its flexibility of use. Rarely have functions in Japanese buildings been so tied to particular spaces as in the West. A space in the Japanese home for instance (kitchen and bathroom excepted) is not so much designated by its form but rather by the activity that it supports at a particular time. The rectilinear grid within which columns occur, the neutral decor and the capacity to amalgamate with or close off from neighbouring spaces give it a flexibility which surprises many Westerners. The very room which I am using to write these words (in a new house but built in a traditional manner) may change its function thrice within a day. When not in use, it is empty and neutral, save for a small wall-clock – like an anonymous cardboard box awaiting the arrival of unknown contents. Given myself and a small table with fold-up legs, it is my

2.16 *Hibachi. Three types of hibachi are shown, as depicted by Morse in 1886. Unlike the Western fireplace, the hibachi was portable and placed on the floor: as such it was central but flexible. Also, they could be individualized and scattered (i.e. decentralized) over the surface of the floor as in 'hibachi arranged for company'. By contrast, the Western fireplace was fixed and part of the wall, and usually had an axial relationship with the room. (Source: Morse, 1972)*

study. In the evening, futons are unrolled to displace the table and transform the space to 'bedroom'. With neither table nor futons in sight but boxes of toys and a fold-up slide-cum-climbing frame, it is a playground for visiting toddlers: when this occurs the 'room' is likely to more than double its size by amalgamation with the next, which is just as flexible. Likewise, at double size, it will be a dining room for visiting members of the extended family on a festival day.

Here, the contrast with the West requires no elaborate explanation. For centuries, whenever income has allowed, the Western house has displayed a hierarchy of rooms from highly decorated to plain, from large to small with a range of materials for floors, ceilings and walls to indicate both function and status.

In most of Europe, no feature placed a room's function and status (the two are closely related) more clearly in the household than the fireplace – by the use of elaborate to utilitarian ironwork, stonework, woodwork, tiles, murals or whatever. In or out of use, winter and summer alike, it was a protruding centre-piece from the line of the feature wall in the (often symmetrical and axial) organization of each room.

In complete contrast, the Japanese family would gather around a small portable fireplace, the *hibachi*, usually placed centrally on the floor. In its most common form, it was a metal-lined wooden box or ceramic pot for burning charcoal. 'The hibachi', wrote Morse, 'is a sort of portable fireplace, around which the family

Fig. 197. — Common Hibachi.

Fig. 198. — Hibachi.

Fig. 199. — Hibachi.

Fig. 200. — Hibachi arranged for Company.

2.16

gather to gossip, drink tea, or warm their hands' (Morse, 1972, p. 216). In other words, although the equivalent of the Western hearth, it was very different. This tradition continued with the *hori gotatsu* and continues with the *denki kotatsu*. In the former, a ceramic pot would sit in a pit on the floor beneath a low table (feet would dangle in the pit) towards the centre of the floor. During the warmer months, the missing floor square would be replaced, the heating place rendered invisible by a *tatami* mat. Even during the winter, the actual heat source would be invisible – under the table. Today, the *denki kotatsu* (a low movable table with an electric heating element attached to its underside) continues the tradition of a shifting, flexible and inconspicuous centre of gravity in most households.

Further, the hearth is only one of several centres in the Japanese house which enjoy some sort of spiritual centrality. These include the *daikoku-bashira* or chief timber pillar of religious significance, and of course the family (Buddhist) temple. The *daikokubashira* is closely related to the Shinto belief in the divinity of trees for it is the tree (trunk) by which a god may descend to the earth or in which he (or she) might otherwise reside. The temple is the place for the spirits of the family's ancestors. In addition, there may be Shinto shrines protecting the house from various aggressors, particularly from fire. In other words, there exists in the Japanese house some kind of decentralized co-existence of multiple spiritual centres with different but equal roles.

Finally, no element speaks louder of the Japanese attitude toward the floor than the mat of which the floor is visually composed. As one steps up to the platform floor, the dominant pattern to strike the eyes is that of the rectangular floor units. I refer, of course, to what is perhaps the best-known element in the Japanese house, the *tatami* mat. *Tatami* appeared in Japan over one thousand years ago but came to cover whole areas in the Shoin style of residence at about the same time as the Renaissance was taking root in Europe, namely in the fifteenth century. Thereafter, it became even more common such that by the Meiji period it was to be found in almost all homes, and today even the so-called 'Western style' houses usually include a *tatami* room. A *tatami* is a soft light-coloured straw mat bounded usually on its longer sides by dark cloth. Each mat measures approximately 2 m by 1 m, this being determined by its capacity to take one person at rest endowing each with a good measure of functional and visual autonomy.

The pre-eminence of the floor over other surfaces is reinforced by being blessed with the lion's share of incoming light; the other surfaces appearing, to varying degrees, shadowy. The size of the *tatami* is also consistent with the placement of the columns and other vertical elements within the building to give the floor mat even greater visual authority. When screens are drawn apart or removed, the pattern of these identical units extends throughout the visible building.

2.17 *A Tatami Floor.*

2.17

However, they are rarely placed in regular parallel sequence which would only serve to create axes, lines and emphasize perspective. They lie mostly with two short ends to one long side and so visually break up the floor into a patchwork of areas. Indeed, mats are usually arranged in a spiral formation. This has the effect of keeping the eye within the space and deters it from moving along a line towards any particular focus (e.g. shrine). The orientation is effectively towards the centre emphasizing the room as area.

If asked the size of a room, a Japanese can estimate easily in *tatami*. This is not an obvious calculation for one has to remember that it is an oblong and not a square unit. A Westerner, faced with the same question is likely to estimate linear dimensions, i.e. wall-to-wall lines. The Western mind is not inclined to think quickly of area.

Where measurements are actually taken, the significance of the wall in the two cultures is again marked by contrast. In Europe, room dimensions are from the inside of one wall to the

2.18 *Some Tatami Floor Patterns. Mats are rarely placed in patterns that emphasize perspective but rather to accentuate area: mats are commonly placed in a spiral formation.*

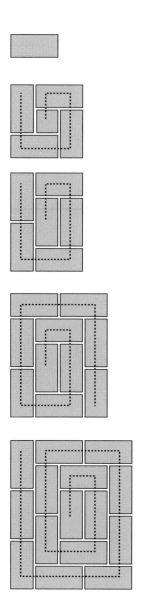

inside of the opposite wall. But in Japan, the measurement is taken from the mid-point of one post to the mid-point of the next, thus 'walls' are effectively disregarded.

It is such phenomena in Japanese and Western building design that have led the Japanese architect and academician, Yoshinobu Ashihara to refer to Japanese traditional building as an 'architecture of the floor' in opposition to that of the West which he describes as an 'architecture of the wall'. (Ashihara, 1983) It is undoubtedly *the floor* that has dominated traditional Japanese architecture while *the wall* has enjoyed the equivalent dominance in Europe. The wall is, of course, a *linear* element in building while the floor is an *areal* one. And in Japan the importance of this is made abundantly clear by the composition of the floor as an elevated patchwork of visually-articulated rectangular units of human dimension.

Lastly, it should be noted that the floor enjoys an independence denied the wall. The floor is a single autonomous platform and nothing makes this point more evident than the wooden sitting platforms that were once commonly found in parks and gardens. To the Westerner, they might resemble a large, low outdoor table. For the Japanese, it was the floor upon which one sat cross-legged or sprawled to view nature beyond as one might from a pavilion, but roofless and therefore also columnless. A wall, however, does not exist independently and define an inside from out. Like the letters of the alphabet, it depends

2.18

2.19 *Floor v Wall. The floor (singular) has been the main Japanese element to define 'inside' (bottom) while the walls (plural) have been the main elements to define 'inside' in the West (top). Screens or blinds are hung in the former to interrupt space between outside and in, while in the latter, holes are cut in the solid to establish connection.*

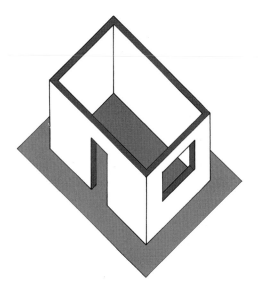

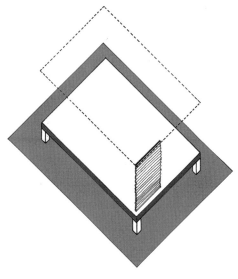

2.19

upon connections with similar elements in order to fulfil its task.

Although focusing upon architecture, the same key words surface in this section as in the last. In the case of Japan, area is again to the fore, this time equating with floor and *tatami*. Both enjoy a high measure of autonomy and form a basis for simple extensions in any direction – a kind of patchwork growth They also offer flexibility of use and surface for shifting centres which are never very conspicuous, sometimes invisible and without obvious hierarchy. In the case of the West, it is the line of the wall which is dependent upon like parts in order to complete the task of spatial demarcation.

While I have written this section mostly in the present tense, infact I refer to traditions. Clearly less and less Japanese live in wooden houses and fewer Westerners live in buildings with a linear front-to-back hierarchical progression of (load-bearing) wall-defined spaces. However, in both instances, millions do. Few Japanese would not have a *tatami* floor in their home and even fewer would fail to treat one with respect. Whatever their home may be, few Japanese would not gravitate to a central and shiftable heat source within it. Similarly, in bleak weather, few Westerners would not be comforted by the warmth of real flames from an ornate central fireplace backed by the solidity of a protective wall. Many are still perplexed when faced with anything other than a solid hierarchical arrangement of rooms. Few would not appreciate a grand

and well-composed building front. And so on. Moreover, increasing numbers in both cultural realms flock to those places which preserve and publicly display these long-established features. Indeed, the last two decades have witnessed the reappearance of many traditional features in the home and greater value placed on those older buildings which have never lost them. Whether we like it or not, the design principles embodied in (the two models) of our respective pasts are part of the cultural baggage which, for better or worse and to varying degrees, we continue to carry with us.

Cities

'The latest edition of the official Tokyo map, running to more than two hundred pages, nowhere mentions the abortive American street plan.* Ask a cabdriver to take you to Yoyogi Street and he will sadly shake his head. To him Yoyogi is a district, not a street.' (*a post-war American attempt to name the city's streets)

Bernard Rudofsky, 1965 (The Kimono Mind, pp. 275–76)

I shall imagine for a moment that I have been whisked in the dead of night from an airport or station to a house in an unfamiliar city. At morning light, I am cast out into the street and have the task of placing myself. I have a map and my eyes to fathom my location.

If in a Western city, I must first look for the street name and the number of the house. The name of the street will be set horizontally on a small signboard which is likely to be attached either to the wall of the corner building or to a free-standing post at the street corner. Either way, it will point along the line of the street. The street is a linear element and its buildings line up on both sides in strict numerical sequence. In all likelihood, even numbers will be on one side and odd ones on the other which is all very linear, logical and sequential. In the wider setting of the city, streets join with streets to form a network or lattice which provides the basic organizational framework. Streets have been named in English towns for at least a millennium and the numbering system in common use today is about two centuries old. For instance, most London houses had street numbers by the late eighteenth century as did many French houses (Garrioch, 1994, p. 37). From maps that I have perused, early numbering in England seems to have been '1, 2, 3 etc' on each side of the street with the modern system of odd and even numbers on opposite sides taking root in the early nineteenth century.

In a Japanese city, however, I look not for a horizontal street sign but for a vertical signboard which is usually attached to the very corner of one or other side of the corner-turning building or wall 'rounding' two anonymous streets. If the corner is chamfered it will probably appear on the diagonal cut across the corner. Whichever, the board will give the number of the 'chome' which is an areal unit, and the name of the 'machi' which is a larger areal unit into which a collection of chome nest. The chome approxi-

2.20 *Street Signs, Lincoln, England. The writing, form and placement of the signs indicate the names and lines of streets.*

2.21 *Machi Sign, Imai-cho, Nara Prefecture. The writing, form and placement of the sign indicates the name and area of the machi and chome.*

2.22 *Network and Patchwork. In the Western city, streets combine to form a network of formed spaces (top) but in Japan, the streets are subsidiary to a patchwork of areas – machi, cho, chome (bottom).*

2.20

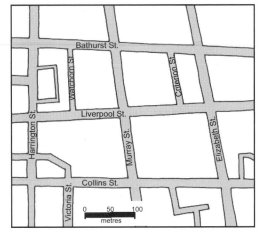

2.21

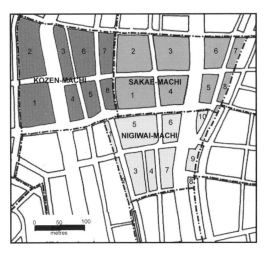

2.22

mates to a Western street block but may not, as with most things Japanese, be quite that regular. It is, however, in contrast to the street, an areal unit. The placement of the sign on a chamfered corner is significant for the diagonal enables the sign to signify more accurately the area. It is not unusual in Japan for a street corner property to have its boundary fence or building wall cut at an angle to allow for better viewing and turning in the characteristically narrow streets and this is especially common in newer suburbs.

Within these *chome* and *machi*, property numbers may not occur sequentially but be dotted seemingly haphazardly (often in order of subdivision or building) over the land's surface. In this situation, anonymous streets may either occur within these areas or as dividing lines between them: in other words they are not the lines of unifying identity as in the West. Thus the *chome* nest within the *machi*, and together form part of a layered patchwork or mosaic which forms the city's organizational framework.

Kurokawa is keen to point out that for many centuries Japanese cities were in fact organized on a street system. For instance, he notes, (by reference to Kazuhiko Yamori's *Toshizu no Rekishi or History of City Plans*) that a change occurred in the late ninth and tenth centuries: from a system in which the streets were 'like rivers separating or encircling communities' to one in which they became the communal focus for people on both sides of the street who were employed in common trades (hence names such as *Konya-machi* or dyers' district and *Kamiya-machi* or paper merchants' district). Only in recent times, according to Kurokawa, has that purported street focus been lost – with new 1962

laws which introduced a system of districts and wards (Kurokawa, 1994, pp. 160–161).

This may be misleading. The street was not the long linear unit of the Western variety. Even in its most regular form, the street existed as *part* of the *machi* area and included portions of cross-streets. The difference is important. In fact, of the many town maps that I have viewed from the Edo period, most show considerable variety in the delineation of *machi*. This is certainly the case in the collection of Edo maps dating from 1849 to 1863 which appear in Shiraishi's beautifully presented *Edo Kiriezu to Tokyo Meisho-e*. Here, while the *machi* name may sometimes be written in the street space, it includes the plots on both sides of the street and parts of the cross-streets within the same areal unit. However, the *machi* are far from regular and occur also in single block widths (i.e. from street to street), two block widths (i.e. from one street through to a third street to include a middle street) as well as in many other irregular arrangements. In other words, the areal or patchwork base of the city is ever present. Indeed, the very suggestion that the city was street-based may itself reflect a (Japanese) perception that has difficulty in appreciating fully the linear nature of the Western street and its links with the organizational structure and imagery of the city.

Some places have adopted sequential street-based numbering (i.e. Western) systems for addresses including the most northernly and newest of Japan's larger cities, Sapporo, the pre-

2.23 *Machi in the Ginza District, Edo, 1861. Few names of machi appear on the street on the original map. The accompanying map identifies more clearly the areas of each machi and shows these to be neither regular nor linear. (Source: Shiraishi, 1993; original in Edo Kiriezu, 1861)*

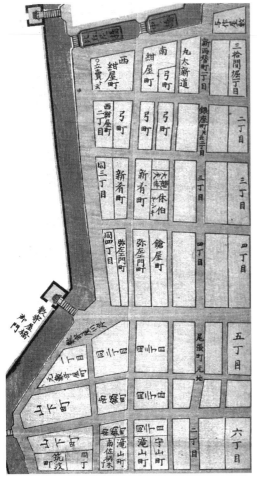
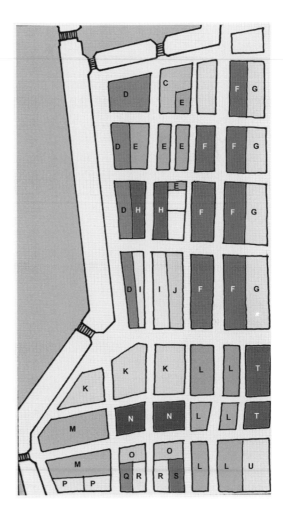

2.23

fectural capital of Hokkaido. However, in most other places, it is different. In Tokyo at least, this is in spite of the Americans who, during their occupation, tried to impose a system of street names: this was resisted, or at least ignored, in favour of areal familiarity (Rudofsky, 1965,

2.24 *Small Subdivisions in Nagasaki. They display numbering over an area rather than along a (street) line. (Source: Adapted from advertising leaflets of the Ryoko House and Nagasaki-ken Jutaku Kyokyu Kosha building companies, Nagasaki)*

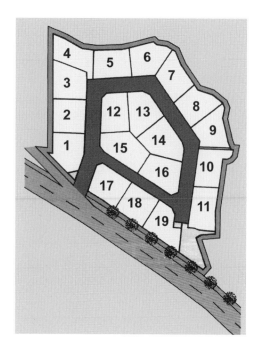

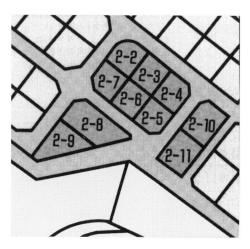

2.24

pp. 275–276). Thus most places persist with tradition and numbers may perplex Westerners even in new subdivisions. For instance, those Nagasaki subdivisions shown below are quite typical. In the first, the road is of a lollipop shape (a 'stick' from the highway connecting with a small 'loop'). The allotment numbers run around the top or outer edge (nos. 1–11) and then in rows to the bottom edge. It is a pragmatic 'across the block' coverage rather than one generated by the concept of a street as a linear spatial focus. The street is seen rather as the necessary route (functional) to connect the plots which are spread across the landscape from one side to the other of the subdivided area. In other words, the plots are conceived more in relation to the larger area of the original land plot than to the street which is placed on the land to serve them. The second example is an even more irregular patchwork.

Another element in the towns of the Edo period which certainly emphasized area was the *kido* gate. During this time the very experience of traversing a town was one of passing through numerous gates across the streets. These gates (often a combination of watchman's hut and gate) separated one area from the next, again to emphasize area as a building block of Japanese urban structure. The watchman's huts were probably forerunners of the ubiquitous police boxes to be found in strategic locations (especially on corners) in each district of the modern city.

2.25 *Kido (gate). A typical form and corner location. (Source: Nishimura, 1985)*

2.25

In addition to the general areas delineated by gates, there might also be one delineated by walls for occupation by a special group. The commonest example was the pleasure quarter or 'city of the night'. In exotic Nagasaki, there were also special areas designated for foreigners. The Dutch were given a man-made island, walled and with a single bridge (and gate) point of entry. The Chinese were confined to a walled and gated hillock immediately to the south of the city (the present-day Kannai-cho). The most famous of all pleasure quarters in the history of Japan was in Edo: Yoshiwara was reached by way of an embankment and was also walled and gated. These areas were thought to require special control by the authorities. In fact, they were but an extreme version of the general areal division

– tethered to the contiguous areas of the town yet displaced from them. In other words, they were pieces of the patchwork but displaced from the main clusters.

It is not irrelevant to leave the city's patterns for a moment and consider those of the country for city patterns are so often born of country ones before them. I have had the opportunity to observe for a great many hours the Japanese countryside from the vantage point of railway carriages. Trains in Japan, especially of the faster variety, spend most of their time, even in the country, travelling over or under the landscape rather than on it. They offer, therefore, either superb views or no view at all and, from above, I have looked down with great fascination at the patterns of fields – although 'allotment' or 'plot' may be a better term, for 'field' seems too generous for what they are. Over a century ago, similar patterns prompted lady-adventurer Isabella Bird to note 'The rice fields are usually very small and of all shapes. A quarter of an acre is a good-sized field' (Bird, 1880, p. 36). Little has changed in many districts.

Small size apart, the first characteristic to strike the Western eye is their clear boundaries. Delineation comes from a raised perimeter walkway, drainage ditch, wall, retaining wall, terrace edge, fence, small windbreak, netting, or, as is often the case, some combination of these. The patterns vary from place to place. On flatter land, plots tend (but only tend) to be more rectilinear – often the result of land rationalization or

2.26 *An Agricultural Landscape. Numerous small plots step and bend with the contours. This photograph dates from the mid-1930s: many cities have since grown over this kind of landscape pattern. (Source: Taut, 1937)*

2.26

reclamation. Where relief is stronger, they are of all shapes and sizes with bowed and snaking edges curving and stepping with the contours. But even on the reclaimed (Dutch-like) flatlands, there are frequently (un-Dutch-like) irregularities (like a distorted Mondrian painting). The smallest plots can be tiny by any agricultural standard – literally just a few square metres. The resulting patterns can be quite extraordinary and an inspiration for any patchwork artist.

In some places the land is dominated by rice cultivation, but in others there are varieties of growth: vegetables, fruit trees, tree saplings, tea, flowers, etc. Everywhere, however, whatever the crops, there are distinct boundaries between the plots which serve only to reinforce the image of the landscape as patchwork. Further, the positions of houses and other buildings and their relationships with the farmed plots are also important in the making of the patchwork. Sometimes, houses will sit in some understandable formation – for instance, on a terrace above swampy ground or in relation to some other physical form. But equally often houses are scattered with no obvious order. Here, each house plot will rise from the surrounding landscape and on it, the house will sit within its boundary walls like some compact version of a samurai's house. Sometimes, the edges of the house will almost touch the surrounding plot walls. Other times the plot will be raised to a considerable and inexplicable height like some truncated castle fortification above its slightly concave rock (more recently, straight but angled concrete) retaining walls.

The characteristic, however, which gives final emphasis to the patchwork is the hidden pattern of ownership. In the older landscapes, the land patches immediately about a particular house do not necessarily belong to it. There is indeed a patchwork of ownership, the result of land divisions upon death, additions through marriages, sales, gifts, transfers in lieu of debts, etc. Thus a house may have many and unconnected plots of various sizes scattered about it, within and beyond its field of vision. It was a phenomenon

2.27 *A 'Fragmented Farm'. This shows just a few of the scattered plots (shaded) held by one farmer in a small hillside village some 20 km from Nagasaki. The dot shows the position of the house. His holdings also include many more plots beyond the boundaries of the map – in all, about ninety plots ranging in size from just a few to*

approximately 20,000 square metres and in altitude from a sea-level swamp to over 250 m over a distance of nearly 2 kilometres. While land consolidation schemes have rationalized much Japanese land, this dispersed and fragmented three dimensional phenomenon is very much part of the Japanese heritage.

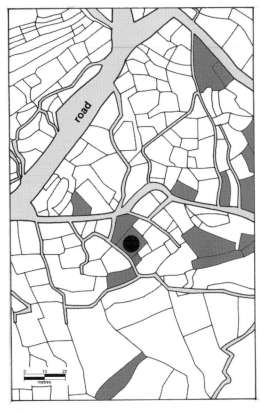

2.27

that made a big impression on architect Bruno Taut when he referred (in 1937) to cadastral plans which 'showed an immense dismemberment of the soil, particularly in the extremely scattered situation of the different properties or leaseholds, some of which, although farmed by the same tenant or owner, would be widely separated from one another' (Taut, 1937, p. 219).

Today, as I look over such scenes, the patches can have a strange sense of equality and autonomy, with each seemingly capable of sprouting rice, fruit, flowers, vegetables or buildings. Indeed, the land surface gives the distinct impression of having been smashed into assorted fragments from which individuals have picked up the pieces and then laid these out randomly yet somehow retained their original ownership. The result is a truly remarkable patchwork or mosaic, part visible and part hidden.

In other words, the equivalent of a Western 'farm' may be a dispersed collection of fragments. It is no simple system equating with, for instance, the linear strips found under collective control in the English medieval strip farming system (and which may still be witnessed at Laxton village, Nottinghamshire, to this day). It is more piecemeal and individualistic and certainly the antithesis of the rational and rectilinear land patterns of the New World and Australia. Thus, fragmentation and discontinuity in the landscape are a part of the Japanese cultural heritage and second nature.

Moreover, it was on this kind of fragmented farming landscape that much city development took place and continues to do so. Thus it is on such rural patchworks that much urban transformation has occurred. Today, from those raised railway tracks that criss-cross the nation and its cities, it is possible to look down on vast areas that are neither true city nor country. They are most definitely both. Only the densest nodes within the so-called cities of Japan have exclusively urban land uses. Likewise, few farming landscapes (as distinct from wooded or mountain landscapes) are free from petrol stations, love hotels, gambling parlours, golf driving ranges and the like. There is no slim zonal ring which separates the built-up city from the farming country. The liveable and farmable 30 per cent of Japan is for the most part a vast amorphous urban-agricultural jumble. As most Dutchmen may be said to be urban and most Australians suburban, so most Japanese are from areas which have a scattered rural or urban presence within their predominantly urban or rural surrounds.

The process of change from rural to urban is one of random patchwork transformation: the established patchwork nature of the landscape merely intensifies. To rice, tea, vegetable, fruit and farmhouse plots are added hospitals, schools, houses, offices, shops, petrol stations, car parks and dozens of other urban and even new agricultural (e.g. Christmas trees) phenomena. Many farmed plots will also support advertising hoardings. These activities are not grouped but quite interspersed. Nevertheless, the definition of each plot persists to emphasize the autonomy of each and the patchwork nature of the whole.

In these landscapes, there are factory and commercial buildings standing over the entireties of their sites with their walls a few centimetres within the blank walls of the site boundaries. There are plots of tarmac for car-parking with neat concrete boundaries and thick white lines about the rectangular parking lots within. There are closely packed but nevertheless free-standing houses each within its own walled territory. (Higher densities are achieved amongst free-standing houses in Japan than amongst many English terrace or row houses, again emphasizing the importance and independence of the plot.) There are apartment buildings and sometimes plots of compressed car bodies piled high with vertical edges to give box-like volumes. There are, of course, remaining agricultural plots whose owners continue fiercely to farm (the land tax system encourages it). And much more. In this rich mix, the tallest building in an area may even be a tall but slim (two-car-wide) parking station within which parked cars rotate on a machine resembling a squashed-up ferris wheel. It will stand straight, blank (that is with no windows but not without a graphic presence) and very tall to peer down over its lower mixed-use neighbours. Multifarious urban and agricultural phenomena sit, stand on and burrow over and into their particular patches with remarkable visual and functional autonomy. 'The evolution of the urban environment in Japan' writes Bognar, 'indicates that the city is created, perceived and understood as an additive texture (text?) in which preference is given to the parts in a network (patchwork?) of "independent" places' (Bognar, 1985, p. 67).

Further, while in many Japanese cities there may be few large areas of flat land, there are

2.28 *A Mixed Urban and Agricultural Landscape. This scene straddles the Shin Ome Road in Higashi Yamato City, some 40 km west of central Tokyo. (Courtesy: Tokyo Metropolitan Government)*

2.28

also, once developed, few slopes as such. There are instead embankments and retaining walls that separate the lots and the connecting roads. Each plot extends absolutely flat over its full area, either cut and filled between embankments, elevated on stilts or even cantilevered out to the extremities of the site over its inclined retaining wall. Come what may, a building will rarely be placed on a plot which is not flat. Thus the landscape, whether hilly or flat, will be transformed into a mosaic of irregular but flat sites and hence a three-dimensional patchwork. The only slopes to be found are the usually narrow streets themselves which serve to connect the independently flat plots. Thus, even this pattern gives continuity

with the past for this kind of patchwork is the urban replacement of an agricultural (mainly rice) landscape that stepped over hillsides in multitudes of small terraces.

In addition, many of the buildings' roofs serve simply as raised ground. Stairs and lifts rise to clothes drying areas, netted play and recreation areas, gardens, etc. Some roofs are complete with fake turf, swings, slides, croquet lawn, plants and shrubs of the edible and ornamental varieties, etc. These raised 'ground covers' often extend over the full area of the plot – ultimate contributions to the three-dimensional patchwork. In Japan, the tradition is, in a very real sense, that of 'constructing the plot' and subsequently 'placing the building' (as distinct from 'surveying the land' and 'constructing the building'). Further, the roof of any structure is potentially another building plot, whatever the level. Hence, a shrine or tea-house may take its place as an independent entity on the roof of a city building much as it would on the ground and in a garden.

There are undoubtedly qualities about this landscape that give the Westerner a frustrating and unfathomable sense of unease. This is, I believe, not so much a result of being unused to the cheek-by-jowl array of contrasting activities or being unable to read the 'written' signs but more a consequence of the visual autonomy of each plot and fragmentation of the whole landscape. Such qualities are quite alien to the ways in which most of the Western world thinks about its cities. Order in the Western city is

2.29 *'Constructing the Plot and Placing the Building'. Suitengu (shrine) stands in its 'grounds' over commercial activity in Kakigaracho, only a short distance from Nihonbashi (bridge) in central Tokyo. The photograph was taken in 1983. (Courtesy: Tokyo Metropolitan Government)*

2.29

underpinned by the notion of street, or even highway as the key visual ordering device.

Since Antiquity, and particularly since the Renaissance, there has been a pre-occupation in Western city planning with axes, symmetry, gateways, grand vistas and monuments and it is the network of streets and squares to which these concepts have been applied. Clearly, these are ideas which are strongly deterministic of the placement and execution of buildings and spaces

in relation to each other. These are long and established practices of intervention and control of city form although more informal (irregular and organic) ideas have joined the more formal ideas passed down from earlier times.

Nevertheless, the essential element about which modern townscape planning has evolved is the street or at least the linear spatial experience. This was central to the now century-old work of Camillo Sitte who may, through his landmark publication *Der Stadtbau* (1889), be regarded as the grandfather of modern 'townscape' planning. For Sitte, the network of city streets and squares provided the collective (spatial) form to which all individual buildings might contribute or detract and which therefore required some form of guidance or control. Foundation works which brought townscape theory into contemporary practice also emphasized linear or sequential spatial phenomena. The notion of 'serial vision' was to the fore in Gordon Cullen's *Townscape* (1961) and, at about the same time, Kevin Lynch (1960) posited the linear path as the key element about which the visual and functional items of a city are organized in the viewer's image. Roger Trancik's *Lost Space* (1986) and Ian Bentley and colleagues' *Responsive Environments* (1985) are more recent urban design works (from the west and east sides of the Atlantic respectively) that continue to emphasize the public domain of streets and squares as linear and nodal formed urban spaces about which buildings should be organized and controlled in the making of urban form. Even Robert Venturi and company in their study of Las Vegas (1972) were preoccupied with patterns of linear order in their exploration of the physical form of the city's highway strip.

In the 1970s 'streetscape' tended, in Australia at least, to replace 'townscape' as the more common term in urban design practitioners' reports reflecting an attitude that emphasized the protection and improvement of the collective form of the street through the conservation of existing buildings, control of the appearance of new buildings and improvement of the street itself. In conservation planning, the keeping of an individual building was seen to lose part of its worth if it was to be kept independent of its (usually street) context. Indeed, in design, 'urban contextualism' is an approach whereby the form of a building is derived from the analysis or at least observation of its surrounding (again mainly street) context and this became very strong in the 1980s especially in the English-speaking world. Brent Brolin's book, *Architecture in Context* (1980) reflected well those sentiments. (Significantly, it is a term borrowed from linguistics where the meaning of a word is interpreted according to its relationship with the wider text.)

Some cities have gone to extraordinary lengths to ensure that contextual criteria, mainly centred upon the continuity of street lines (alignments, heights, patterns), are followed in new design, albeit sometimes with dubious results. Even in the relatively mixed form city environments of Australia (compared to the more consistent European ones), design guidelines have been attached to city plans (e.g. Adelaide) to cover (in addition to the above) such items as roof form, materials, building details, retention of old street facades, etc. The chief concern in such cases is for a consistent visual language which has at its heart the linear street and, in turn, the network and hierarchy of linear streets, as the primary formal element about which urban design must revolve.

2.30 *Continuity of Street Form: Adelaide.*

2.31 *Continuity of Street Form: Melbourne. In Adelaide (top) the street-front sections of old buildings have been retained with tower forms behind. In Melbourne (bottom), although the styles of the two infill developments are very* *different, the continuity of building alignment and height along the street is maintained. (The latter buildings are part of the Royal Melbourne Institute of Technology.) In both cities, the authorities wished to maintain the linear form of the street as part of rectilinear street networks. (For a plan of Adelaide's streets and squares, see figure 3.79)*

2.30

2.31

50

2.32 *Street as City Image: Boston.*

2.33 *Street as City Image: Lisburn.*
*From the birth of the postcard in the late
nineteenth century until after the Second World
War, streets as formed linear spaces were the most*

*commonly used views for projecting the faces of
Western cities and even small towns to the world
at large. Two typical views are Washington Street,
Boston, USA (top) and Bow Street Down, Lisburn,
Northern Ireland (bottom).*

Washington Street Downtown Shopping District, Boston, Mass.   B-27

2.32

BOW STREET DOWN, LISBURN.

2.33

51

Further, this notion of the city as a collective structure of linear spaces is not some wishful figment of the professional designer's imagination. It is one that is ingrained in Western culture and nothing brings home this point more clearly than a perusal of old postcards of city scenes. Following the birth of the postcard *circa* 1890, the vast majority of popular picture postcards had the common street as the main subject for many a decade – in fact, until about World War II. Pictures would simply bear the name of the street and city as title with the camera having been lined up from some point at the centre of the space to take-in the lines of buildings on both sides. Thus, the collective setting of the street was considered to be the most appropriate scene to act as a city's ambassadorial image to the wider world.

In the West, it is ideas about the collective form of city spaces, particularly streets, that continue to underpin notions of good city form. Consequently it is the likes of London's Regent Street and Venice's Piazza San Marco which feature in relatively recent urban design primers such as Ed Bacon's *Design of Cities* (1978) and Cliff Moughtin's *Urban Design: Street and Square* (1992). It is even axis, monumental circus, square and building that feature at the centre of London's much criticized flagship of private development – the Docklands. The central ideas in these works are based on established ideas of linear spatial form and associated conventions of urban grammar.

These are, of course, quite the antithesis of the Japanese notion of the city as a patchwork of relatively autonomous plots. In a patchwork model, the street primarily forms a kind of left-over space which serves as the route or service conduit between plots and is born of the necessity to move people and things from one plot to another, although there are other roles. There are those of accommodating local activity (mostly in the form of spill-over activity from the buildings themselves) and as a communication channel (in the sense of transmitting information) and much more will be said of these in later sections. In the network model, the streets are more the public spaces which command a collective respect and stage-set response from the individual developments that line them. In the former, the emphasis is on essentials. In the latter, while no-one would deny a practical role, there is also the very important dimension of visual address. Such a model is rather more deterministic of pattern and form with the Japanese model offering greater flexibility. Thus, we are again comparing a way of thinking that is linked to line (or, collectively, a network of lines) with one that revolves about areas (or collectively a mosaic of patches).

City Maps

Maps are a special kind of city portrait, usually of practical intent. They are made to assist the 'man in the street' (or 'on the plot') to find position, property and place. Techniques of map illustration mirror the way a community thinks about the space of the city and places within. Thus differences in the ways that cities are presented on maps must inevitably reveal something of how cities are perceived in different cultural realms. Generally, older and/or popular maps are most interesting, in contrast to official modern maps for which more or less standard (and essentially Western) conventions have been adopted almost everywhere.

In looking over city maps of the Edo era, several characteristics are likely to surprise Western eyes when compared with our own maps of a similar vintage. The first is that streets are often devoid of writing while plots are very full. This follows from the simple fact that long linear streets did not provide the formal framework of organization in Japan and did not generally therefore support names, consequently there was usually little to write in them. The street was an anonymous 'in-between' space: an exception might be one leading to a special place such as an important temple or shrine, in which case it may bear a name indicating its function as an approach.

On many maps, there will be at least some writing resembling street names, in that the nomenclature of some *machi* appears on the street. Closer inspection will, however, only reveal that this does not refer strictly to the street upon which it is written. For every street that bears a name, there is a cross-street without one. And the names of many *machi* are not written on the street at all but on the blocks between the

streets. Indeed, *machi* often run from one street to another over one, two or even more blocks. Thus, name changes from one side of a street to the other are commonplace. As inferred in the last section, the term '*machi*' does not translate easily into the English 'street'. We are not looking along a single linear strip of frontages but at patches which encompass both the areas of adjacent land plots, streets and cross-streets. This is clearly not your Western network of streets.

The second Japanese characteristic likely to raise a Western eyebrow is that the map has to be rotated through a full 360 degrees in order for its written and pictorial information to be absorbed. The information faces in all directions. On the Western map, every effort is made to line up the writing in a single direction, though because of cross-streets, the map will usually have to be turned through 90 degrees (but only 90 degrees and in a consistent direction) to read the names. This follows partly from Western letters having to be written horizontally and line up along the street. Ironically the more flexible Japanese script would allow the Japanese to achieve the Western map makers' desire for a unidirectional map since their script can be written both horizontally and vertically. In fact, while Japanese maps embraced both vertical and horizontal script, they still insist on the reader rotating the map full circle! No symbol shows this more than the orientation pointer itself. In the West, we have emphasized north, to the extent that only the 'N' point often appeared at the end of a single arrow

2.34 *Edo Period Map – General Characteristics.*
This 1861 map of the Tsukiji district of Tokyo
displays: a multi-directional orientation sign;
irregular machi areas; plots without buildings
excepting an important temple complex; names
on plots rather than streets; and script to be read
through 360 degrees. Generally, it is ground that
dominates the map. (Note also the small black
squares on the streets indicating the location of
watched gates – as described in the last section.)
(Source: Shiraishi, 1993; original in Edo Kiriezu,
1861)

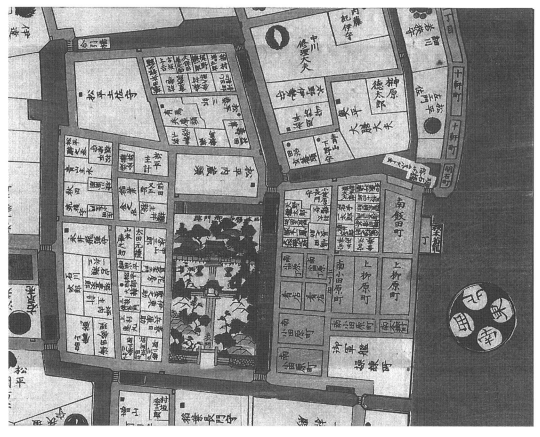

2.34

(and then more or less vertical on the page). The
common direction finder on a Japanese map was
a circle with the four points of the compass
receiving equal emphasis: each character is written in the direction that it represents. Further,
north rarely coincides with the 'top' of the map.

The third unusual Japanese characteristic, and
entirely consistent with the second, is that where
building complexes (usually temple compounds
or shrines and their approaches) are shown, then
aspects of their component buildings, walls
and gardens are also portrayed to face all sides of
the map. Further, they are often shown by a
mix of drawing techniques, with images that
approximate roughly to perspective, volumetric,
elevational and even aerial views sharing the

2.35 *Edo Period Map – Portrayal of Building and Landscape Elements. These have been redrawn as they appeared on a mid-nineteenth century map of Sensoji (temple), Asakusa: they appear in a variety of ways and from several directions – according to how they are commonly experienced. (Source: Adapted from Shiraishi, 1993; original in Asakusu-ezu, 1853)*

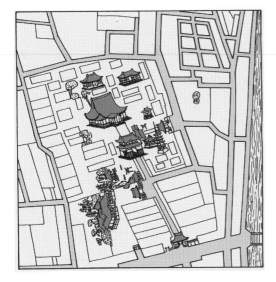

2.35

same map, or even plot. This is again in marked contrast to most Western maps which, in depicting buildings in the vertical dimension, would generally show them consistently from a single viewpoint. Also, Japanese maps commonly combined the city in plan form (plots and streets) with the surrounding landscape, especially hills, in the third dimension. Viewpoints were forever changing with features usually drawn as seen from the routes from which they (hills, trees, gates, shrines, temples, walls, etc.) were most commonly seen. Thus, the maps result from the way in which landscape is experienced.

Lastly, while buildings that do appear are likely to face in different directions, very few buildings are shown at all. Most plots are devoid of buildings thus it is the plots that dominate the maps. The few scattered buildings selected for portrayal are usually important temples and shrines. The equivalent Western map is likely to show all building footprints with perhaps elevations of a few important ones.

To a Westerner, the Japanese maps may be seen to fragment the landscape. The Japanese maps are rather like a cubist painting where one can see on a single surface, many aspects of a three-dimensional object which could not be seen from a single static viewpoint. Considered another way, they may be seen to integrate the landscape for they show it, as it is commonly experienced by the majority of those who move through it. In other words, it is more a product of experience than the Western map which is more one of intellect.

Ashihara has made some related observations about maps. Using more extreme examples, he showed the famous Nolli map of 1748 Rome which depicted buildings and spaces (streets, plazas and even the interiors of public buildings) in black and white alongside an old Edo map (Ashihara, 1983, pp. 58–59). In one version of the Nolli map, buildings are shown as the positive or (black) figure while in the second it is the spaces which are portrayed as the positive: this reflects the strength of the form of buildings and spaces as well as an equality between the mass of the buildings and the void of the spaces in the making of European, and particularly Italian, city landscapes. His Edo map, on the other hand,

2.36 *Modern Multi-directional Map. Old ways persist in many popular maps. This illustration is taken from a tourist map of Kyoto and shows the Higashihonganji (temple) complex and its environs: buildings are represented in plan and elevation and face in all directions. (Source: Ekimae Shuhen Guide Map published by Kyoto Ekimae Shinko Kabushiki Gaisha)*

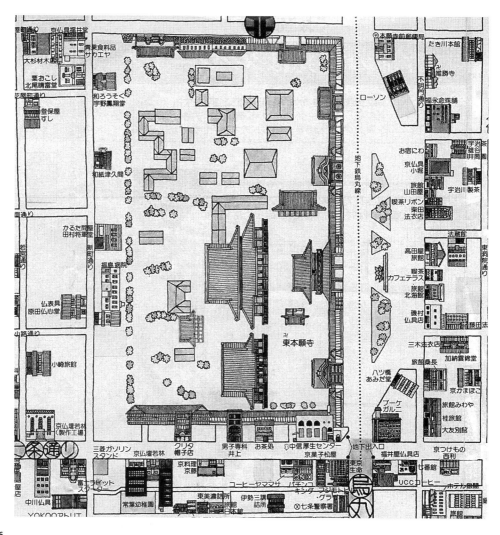

2.36

shows only the plots and anonymous streets reflecting the importance of the land over buildings and, perhaps even more important, the irrele-vance of the figure-ground diagram as a tool for depicting space in the Japanese city.

In Japan, plots bearing family names or areas

2.37 *A Seventeenth Century English Map. This part of a larger map shows the footprints of all buildings plus elevations of a few important ones. Buildings are viewed from a consistent direction. Built form dominates the map. (Source: Barker and Jackson, 1990)*

2.38 *1748 Nolli Map of Rome. Either buildings or spaces may be shown as the positive figure.*

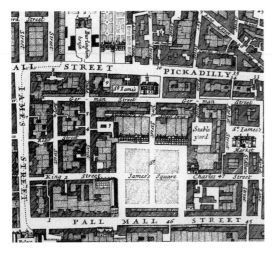

2.37

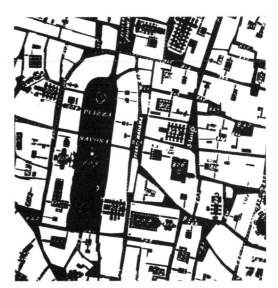

2.38

bearing *machi* names were visually prominent as were street names on Western maps: and multiple viewpoints prevailed as compared with essentially single ones. Further, this graphic representation by the Japanese of their cities seems a very appropriate portrayal of place in a country where the land was (and is) perceived as so much more important than the see-through combustible buildings which stood freely (literally like pieces of gigantic furniture on legs) on plots bounded by high and substantial perimeter walls. Indeed, the common buildings of a city were subsumed by the land over which they relatively fleetingly floated.

In the West (or at least in the old West of Europe and England), buildings were made of the land (stone, and brick), rooted in it (deep foundations), and stood to dominate it. At the same time, they were components in the making of positive spaces in the form of streets and squares.

2.39 *'Rooted' and 'Floating' Buildings. These diagrammatic sections represent a building rooted (deep foundations) and made of the land (stone or brick) (left), and one hovering over its plot behind high perimeter walls like a giant piece of furniture (right).*

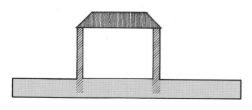
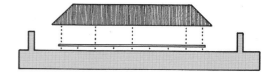

2.39

Thus, the themes which emerge from observing maps only continue those from the previous sections: in short, they again emphasize area (plot and patchwork) and plurality of prospect rather than line (strong building lines and spatial network) and single lines of sight.

Today's popular maps are also revealing. Because of the haphazard nomenclature and numbering systems of most Japanese cities, maps are a common feature of regional and local newspapers, magazine and even billboard advertising. Similarly, it is quite common to be given a map (often faxed these days) on invitation to a Japanese home; and maps appear not infrequently on the backs of business cards. For Roland Barthes, the phenomenon of the hand-drawn map made such an impact during his short Japanese stay that he made them the subject of an article: the Japanese, he wrote, 'excel in these impromptu drawings' (Barthes, 1982, p. 34). The advertisers' maps are but the public equivalents of these private ones and again offer some insight into city structure and its perception.

First, I refer to a map designed to inform pizza lovers of their local pizza palace. The map shows just three primary elements: the areas of the *machi*, the major routes and the pizza building itself. The scores of streets in the area of the map are completely eliminated with just three major road routes and one railway remaining. None of the roads are named or even given a route number. There is no north point or similar direction sign. The boundaries of the *machi* are marked and the name of each is placed centrally within each area. The vital element, the pizza house, is named and marked with a conspicuous red dot. This map is very much a '*tatami* view' of the city: the precious mats, the anonymous or non-existent corridors and a centre (as determined by the task at hand). Further, it is a much distorted map for the *machi* are shown inaccurately both in area and distance to one another. It is a highly stylized map of areal relationships minus the connecting 'streets'.

The most common of the popular direction-finding maps is that which shows selected streets and a few landmarks – and the destination point which is the object of the map. On these maps, there are rarely indications of formal street qualities (e.g. flanking buildings) or name, just route; and

2.40 *Maps for Pizza Eaters. They show the machi areas, anonymous routes, and, of course, the pizza place itself. (Source: Advertising leaflets of Pizza-la, Nishijin, Fukuoka and Pizza-M, Showa-machi, Nagasaki respectively)*

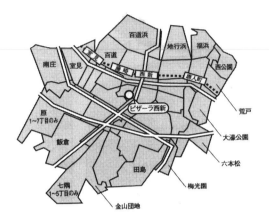

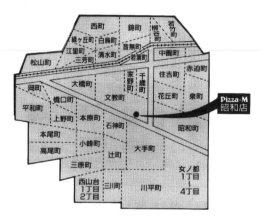

2.40

the landmarks are unlikely to be highly visual (in the Western sense of tower or similarly prominent visual feature) but rather some known prosaic function (such as a bank or police box) as points of reference. Streets are usually represented by anonymous broad black single lines and are carefully selected, straightened, re-orientated and re-scaled. While, in reality, many of the streets do connect, they are severed on the map, so decimating the network. Further these severances are usually finished with rounded ends giving, to Westerners, an impression of cul-de-sac. The points of reference are represented by squares, big solid dots or sometimes symbols. Finally, the rounded street ends usually stop short of the map boundary. The only indication of the relation of the map area to the wider city may be an arrow or two pointing to other known places (e.g. 'to the Aquarium' or to the name of the next town).

The map showing Nagasaki's Yokoo district illustrates these characteristics. For the area concerned, some seventy plus roads are reduced to seventeen and greatly stylized in the process. Six prosaic places are selected (local park, bank, supermarket, school, police box and fire station) as points of reference. Distances are halved or doubled relative to each other depending where you are on the map. Meanders are straightened. In Christopher Alexander's (1966) terms, the lattice has been reduced to something resembling a tree. And because the roads are truncated short of the map's edges, the graphic gives a sense of detachment and autonomy from the wider city.

Indeed, this ubiquitous form of map reads like a large self-contained *kanji* character within a square, which should not surprise for it is devised in much the same way. *Kanji*, as earlier explained, have an iconic parentage. With time

2.41 *The Kanji-like Map showing Nagasaki's Yokoo district. The upper map shows the kanji-like figure of the advertiser. The lower map shows the complexity of the area before the process of minimalist reduction: this map includes the same points of reference as the first. (Source: The kanji-type map is extracted from an advertising leaflet of Kawahara Jutaku Sangyo, Nagasaki)*

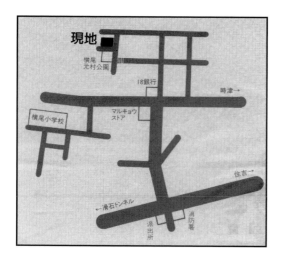

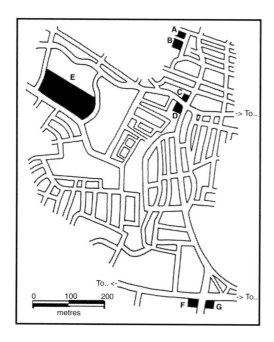

2.41

the more literal early pictograms were reduced, simplified and stylized. In other words, parts of objects were omitted and the relationship between the remaining parts became distorted. Lines were rounded and squared. And so on. In the process of map-making, the surface of the city undergoes similar transformation to result in a graphic that bears the same strikingly bold and autonomous qualities. Thus endless complicated networks of roads are reduced to simple character-like figures to connect a few familiar reference points which offer some sense of areal relationship within the map.

A map detail which is perhaps worthy of note is that where points of reference are represented by solid round dots, these can appear quite independent of the streets. Dots, I have noticed, are not always placed consistently at the street frontage (as might occur on a Western map) but at varying distances from it. Comparison with accurate maps reveals that the dots correspond more to the centre of the plot or building being depicted. This is but a small observation but it is yet another indicator of the Japanese tendency toward area rather than line.

In the West, popular mapping of the city is by no means the same day-to-day occurrence. It is not as necessary as an address can usually be found easily by way of logic or a standard street directory. However, within the built-up city at least, any localized Western map destined for public view is almost certain to be more literal with the street clearly to the fore and portrayed as much more than a simple route. It is likely to give at least some indication of the place as a linear space. Street-making buildings and land-marks (more visual than functional) are located with some sense of scale and orientation. Bends and links in the street are likely to be retained. Where the map is clearly bounded the streets will continue to the boundaries to give a strong sense of being part of a larger and continuous city network, and that what we see is conveyed as a small part of a greater whole.

To conclude, I shall recall an experience which, at the time, took me by surprise but offered some lasting insight. A man drew me a map indicating some of his landholdings – of scattered plots of mixed shapes and sizes over complicated terrain. He started by drawing a number of his dispersed plots (house plot first working out from his obviously personal point of reference), after which he started to connect them by road and path. In other words he was able to conceptualize the fragmented relation-ships of the plots over the area of the land in iso-lation from the connecting roads and paths. All I can say is that I have never seen a Westerner start drawing a comparable map with anything but streets and roads – lines.

Times, Patchworks and Linear Spaces

Whenever I ask a Japanese the question of how many metres or kilometres it is from one city place to another, the reply is never forthcoming as I had hoped. No matter how much emphasis I put on 'kilometres' or distance, the question is always transformed, reinterpreted, for the response is always in time. That the Japanese think of the 'size' of their cities in terms of travel is hardly an original observation. It is a phe-nomenon noted by probably hundreds of writers and journalists over many decades. In Japan, the time (or at least 'connection') map rather than distance or topographic map is common-place and this is of considerable interest to us here. While in our age, Western city dwellers also think increasingly of time over distance, there remain differences which are deep-rooted. The preoccupation with time reflects a different way of 'seeing' the city – fragmented, scattered, discontinuous. The Japanese way of seeing is not a recent consequence, as some might have us believe, of dense city living, subway and stilted travel. Rather, I would suggest, it is the other way round: their preparedness to tunnel under and fly over their cities (and indeed under and over their entire country) has grown out of an older way of thinking about space which is deeply rooted in the culture. In the narrow Western senses of architectural formed space and geographic (scaled topographic) space, the Japanese way of thinking is a-spatial. It should therefore come as no surprise to discover that they have been the most eager and prolific pro-ducers of time and other maps that deliberately ignore or at least distort topography, direction and scale, and that this practice goes back over centuries.

Bernard Rudofsky includes, in his *Kimono Mind*, a fragment of a remarkable map from the early eighteenth century (Rudofsky, 1965, pp. 220–221). The original map in its entirety shows the whole of Japan and is very long and very thin – some 28 feet long and 7 inches wide. The highly irregular coastlines to the Sea of Japan and Pacific Ocean have been straightened into borderlines and within this rectilinear land, roads run parallel to each other. Large mountains are stylized in the form of Fuji and territories are indicated by way of family crests in rectangular patches. Some rivers are shown though these appear often to stop abruptly at arbitrary points. Along the roads appear the names of important towns with distances written between. And, if the short section of map that is reproduced by Rudofsky is indicative of the whole, then pictures of special places (in this case, Edo) occupy significant rectangular chunks of the map surface rather like the places depicted on the board game of Meisho Sugoroku. In Western terms, the map is patchy, massively distorted and greatly discontinuous, if highly ingenious.

Meisho Sugoroku was a board game from the Edo and Meiji periods in which one travelled to famous places. The board was a patchwork of pictures of these places arranged in a multi-directional manner around the board (usually in a spiral and facing outwards). As on the Sugoroku board, the city, writes Hidenobu Jinnai, 'is com-

prehended . . . as a sequence of points each bearing some single strong impression' and this summarizes, he believes, 'the Japanese understanding of a city' (Jinnai, 1987a, p.42). It is a collection of memorable patches between which there is void and therefore, if one moves between these places, it is across time rather than topography.

This is in the nature of that classic map which distorts scale, ignores direction, lacks topography and reduces the city to route and points. I refer to those masterpieces of minimalist mapping – the subway or underground maps which were first made famous by the London underground. Here, routes, stations and liveries are the total information. The Japanese go one further in that they also include time. Combined underground and surface railway maps of the big cities are readily available. Peter Popham describes a weekly publication aimed at Tokyo house-hunters as: '. . . a beautiful thing. It's two feet wide and about eight inches high. Every national, private, and subway station in the whole megalopolis can be found there, but what really makes it special is that you can tell from a glance exactly how many minutes any given branch-line station is from any terminus. That's why they call it, using English, a "Time Map"' (Popham, 1985, p. 55).

In the West, it is only when we have descended below the surface of the city that we have readily felt free to abandon topographic conventions. Sub-surface, there really is no topography, no visible setting or landscape, there are vast stretches of immeasurable darkness and, by contrast, short stretches of station which provide the only exterior points of visible setting and human activity. Only in this subterranean blackness have physical absolutes been abandoned without fear of betraying the 'reality' of the landscape. For the Japanese, however, it has long been standard practice, even on the visible surface. In other words, the surface experience for them, is not unlike that of the underground: the surface is discontinuous.

For the farmer, of whom I earlier spoke, his fragmented scatter of plots is collectively his (singular) farm with the intervening plots a kind of (also singular) void. Likewise, for the city dweller, his or her domain of experience is a patchwork of discontinuous plots, each of which has a certain autonomy. The patches which make one's city are those which are experienced directly. The areas between resemble underground black space. The patches are urban oases – places surrounded by cluttered void and connected by anonymous route. Thus, a route connects places but, of itself is both formless and placeless. 'Tokyo', writes John Thackera, 'is a place-by-place place – how each location relates to the last remains obscure. Lacking vistas and grand plans, you have no sense of travel between points: rather, you leave an experience and start another somewhere else. The intervening motion is out of place and time' (Thackera, 1989, p. 66) .

In the West the surface has been considered as a continuous and consistent (whole) physical setting. The history of the European city is that buildings have related to each other to make continuous public spatial form, mostly by way of streets and squares. This form has been manipulated (by designers and others) according to two rather different bodies of thought. One is classically-inspired resulting in formal space with geometric order while the other is that inspired by more irregular (ironically unplanned) 'organic' urban forms made virtuous by Camillo Sitte and theorists of a similar vein. Both, however, see the spaces of the city as formed and finite and to be imbued with a strong sense of place. They are much more than mere routes even when devoid of people and activity. They are always places. It is against these traditions that Western planners have become pre-occupied with issues of 'landscape continuity', 'streetscape' and 'contextual fit': and that they became alarmed at 'missing teeth' (i.e. gaps) in the continuity of buildings along the street. Where there are several missing teeth there is a crisis of Trancik's 'Lost Space' and the urgent need for repair through control, incentives and design guidelines (Trancik, 1986, pp. 3–20). These have not been such major issues in Japan because the city is anyway a disconnected plot-by-plot affair. In the Japanese patchwork, there is no string-of-continuity to be broken. To disregard these issues in the West, one has to wrench oneself away from a very large slice of cultural heritage, although contemporary forces at work in cities together with contemporary theory in science and philosophy are

2.42 *Early Renaissance Model of an Ideal City. Filarete's 'Sforzinda'.*

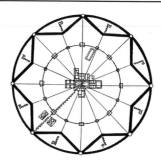

2.42

slowly but surely prizing architects and planners away from their established notions of good city form.

The fact is that for all (two millennia at least) but a relatively short and recent period of history, the West has treated space as something that is absolute and independent of time (and for all practical purposes continues to do so in all but the most theoretical of situations). Accordingly, preoccupation has been with 'accurate' representation of place and relationships. Concepts of space and form have revolved around geometrical relationships, fixed focal and viewing points, linear perspective, plan and elevational symmetry, controlled vistas and so on. Such ideas of the city are, however, allied to a notion of the universe which is essentially mechanical in nature (Newtonian physics) and backed by a belief in a single primary force or centre (monotheistic Christianity and its idea of a single creator). Buddhism, on the other hand, has treated time and space as inter-related – i.e. more in the manner of modern physics and relativity. Fritjof Capra (1991) describes the Eastern concept of space as 'relative, limited and illusionary' which is closer to the way in which the Japanese think of and record their cities. Here, there are points or centres of activity whose relationships are not fixed in space but changeable according, if you like, to the conditions of connection and the mood and mind of the observer. This is, for instance, the antithesis of the planned Renaissance city fashioned as a mini-mechanical universe where all parts have measured and interdependent relationships which are constants and independent of the observer.

There is another and deeper layer to the form of the Japanese city, and that may be related to the country's native religion. Shinto has co-existed with Buddhism in a loose marriage since the latter's spread from Korea and China in the sixth century. Shinto is polytheistic with spirits residing in all things, living, non-living and in particular places. The country and especially the cities are littered with shrines representing countless gods, each of which is different, equal and largely autonomous. One is likely to encounter shrines of many shapes and sizes (from the scale of a birdcage to that of a stately home) on the streets, under bridges and freeways, on rooftops, in gasoline stations, in the family home and in the many green and concrete folds and creases that Japanese cities embrace. Thus the city is itself a variation on the theme of the Shinto landscape – discontinuous, of autonomous parts and of disparate scales.

Chapter 3

Aspects of Form: Street and Related Scenes

Writer and journalist, Peter Popham, grew up in London, spent his university years in the English regional 'capital' of Leeds and later moved to Tokyo, from where he emerged as a respected commentator upon architecture and cities. To him 'Streets seem to have little significance in the Japanese urban scheme of things to warrant the prestige that names confer' (Popham, 1985, p. 48).

A key aspect of the previous chapter was the relative prominence of the street in the Western scheme of things and this is particularly apparent in the organizational and aesthetic ordering of cities.

If we step back into the Edo period (1603 to 1867) we discover that the Japanese urban scene was dominated by three types of building which reflected society's class divisions of the time. Each displayed a particular set of characteristics both in itself and in its relation to the wider city and streets.

The first type was the *buke-yashiki* residence in which one or more buildings stood within a garden withdrawn from the world behind high walls and big gates. By today's Western standards, it would be perceived as a rather defensive and somewhat suburban form. *Yashiki* quarters were the domain of the samurai or warrior classes.

Second, was the *machiya* or townhouse which functioned as residence plus shop, office, warehouse and/or workshop. These were the dwellings of merchants and artisans. The building

or buildings forming a *machiya* complex ran back from the street line covering most of its site and enveloping one or more gardens of pocket dimensions.

These building types are not commonly stumbled upon today in their original form, although examples do remain in many Japanese towns and cities, and even whole groups of such dwellings remain in some. Nevertheless, they occurred in certain patterns of location and subdivision that have powerfully shaped present-day patterns of urban form. (Professor Hidenobu Jinnai's studies of how Tokyo is shaped by the *yashiki* and *machiya* developments of Edo are particularly interesting and available in English translation (Jinnai, 1995).) Further, they established certain characteristics and qualities of building-to-street relationships which undoubtedly persist in modern Japan's city form. These models also provide the backcloth of urban experience which continues to influence Japanese urban spatial values, perceptions and aspirations to this day.

Third, was the tiny rowhouse or *nagaya*. This was the commoner's house and, in the big cities at least, perhaps the most numerous of all dwelling forms. However, because of its cramped form, it did not occupy extensive areas. While a few examples remain, its main legacy may be seen in the narrowest of city lanes and, to an extent, in some modern blocks of apartments or flats. For rather obvious reasons, it was not a model to be emulated: it may have repeated in compressed form some of the spatial and material characteristics of the *buke-yashiki* and *machiya* dwellings, but offered only a fraction of the amenity.

Thus, as background, an introduction to these building types forms the early parts of this chapter, followed by miscellaneous observations of other aspects of street form. These include the importance of signs and activity in the making of 'place' in the Japanese city, the nature and juxtaposition of different kinds of streets including arcades, the special role of bridges and last, but certainly by no means least, the dominance of the horizontal and the centrality of the periphery as city traditions.

Traditional Urban Typologies

Buke-Yashiki Quarters

The yashiki is a product of architecture distinctly Japanese. It's meaning is 'spread-out house'.

Let the reader imagine a space of several miles square covered with yashikis. To walk through the streets . . . was a monotonous and gloomy task.

William Elliot Griffis, 1876 (The Mikado's Empire, pp. 393 and 397)

The first old Japanese street along which I had the pleasure of walking was in the small Kyushu city of Shimabara. It was in the former samurai quarter in the shadow of the city's impressive albeit mostly reconstructed castle. By 'old street', I mean one that had retained not just the mere route and width but walls and floor to give a reasonably authentic sense of an old form. The

experience was like being channelled through a pygmy canyon. On each side were high, mostly stone walls interrupted occasionally by solid and usually higher gates: between the walls was a flat earthen floor, perhaps 6 m in width, with a central water channel. Behind the walls and gates were unviewable plots and their free-standing houses. Parts of the house roofs were visible amongst the greenery above the walls but little else of the buildings. Though far from unpleasant, it was a long, straight, narrow and thoroughly plain affair. It gave an impression of the minimum deemed necessary for movement and other utilitarian needs. It felt as if the plots had once lain immediately alongside each other but somehow been prized begrudgingly apart to cater only for the necessity of moving from one plot to another. In my notebook of the time, I described it as 'necessary left-over space'.

Of course, I subsequently learned that this long, straight, plain and narrow form was not untypical for these quarters although walls, while always high and thick, were not universally of stone. They were often built of timber, lathe and plaster with tiled tops.

I later came to see more picturesque versions of the same basic arrangement in that the streets were forced to incline or even step and curve on account of terrain. Also, they sometimes displayed a greater range of colours both in the walls and in the vegetation that protruded above. But in spite of these added picturesque touches the street spaces between the walls were no less

3.1 *Street in a Buke-yashiki Quarter. The cross section is typical of streets in these quarters with high walls and flat floor: the central water channel is not so common. The street is in Shimabara, Nagasaki Prefecture.*

3.2 *Street View of Walls and Building in a Buke-Yashiki Quarter. (Also, Shimabara, Nagasaki Prefecture.) Only the roofs and trees may be seen over the wall.*

3.1

3.2

basic in section – flat floor, drainage channel and strong side walls – and no less 'remote' from the flanking gardens.

Within each garden, the house stood free. Wearing a roof of heavy thatch or tile, its timber feet stood lightly (in older examples) on stones over the ground. Between roof and ground 'floated' the timber and *tatami* floors supported on timber stumps. *Amado* (timber screens) and *shoji* (the famous rice paper screens) hung between interior and garden. When drawn apart or removed, the eye might gaze out upon the garden but be contained by the wall to put the street well and truly out of sight and mind.

The premises I describe are those belonging to the warrior classes, and known as *buke-yashiki*. They occupied entire quarters of all substantial Japanese towns and cities through-

out the Edo era. As capital and national stronghold, Edo had the most extensive area with *buke-yashiki* occupying 70 per cent of its area. On the other hand, a commercial stronghold such as Osaka would have had proportionally a much smaller area.

This building form and layout was to be seen in at least three sizes: in the houses of *daimyo* (or aristocratic lords), *hatamoto* (middle ranking warriors who had the privilege of audience with the Shogun) and *gokenin* (lower ranking warriors who did not enjoy such privilege). Nevertheless, these were, in a broad sense, variations on a common theme. 'Even when adjusted to fit their smaller lots', writes Jinnai, 'hatamoto residences in Tokyo's Bancho district incorporated almost every element of the larger residences into their own more compact establishments, taking on the

3.3 *House on a 'New (Tokyo) Street' described by Morse in 1886. It shows a continuation of the buke-yashiki tradition. The boundary fences may have contracted inwards to 'squeeze' the house upwards but the high all-round enclosure remains to dislocate the plot from its surroundings. (Source: Morse, 1972)*

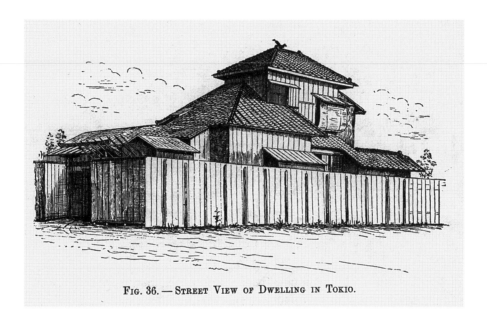

FIG. 36. — STREET VIEW OF DWELLING IN TOKIO.

3.3

air of mini daimyo mansions' (Jinnai, 1995, p 44). Likewise *gokenin* residences at an even lesser scale were modelled on those of the *hatamoto*. Further these residences were grouped into areas which were entered along gated streets. Gates apart, this character continued in new suburban areas long after the samurai disappeared following the Meiji restoration and, to an extent, continues to this day.

A 'house of one of the better classes' in a Tokyo street is described by Edward S. Morse in his 1886 classic, *Japanese Houses and their Surroundings*. It 'stands on a new street, and the lot on one side is vacant; nevertheless, the house is surrounded on all sides by a high board-fence

. . . The house is shown as it appears from the street. The front-door is near the gate, which is shown on the left of the sketch. There is here no display of an architectural front; indeed there is no display anywhere. The largest and best rooms are in the back of the house; and what might be called a back-yard, upon which the kitchen opens is parallel with the area in front of the main entrance to the house . . .' (Morse, 1886, pp. 54–55).

I might point out this is quite the antithesis of so many houses that appeared at about the same time on the opposite side of the Pacific in the United States. Take for instance the San Francisco houses shown below. Similarities

3.4 *Flamboyant Frontages on San Francisco Houses. The faces of these houses to the public street are both ostentatious and cosmetic: the side and rear walls are private and plain.*

3.4

between the Tokyo and San Francisco houses go no further than their main material which is timber. On the San Francisco house elaborate decoration is piled thick and high across the building's street frontage behind which there is a less than plain appearance. Indeed the whole design is about as close as domesticity can get to one of Venturi's 'decorated sheds', for which the archetype was the Wild West store or bank with its cosmetic billboard-like 'rhetorical front' and utilitarian shack-like 'conventional behind' (Venturi, 1972, p.90–91). The houses show a frontal profusion of classical detail culminating in a massive cornice to mask the entire roof pitch behind. The San Francisco house is in a street of such houses. Today, they stand ostentatiously as remnant public faces of frontier nouveau riche and as caricatures of Western street frontality.

Morse, in his description of the Tokyo house emphasized the best rooms as being towards the back of the house and, I might add, towards

the centre of the plot. This is also a common Japanese characteristic. While it is often hard to say precisely where the heart of a house is, one can be reasonably certain that it will not appear ostentatiously at the front or near the entrance. The Japanese house revolved about an obscure centre reached by an indirect route, while its Western equivalent progressed linearly and hierarchically from grand to humble, from show to utility, and invariably from street (i.e. front) to back.

Over the century since Morse's writing, Western and Japanese house designs have moved closer together. In Japan, it has consciously been towards a 'Western Style' house. In the West, it has been a case of adopting characteristics flowing from its own Modernist-Functionalist movement which happen to bear strong resemblance to several traditional Japanese design characteristics (namely, continuity of indoor and outdoor space, free-flowing internal space and flexibility of use).

Nevertheless to walk through today's typical Japanese suburb is to experience something distinctly different to that gained from a walk through the equivalent in America, Australia or England. The differences which I infer go far beyond the often-mentioned but obvious ones of density and distance between buildings. In *The Aesthetic Townscape*, Ashihara (1983, pp. 40 and 42) shows typical suburban residential townscapes in Japan and America. The Japanese example shows a plan of an irregularly shaped

3.5 *Street, Plot and House – in Typical Japanese (left) and American/Australian (right) suburbs.*

3.6 *A Typical Residential Street in a Japanese City.*

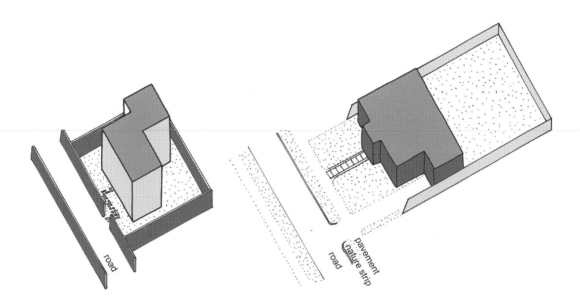

road

pavement
nature strip
road

3.5

3.6

3.7 *Nagasaki Hillside Suburb – Plan. This small part of the suburb of Hayama shows houses, flat 'platform plots' and steep streets, some of which are in the form of steps. (Courtesy: Nagasaki City Council)*

3.7

house within a rectangular (almost square), fenced and gated plot. He has an accompanying photographic view of the street which is narrow, high-walled and utilitarian. By contrast, he shows in the American suburb a frontal building in an unfenced area facing a tree-lined street. In fact the typical American house sits on a rectangular block, rather longer than it is wide, unfenced to the fore of the house and fenced behind. I have witnessed such contrasting scenes over countless hectares in scores of places in the respective countries. In Japan, the garden fences may have closed in on the house since Morse's time but the spatial experience of the modern suburb from the viewpoint of the public realm remains essentially that of a squeezed-up version

of its distant samurai ascendant and of that subsequently depicted by Morse.

The Japanese characteristics described are exaggerated in areas of sharp relief. Nagasaki is a classic hillside city with extensive suburbs clinging precariously to staggeringly steep slopes. When construction occurs in some of the older inner suburbs, building materials are still back-packed to the sites on a local breed of pony particularly suited to the task. Yet in this city, and several others like it (urban flat land can be a rare commodity in Japan), house plots remain flat and walled in spite of the contours. Such plots sit above retaining walls to form plot-by-plot terraces. Sometimes, they are cantilevered out from their retaining walls which rise sharply from the street below. Thus the internal site relationship of the house to plot is constant (and in direct descent of the *buke-yashiki*) while the street alone bears the transformation (slope or even steps) demanded by the contours. Here, the streets can take on an even more canyon-like appearance. Indeed, so little remains of the earth's natural surface that, given Japan's generous rainfall, drains must assume generous dimensions. These, together with power poles, fire hydrants and wire fences, protecting the drains from late-night sake-soaked salary-men, only add to the utilitarian image of Japan's residential arteries. It is a bizarre and eerie landscape crossed and cut by dank and dingy ravines of tarmac floors and grey concrete walls. For the pedestrian, the edges of the platform plots

3.8 *'Canyon Street' below Elevated Plots,*
Sankeidai, Nagasaki.

3.8

project out above the head, like dwarf versions of *daimyo* fortifications. In these places, the flat walled plot is the unfettered constant. Its autonomy is sacrosanct. Concessions to contours occur not on the plot but in the 'street' to reinforce the latter's leftover status.

The plot-by-plot insularity is extraordinary in spite of the crowded landscape of narrow streets and relatively small lots. At the same time, it cannot simply be explained as the product of limited space and extreme topography. I have witnessed stilted plots on open, flat and isolated ground. The plot is raised to hover overhead: the pedes-

trian views the plot as a toddler might view a giant table from below: on top, the house stands freely within the walled plot, the inhabitants seemingly oblivious to their elevation. Even more extraordinary to the Western eye is the inverse arrangement of plot over house, for I have also seen the platform extend over the ground plot which is complete with house. It is a variation on the theme of stacked real estate where each high-rise deck is occupied by an independent suburban house much as cars occupy parking spaces in a multi-storey carpark: Koolhaas shows such a notion by way of a cartoon from a 1909

3.9 *A Stilted Plot. Though the plot is dislocated from the true ground the spatial relationship between house and plot remains constant : the house is centrally placed on a flat plot behind walls.*

3.10 *House Plan with Utility Areas Closest to the Street. One has to pass through the utility zone to reach the 'living heart'. (Source: Adapted from plan of Kenko Jutakubu – Iwatani Home)*

3.9

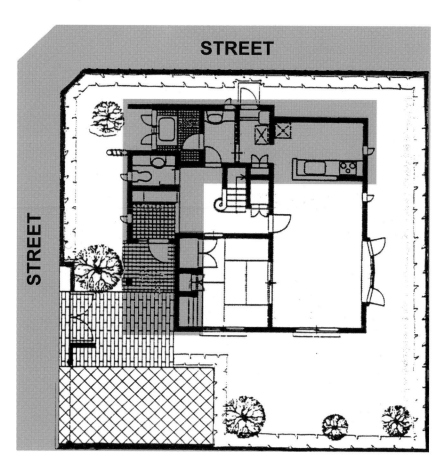

3.10

issue of *The Globe* newspaper (Koolhaas, 1978.) These stilted and near-subterranean sites may not quite be typical but they do reflect that attitude to plot and space that emphasizes the autonomy of the plot, the secondary status of the street, and the fragmented nature of the overall landscape. But again, this making of flat plots on difficult landform is a Japanese tradition

– so many agricultural plots have been terraced from steep hillsides or reclaimed from marsh: lake or sea. In other words the construction of these seemingly unnatural plots is an urban extension of an old rural practice.

Some recent suburban subdivisions do project new images. Their self-conscious 'Western-style' images seem, at first sight, removed from the shielded grey family homes of only two decades ago let alone more distant *yashiki* days. Roofs are now shallower. Colours are lighter and brighter. Glass is used more extensively. Many houses show clean-cut compacted two-storey variations of what appear to be American models. Inside families may sit at high tables to eat their fare and climb rather than crawl into bed. But even here, appearances can be deceptive.

There are some obvious continuities with tradition such as the inclusion of a *tatami* room, Japanese-style bath, etc. (although these may not be apparent from the outside). There are also some less obvious and, from the standpoint of this work, more significant continuities. Plots are barely longer, often shorter, than they are wide (i.e. more or less square). Houses will tend to sit centrally on the block. The perimeter is likely to be high fenced or hedged. The house form is likely to be contrived into something irregular and seemingly larger than it really is (like the Japanese garden). In many houses, their service rooms and elements (toilets, bathroom, built-in cupboards, etc.) line up on the ground floor closest to the public street. Thus, on entry, the outside porch (recessed) and the 'inside' *genkan* (where shoes are removed) take the visitor effectively through a utility zone to the protected heart. Porch and *genkan* may be paved in the same material emphasizing that part of the house inside of the 'front door' as an extension of the outside. Inside rooms are almost certain to be connected by openings to the outside rather more

generously than their equivalents in Western houses (even upstairs to balconies) and these are likely to be occupied by sliding screens. Should there be a floor level window that is visible from the street, which is increasingly common, then blinds may well hang low to give views of floor and feet to passers-by. Also, however small the plots may be and however close the houses may be to each other, the buildings stand within their own autonomous plots steadfastly detached from each other on streets geared to utility.

In other words, there remains considerable *yashiki* spirit and habit within and about even those countless free-standing Japanese family homes which adopt Cape Cod and other American suburban fashions for their external image. Again, Jinnai in his study of Tokyo's urban morphology emphasizes how 'mansions since the Meiji era (have) inherited the images of small-scale *daimyo* or *hatamoto* residences' while 'the houses we see everywhere in Tokyo today – independent homes with small yards – belong to the tradition of residences for low ranking warriors' (Jinnai, 1995, p.48). If this is true for Tokyo, then it is even more the case for the homes to be found in smaller provincial cities where space is not quite at such a premium and perhaps values inclined to change rather less rapidly.

Machiya Quarters

Looking at the bustle of the town, we also got used to its way of life and the many stores and workshops that lined its streets in an unbroken chain . . . The displays of every kind of merchandise, as well as the entire interior life of the store and workshop were open to the eyes of the passers-by . . . A little way back the matted living-part adjoined the shop . . . When the paper sliding doors were pulled apart one could often see the family at their meal or the children at their studies. Sometimes you could see right through these rooms into the small garden beyond.

One night, we drove home very late and all the houses that at day-time were so free and open had been shut up like wooden boxes. Without exception all the wooden shutters had been drawn close . . .

Bruno Taut, 1937 (Houses and People of Japan, pp. 43–44 and 45)

The second long-established building type of importance in Japanese cities is the *machiya* which translates into the Western townhouse. *Machiya* normally stood independently but side-by-side more or less continuously along streets. Where there were breaks between buildings, high walls with roof-like capping would fill the gaps. Here, the common development pattern was not of squarish but rectangular plots with narrow frontages relative to their depths (usually three or four times deeper than they are wide). In extreme cases, however, they may measure only 4 m in width yet extend back from the street for as much as 40 m: this formation earned some of Kyoto's *machiya* the nickname of '*unagi no nedoko*' or 'eel's bedrooms'.

In the Edo period, just as *yashiki* quarters were the domain of warriors, so *machiya* were synonymous with merchants. The building was usually more than a house incorporating shop, office and/or workshop. Unlike in Europe where downstairs shop and upstairs living was common, in Japan it was usual for the house to stretch backwards behind the street-front shop area with a storehouse at the rear. There remain numerous scattered examples, some groups and even a few whole districts which retain the machiya character from Meiji and even Edo times. One such district is Imai-cho in Kashihara city, Nara Prefecture, where nearly all buildings date from these and Taisho periods. It has miraculously escaped serious fire for four centuries with much of the old townscape still intact: 80 per cent of buildings date from the Edo period. Again, I have walked such streets in several cities (including Imaicho) and been privileged to have entered numerous interiors.

The spatial characteristics of *machiya* generate a remarkable sense of isolation from their usually dense urban surrounds. Within each plot, the lines of sight can be quite restricted – essentially from one internal space to the next and from under the roof to tiny garden. Excepting glimpses of very near rooftops, views out to any fragment of the wider city are not easily come by and this high level of introspection links *machiya* strongly in spirit to the *buke-yashiki* even though the latter achieves similar ends by inverting the relationship of building-to-space. The timber *engawa*

3.11 *Machiya Street Front, Fukuoka. (Photograph: Michiyuki Hirashima)*

3.11

(a kind of verandah space) which mediates between trees and *tatami* on the perimeter of the *buke-yashiki*, likewise hovers between shrubs and straw mats in the *machiya* complex but inwards towards a garden. In both instances, the garden views are contained. All this is assuming that the screens towards the street-edge are closed.

Machiya are, for much of the time, in mysterious retreat behind multiple but plain timber,

bamboo and paper screens. When closed and stripped of accessories, there is no invitation to enter individual premises and the street is left as a dull utility. When, however, banners and lanterns are hoisted and draped outside, the street is at once more welcoming although there may still be a considerable element of mystery in entering particular buildings. With screens drawn or even removed, at least part of a building's interior becomes open and visible to the street and vice-versa. Of Edo, Frank Lloyd Wright wrote, 'The lower stories of buildings lining the labyrinth of earthen highways and byways are all shops and wide open to the street from side to side' (Wright, 1932, p. 206). The highways and byways may no longer be so earthen but the spatial qualities to which he refers, remain a common part of today's urban experience.

Even today, in older districts, building interiors may flow over on special occasions onto the streets. For instance, at festival times platform or mat may extend from the building effectively to annex part of the street. Annexation is not too strong a term for shoes are abandoned on the street at the point of stepping onto the temporary extension. More commonly wares and signs will spill out onto the street edge itself to extend the sales space. On the other hand, there will be earth floor sections adjacent to the street and under the roof of the building where shoes will remain firmly between foot and ground. Thus, in the words of Bognar, 'there is no clear distinction

3.12 *Machiya Plans. The routes through the sites are at ground level but under the roof : screen-interrupted areas of raised tatami extend through most of the buildings and open to small internal gardens. (Source: Adapted from Yagi, 1992)*

3.13 *Annexing the Street. Two Kyoto examples of buildings claiming part of the street or alley at (Jizo Bon) festival time. (Source: Kato, 1993)*

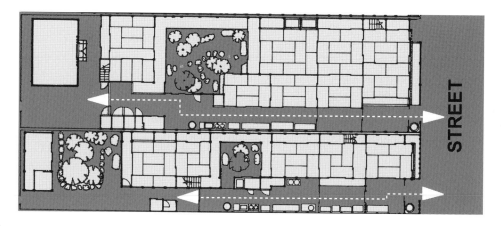

3.12

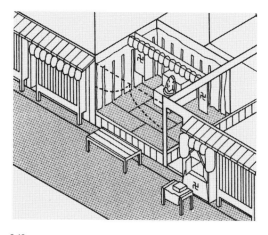

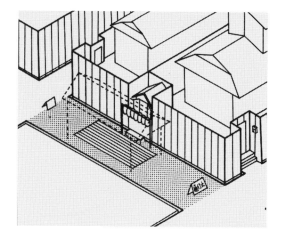

3.13

between building and city, interior and exterior, private and public, turning such street architecture into the most ambiguous urban formation' (Bognar, 1985, p. 71).

The relationships of *machiya* to street space is complex. For a Westerner, walking the streets of

an old *machiya* district can spark highly ambivalent feelings. On the one hand, the scale suggests intimacy: most streets are narrow (5 or 6 metres is not uncommon) and it is easy to feel that one is trespassing on private ground. On the other hand, with screens closed, the same street can

3.14 *Old Shop-dwelling Open to the Street. This Fukuoka machiya is fitted with metal roller front and neon sign (just visible).*

3.14

so easily convey an impression of neglect – an utterly utilitarian channel abandoned by the very structures which flank and depend on it for their livelihood. Such ambivalence may again be explained by reference to long-standing Western practice where it has been normal to put a handsome face to the forever public street.

While original *machiya* may be relatively few, their legacy lives on in so many commercial streets in contemporary Japan. Metal grills and shutters may, to a large extent, have replaced the sliding timber frames and neon has joined banner and lantern signs. But signs continue to proliferate and disappear (or at least switch on and off) between opening and closing times. Wares and shopkeepers make their morning advance

from beneath buildings to squat on street-space and retreat at night. Further, such is the power of neon and modern electronics that many a Japanese street undergoes daily transformation from the flick of a switch or programmed electronic circuitry – from a place that is depressingly dull or even disgracefully decrepit by day to one that can be a stunning fairyland by night. This is the way of many *sakariba* (entertainment and bar districts) which merely take advantage of today's technology to extend the tradition of the 'glowing "advertising"' which so fascinated Wright.

Perhaps mindful of the Western disdain for excessive signs, he wrote: 'The illuminated sign is ancient (in Japan)' (Wright, 1932, p. 205). Thus, traditionally, there have been two key and often

3.15 *Machiya Closed to the Street. A Street of closed buildings can be a rather dull affair, even in one relieved by a central water channel (stream). Here, in Konyamachi, Nara Prefecture, wooden and metal 'fronts' are side-by-side.*

3.16 *A Fukuoka Machiya viewed from the Street. It exhibits a very plain exterior.*

3.15

3.16

colourful components of the Japanese (*machiya*) street setting. First there was information made up of large banners hanging either flat to the building or at right angles to it on steeply inclined poles and hanging lanterns (also containing information) plus smaller banners about entrances and openings. Second, there was the activity made up of people (children were dressed particularly colourfully which is also a tradition that persists) and their wares. These semiotic and

human components long dominated the Japanese street scene. With these in place, there was vibrance albeit of a temporary nature. Once removed the street reverted to its basic condition of sombre and grey-brown utility.

So from the street, *machiya* quarters could appear either as fascinatingly festive, bright and active or as deadly dull and functional. If the former, the building played only an indirect role as facilitator of visible activity and communication:

3.17 *Under the Roof of the Same Fukuoka Machiya. This view is of the area adjacent to the street and taken from the upper level. There is a substantial area of ground between street-front and the 'true' tatami interior (visible in the foreground).*

3.18 *Decorated Fronts of a Western Variety? Yes, but they are far from 'home'. These buildings are at Huis ten Bosch, Nagasaki Prefecture, where a mock-Dutch town has been built. Frontages are ornate and devoid of advertising: and a solid wall separates those dining inside and outside the cafe.*

3.17

3.18

here, any likeness with the *yashiki* is null and void. But if dull and functional, then similarities are apparent even though one is walled and the other veiled.

It is also these impressions of neutrality, utility and, to some degree, mystery together with those of relatively insubstantial and indeterminate street edges that place the *machiya* street at odds with its Western counterpart. The traditionally solid and ornate facades of Western street buildings are closely linked to the idea of the street as a formed linear space which, in turn, was much reinforced by the development of linear perspective in the early Renaissance. It is impossible to think of established European streets without also thinking of the building fronts that make and grace them (e.g. Amsterdam's Heerengracht or Oxford's High Street). Though something of a cliché in recent years, they are nevertheless the urban stage sets before which citizens and visitors

alike anonymously or otherwise act out their lives.

Thus, it may be said there that while Western buildings have put cosmetic faces between private interiors and public streets, their Japanese counterparts have worn (multiple) veils or, in the case of *yashiki*, disappeared almost completely behind walls. As a consequence, in the West, it is so often the permanent physical setting that is so memorable about a place, while in Japan it is the transient activity and display.

It is worthwhile considering for a moment the English word 'facade' which refers, of course, to a building's front. It entered the English language only in the seventeenth century from the Italian '*facciata*' following the influence of the Renaissance and means literally the face or principal front. Face is, in turn, synonymous with appearance, aspect, outward show and in this context, street frontage. Likewise, it is pertinent to note that in architectural books which include glossaries of Japanese terms, equivalent words are not really to be found.

Indeed, the modesty of the *machiya* veil is contrary to the ostentation of many Western facades and, in this context, it is worth turning to Atsushi Ueda's description of the typical Kyoto townhouse. He contrasts the public plainness of the building at the street-edge with the private richness at the heart which is deep on the plot. One moves from an unassuming and unnoticeable 'front' which is 'easy to dismiss at first glance as a modest structure to increasing finery in the secluded depths of the building. The further back you go, the finer the house, the finer the garden, indeed the more refined the whole house appears to become' (Ueda, 1994, p. 107).

I cannot help but contrast this entire pattern with my daily experience of home in Australia. My turn-of-the-century townhouse in central Hobart has a street facade which is the most elaborately presented part of the house – though still relatively subdued compared to the street-front excesses of earlier Victorian years. The back enjoys no special treatment whatsoever: it is entirely workmanlike. Inside the room nearest the front (i.e. street) door is the most elaborate with other rooms descending in their levels of decoration with distance from that point and from front to rear.

Nagaya

Row houses have existed in Japan's cities for a very long time. Picture scrolls of twelfth and thirteenth century Kyoto and Nara show rows of small houses, each standing up to the street edge under a common plank roof with small gardens to the rear. A wide door opens to the street in which *noren* (short curtains) are hung and there are high lattice windows to one side.

In the Edo period row houses were also common in Japan's cities. In Edo itself, the most usual pattern was for dwellings to line up along small alleys (just 1 m or 2 m in width) behind and between *machiya*. The centre of the alley would be marked by a plank-covered drain. Because of their cramped sites and generally shielded locations, they would not have appeared as numerous as they really were, though they housed the greatest number of people. *Nagaya* were the homes of artisans and labourers, and their alleys were semi-private and often dead-ends.

Domestic activity, especially cooking and washing extended into the alley space. Toilet and water supply, usually in the form of a well, were shared. The homes themselves were generally not more than 4 m × 3 m with one-fifth of the space at ground level (entrance and utility) with another 15 per cent as storage cupboards leaving 65 per cent as the raised floor (*tatami*) flexible living space. Another often shared facility was the Inari shrine which, it is sufficient to say, guarded the

3.19 *Plan of Nagaya Alleys. It shows the entrance between larger buildings (machiya – marked F) to the nagaya (alleys and houses – marked N) behind. (Source: Adapted from drawing, Shitamchi Museum)*

3.20 *Looking Down on a Nagaya Alley. It shows the gate, well and shrine. (Source: Shitamachi Museum)*

3.21 *Nagaya: Plan of Three Dwellings. (Source: Shitamachi Museum)*

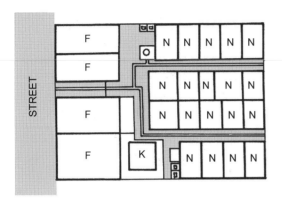

3.19

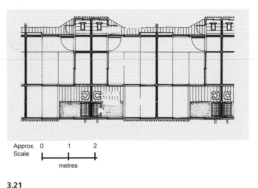

Approx. Scale

0   1   2

metres

3.21

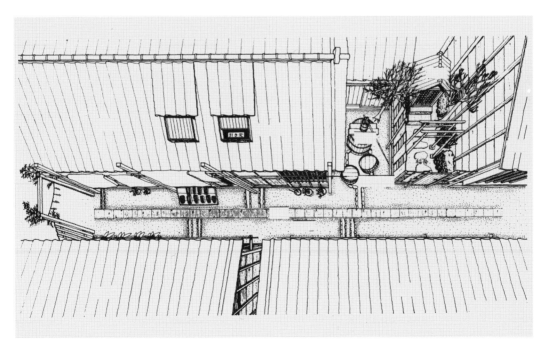

3.20

inhabitants against many dangers and gave hope for a better life.

The alley was usually gated, at which point there was a multitude of nameplates and signs

3.22 *A Reconstructed Nagaya Alley in the Shitamachi Museum, Tokyo.*

3.23 *Morse's 'New Style' Row Houses. These are entered from the street and date from the Meiji period. (Source: Morse, 1972)*

3.24 *A Nagaya-like Alley Today in Tsukishima, Tokyo. Although two storeys, it bears some nagaya-like spatial qualities.*

3.22

3.23

3.24

indicating the people and services to be found there. The dwellings were mostly single storey through to the Meiji period, after which two storeys became increasingly common. Given the semi-private nature of the alley, and its use for domestic purposes and potted plants, it was something of the *machiya* street and the *machiya* garden rolled into one at a greatly reduced scale. Writing in 1885, Edward Morse would have been referring to this kind of dwelling when he

wrote of 'a number of tenements occurring in a block with the entrance by means of a gateway common to all' (Morse, 1972, p. 52).

In the warrior districts, row housing would sometimes substitute for the wall to provide part of the defensive street edge for larger establishments and house the household's retainers. Entry in these cases was also via a common gate into the compound. Morse referred also to 'a new style of building in Tokio, in which a continuous row of tenements is under one roof, and each tenement has its own entrance directly upon the street' (and not from a narrow alley). A tiny garden was common at the rear. In his accompanying drawing, the 'new style' seems to be a variation on the theme of those depicted in the medieval picture scrolls, to which I earlier referred. It is probable that in many cities, both types of row house (i.e. those facing semi-private alleys and those facing streets) had co-existed.

These patterns changed somewhat with the coming of gas-fired cooking and individual water supplies, namely in the Taisho period. It was at this time, according to Jinnai, that domestic activity tended to retreat into the house itself and single storeys transformed (by replacement or extension) into two (Jinnai, 1995, p. 62). While governments have attempted to rid Japan's cities of these kinds of dwellings through land re-adjustment and renewal schemes, there remain extensive areas of narrow lanes which continue to bear the spatial qualities of the *nagaya* alleys. The houses along these, like *machiya*, retreat behind veils with plenty of potted plants and washing as the remnant protruding items of domesticity.

However, if one steps into a modern city apartment block in a commercial area (such as I have occupied temporarily) it is evident that some qualities are enduring. Firstly the block is likely to be mixed use with a commercial ground floor as well as scattered commercial units above. There are lists of occupiers and signboards at the entrance which itself is likely to be shadowy and recessed. At this point there may well be a caretaker's office keeping a watchful eye on the comings and goings rather like the watchposts by the old *kido* gates at the entrances to each area in Edo city patchworks, including *nagaya* alleys: and, as then, the occupant may also sell a few convenience items on the side. While lifts are now common, the entrance, stairs and access decks are themselves most likely exposed to the elements. The flats retreat behind their service areas (where light is admitted through sliding frosted glass) with only the *genkan* opening to the deck via a solid door. At this point shoes are removed and the surface changes even if the rise may be negligible.

From within the flat, it is common to find windows of frosted glass that mellow the admitted light and eliminate the distant view: clear glass is more likely to be reserved for the balcony window where the view is normally contained by a solid wall to give the traditionally-valued short view of the garden in the form of potted plants. Here, while the sound of the city may be difficult to repel (as in the *nagaya*), one is visually cocooned in a somewhat secretive cell as if hemmed in by dense building, which may or may not be the case.

Another form of flat is to be found in low (2 or 3 storeys) blocks which squeeze their way down the length of long thin blocks. The street is dominated by the entry stairs behind which strips of access balcony and dwelling space run in

3.25 *Contemporary Nagaya – Horizontal? The front of a long thin two storey block in which narrow access ways and tiny apartments squeeze down the plot.*

3.26 *Contemporary Nagaya – Vertical? The horizontal arrangement is upended with an even greater ratio of circulation (stairs, lifts and landings) to floor area.*

3.25

3.26

parallel widths that do not seem to differ greatly in dimension. And an upward variation on this theme – a kind of vertical *nagaya* – is the slender block which rises as a cluster of three pencil-thin tubes of stairs-lift-balcony, apartment stack (one per floor), and fire stairs.

Streets, Signs and Circulation

An ideograph does not make on the Japanese brain any impression similar to that created in the Occidental brain by a letter or combination of letters, – dull, inanimate symbols of vocal sounds. To the Japanese brain an ideograph is a vivid picture: it lives; it speaks; it gesticulates. And the whole space of a Japanese street is full of such living characters, – figures that cry out to the eyes, words that smile or grimace like faces.

. . . most of the amazing picturesqueness of these (Japanese) streets is simply due to the profusion of Chinese and Japanese characters in white black, blue or gold decorating everything, even surfaces of doorposts and paper screens.

Lafcadio Hearn, 1894 (Glimpses of Unfamiliar Japan, p. 4)

Content versus Context

The memorable places in Western cities are invariably those with a strong physical context or collective built form. They are not necessarily places of great size or powerful geometry such as London's Trafalgar Square or Paris's Place Vendome but may be of modest scale and picturesque irregularity such as a street in Amsterdam's Jordaan quarter or Stockholm's medieval island centre. Nevertheless, appreciation depends much upon vision and partly on intellect. Not so in Japan. It is the intensity of activities, the colour of events and the profusion of signs which collectively leave the lasting and livelier though far-fuzzier impressions. This power of content (people, activity and signs) over context or setting

in Japan cannot be underestimated and has long surprised Westerners whose urban experience is generally rather different.

Writing in *The Listener* almost thirty years ago the late Sir James Richards wrote: 'The dynamic quality of Japanese cities is created by layer on layer . . . of moving objects and incidents, inextricably interwoven, each justifying its presence . . . by the way it involves people' (Richards, 1969, p. 593). This is, I might add, one of the earliest examples of a post-war Western design critic seeing beyond the messiness of the urban form and recognizing positively the role of animation and dynamism in Japanese urban place-making.

It is this experience of content that has led Bognar to conclude that in Japanese cities the 'relationship between man and (spatial) reality . . . is more phenomenological than objective, based more on the functions of intuition, imagination and memory, as well as active physical involvement, than dependent simply on vision' (Bognar, 1985, p. 70).

In an essay on 'Walking in Tokyo' film and literary critic Donald Richie evidences this view when he compares Japanese with European street experience:

In Europe, one is part of the display – to see and be seen, to look and be looked at. The street is a stage. How different Japan . . . You, the walker, are not the actor.

Rather, you are an active spectator. The display is not you and the others about you. The display is the

3.27

3.27 *Street Display, Sasayama, Hyogo Prefecture. Signs, goods and people have traditionally been the place makers in Japanese towns against a neutral and sombre backcloth of building.*

3.28 *Street Display, Nara City. Today, scale and materials may have changed in many places but signs, goods and activity are even more dominant.*

street itself. The direction is not from you to it but from it to you.

Shops line the street, open up, spill out. Clothes on racks and sides of beef alike are shoved onto sidewalks. The fish shop's scaly glitter is right there, still gasping. Baby televisions piled high blink at you eye to eye . . . on the Tokyo street, there is the raw profusion of consumption itself.

He continues: 'even in more sedate avenues, such as the Ginza, where goods stay indoors, the display continues. Signs and flags proclaim: kanji . . . grab and neon points. Signs, signs everywhere, all of them shouting, a semiotic babble, signifiers galore, all reaching out to the walker . . .' (Richie, 1987, pp. 53 –54).

Consequently, the perceptive Barthes deduced from his short Japanese stay that: 'you must orient yourself . . . not by book, by address, but by walking, by sight, by habit, by experience; here every discovery is intense and fragile; it can be repeated or recovered only by the memory of the trace it has left in you' (Barthes, 1982, p. 36). This emphasis on content and experience over setting in Japan is, however, not merely a product of its modern age. It has been this way (and I hope by now the evidence is beginning to convince) for centuries.

Richie in the latter part of his 'Walking in Tokyo' essay actually recalls Hokusai's and Hiroshige's wood-cut views of Edo connecting past with present. 'All of that detail, all of these particulars, all that decoration, the sheer movement of it (captured by the great printmakers) – it

3.28

is all real and it is all here now' (Richie, 1987 p. 60). Indeed, street scenes by these and many lesser known artists show scenes in which buildings are greyly inconspicuous. Prints such as Hiroshige's 'View of Nihonbashi Tori I chome' and 'Silk-goods Lane, Odenma-cho' show some

3.29 *Focus on Activity with Setting Obscured. This scene is on a shrine souvenir card and shows the commonly used technique of concealing built form (which was any way neutral and grey) in favour of activity, signs and people (which were animated and colourful). (Source: Shiraishi, 1993; original in Edo Kirie Zue)*

3.29

of Edo's best-known streets yet the scenes would hardly make pictures at all without people, parasols and signs. These provide the stream of colour within the uniformly grey-brown channel of street floor and buildings. The subservience of the built city as visual setting is brought home even further in those numerous Japanese scenes which so shroud the buildings in cloud that built form disappears from sight, with activity (especially processions and crowds), goods and signs generating the sense of place. Yet because these are the focus that sense is inevitably unstable.

In Japan, flanking buildings are not essential to the processional way and this is emphasized by the shrine where 'the festival way' is defined by a series of *torii* (free-standing portals, each consisting of two posts and two cross beams): the disposition of buildings along either side may pay scant attention to the route. Come festival time, stalls may be erected along it, but these are a temporary phenomenon and would occur in quite the same manner even if the event were in open country (as some are). The uphill climb in Nagasaki from the river to the city's most popular shrine, Suwajinja, is an example of a *torii*-defined route which relates somewhat tenuously to the buildings about it. It is a well-delineated route (by way of stone lanterns, gates and flag-stone paving) which ascends the steep slope via many steps and areas of flattened hillside. It is the location for the city's famous Okunchi festival. However, the buildings to either side are far from regular.

To the Westerner at least, it is always of interest to watch the filming of festival events in Japan for the camera rarely strays from the

3.30 *Lower Part of the Route from Nagasaki's Suwajinja (Shrine). While the route is well-defined by torii, lanterns and paving, the relationship with the buildings on each side is rather more tenuous.*

3.30

activity and the display to the setting even where the latter might seem to warrant greater prominence. In Europe, coverage of equivalent events would lose much of the occasion if the physical setting containing the activity were to be so disregarded. It is part of a way of seeing which has been deeply engrained in the Western psyche for a very long time. In Bellini's 'Procession of the True Cross' from the early years of the Renaissance, the procession would be nothing without the detail of its setting, namely the great Piazza San Marco. Similarly, in Carpaccio's 'Miracle of the Cross at the Rialto', the proces-

sion and even the bridge itself depend upon the wider urban setting for their power. Today it is little different: the spirit of any event in or through the streets and squares of an old European city could not be truly captured if the cameras were to neglect the physical space and setting. By contrast, street settings in Japanese cities will often be thoroughly eliminated by signs, lanterns and decoration.

By contrast, a walk through many an English market place even on a quiet (non-trading) Sunday can still be an uplifting experience simply because of the form of the space and strength of

3.31 *Map of Approach to Sewajinja, Nagasaki. (Base map: courtesy of the City of Nagasaki)*

3.33 *Market Place, Newark on Trent, England. The physical characteristics of the space make it a pleasant setting even when the stalls stand abandoned and there is no activity.*

3.32 *Tanabata Kazari (Festival), Taito-ku, Tokyo. Here, buildings play less than even a backseat role: they are barely visible through the remarkable array of signs and streamers. (Courtesy: Tokyo Metropolitan Government)*

3.32

3.33

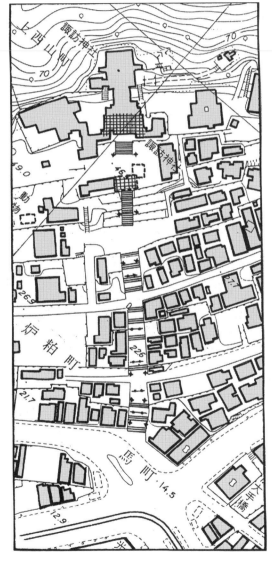

3.31

the setting. Even when deserted stalls stand sadly like skeletons, the setting can remain all-powerful.

An example is the previously mentioned Nottinghamshire town of Newark where the irregular but generally rectangular space is formed by buildings from the fourteenth to present centuries. Significantly, it is the Renaissance-inspired eighteenth century classical buildings, particularly John Carr's Town Hall (1770) and the Clinton Arms Hotel which are most frontal and eye-catching. The square is entered from three major but relatively narrow streets, only

3.34 *Signs in the Asakusa Theatre District in the Early Showa Period. This postcard scene is of 'Asakusa Koen Rokku' or Sixth District, Asakusa Park and shows buildings again largely hidden behind signs.*

Picture Halls in Asakusa Park

3.34

one of which occupies a corner position. Otherwise, it is entered from narrow lanes and yards, of which all but two tunnel through the surrounding walls of buildings. This gives a powerful sense of enclosure, history and richness of physical setting to the large, cobbled space of the market.

In Japan, however, once the activity has retreated from a city space, whether it be an old shopping street, a new taxi-filled station square, or something else, that which is left is rarely of consequence as an experience.

The treatment of early cinema facades in Japan is another indicator of the strength of the country's 'content tradition'. In the early part of this century, the fascination with the movie cinema was no less than in the West. Accordingly, many Japanese picture theatres adopted ornate facades after the fashion of the West where, of course, exotic facades were both advertisement and street-set. In Tokyo's Asakusa amusement district old postcards reveal that the already exuberant and fanciful fronts were subjected to the same banner-strewn treatment that

3.35 *An Edo Theatre Street. Behind and beyond people and signs, there is little of the buildings to be seen. (Source: Jinnai, 1987)*

3.37 *Roof-top Signs Today in Nakasu, Fukuoka.*

3.36 *Roof-top Sign in Eighteenth Century Kyoto. Neither the giant multi-directional and roof-dominating sign nor the sign-swamped frontage are new in Japan. This view is an extract from a street scene attributed to Shijo Shibai of the Maruyama School of artists. (Source: Yamasaki, 1994)*

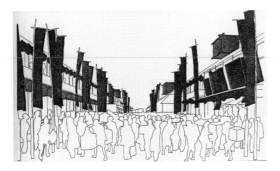

3.35

3.37

3.36

might obscure a modest *machiya* veil at festival time. Thus in these cinema districts where banners and building fronts were rival transmitters to the street, dynamic information triumphed over exuberant but static building. Indeed, some interesting graphic analyses of Asakusa theatre streets have been done using old prints and photographs from the nineteenth and early twentieth centuries. Within the street view signs are simply highlighted to obscure most of the buildings

along the street. If people (as activity) are included with the signs, then there is little actual building to be seen within the picture. Edo period signs are particularly interesting in that these include vertical banners at right angles to the building, squarish signs flat to the building, lantern signs and even large square roof-top signs – all precursors of today's babble of street information.

Nearly twenty years ago, Ashihara turned his attention to signs and modern Japanese streets.

3.38 *Street Signs in Ginza. The experience of the street-edge is one of signs. (Photograph: Leigh Woolley)*

3.38

He examined signs in Tokyo's glitzy Ginza Avenue and quantified their dominance. Along the two sides of an almost kilometre-long stretch, he found that there were two tall vertical signs (some are themselves vertical clusters of smaller signs) for each 9 metres of street. Further, for each metre of street length, there were over one and a half square metres of sign. Walking 3 metres from the street edge, virtually all of the building facade is obscured on that edge: at 6 metres, about 50 per cent comes into view (Ashihara, 1983, pp. 78–80) These figures are for buildings on which signs are well-spaced on the upper frontages and, I might add, do not include the giant roof signs which weigh heavily above.

Signage in cities has progressed since then and there are many areas of Tokyo (Shinjuku, Shibuya, Ikebukuro and Akihabara to name

but four) and of other cities (such as Osaka's Dotonbori district) which can easily outdo the still colourful but relatively sedate Ginza. Vertical and roof signs have been joined by massive flat and animated ones, not to mention large-scale screens complete with sound – in effect, street cinema. Also, since the majority of city streets are only 6 to 12 metres wide and do not have Ginza's consistently high buildings, it is impossible to step more than a few metres from the street edge (too narrow) or encounter those high building levels where signs are more generously spaced (fewer of them). Thus the dominance of signs is only amplified. Further, since most signs are commercial, their intensity is, in part, a reflection of the flow of people beneath and between them. In other words, the vortices of the city can be measured in signs and people. The buildings, while essential, are visually irrelevant, unless themselves the sign. Further, modern computer and electronic wizardry can only intensify such scenes.

Thus the Japanese street is a pulsating channel of information where content triumphs overwhelmingly over context or form with signs to the fore, as they have always been. Indeed, the prominence of the sign in Japan cannot be disassociated from the nature and power of *kanji* themselves and their place in Japanese culture. First, each *kanji* has a measure of independence and is capable of direct meaning. Second, most are pictographic or ideographic and combine easily with pictures. Third, the transcription of

3.39 *Signs attract People and People generate Signs. Kabukicho, Shinjuku. (Courtesy: Tokyo Metropolitan Government)*

3.39

these characters is a highly respected, old-established and widely pursued art form. *Kanji* can, at their best, be stunningly beautiful. Fourth, there are *kanji* for every occasion with at least four major and countless minor variations from the more rigid (*reisho* which might be associated with things Chinese) to the soft and flowing (*sosho* which might be associated with things refined and feminine), and including specialized versions with very particular associations (e.g.

sumo-moji with the sport of Sumo). These qualities all offer contrasts – some sharp, others by degree – with those of Western letters.

Further, as many linguists have noted, *kanji* stand independently of speech while Western letters are the servants of the spoken word (as abstract phonetic representations). In other words, *kanji* enjoy an independence which gives at least an equality with, if not a superiority, over the spoken word.

Finally, the linear thinking that underpins Western writing (namely, the total dependence upon sequential and unidirectional connection and punctuation) surfaces also in Western notions of city form. Western planning has for long been preoccupied with the composition of wholes: individual buildings are viewed as parts of a wider system of urban language, the basis of which is sequential connection and punctuation (mostly along streets). This has persisted at least from the early Renaissance through figures of both formal (e.g. Hausmann and Burnham) and more picturesque persuasions (e.g. Sitte and Cullen) to remain alive as conventional Western wisdom in contemporary practice.

In the West, the object is the building (and particularly the facade) as an element in the city's collective form with symbols and information controlled and relegated to minor and subservient places in the overall composition. This is especially the case in Scandinavia, Western and Southern Europe and the UK, where it is possible to walk through entire city districts in which lettering and signs are strictly controlled and building fronts above ground floor are substantially sign-free. (Or rather, they are free of applied signage for I realize the building may itself 'speak powerfully'.)

I might add that this Western antipathy to signs in city streets is far from new. In Europe, there have been attempts to restrict the number, types and size of signs in cities for at least 300 years, with the French seemingly to the fore. Garrioch (1994), in an interesting discussion of city house names and signs over four centuries quotes a number of sources to leave the reader in no doubt of the strong desire amongst civic officials to bring order and taste to city streets through the control of signs. He refers to various instances in London, Paris and elsewhere through the seventeenth and eighteenth centuries, namely, since Renaissance.

Thus, while the European street is a primary and positive form to which the sign must be subordinated, the Japanese street exists as the neutral and utilitarian container which is subordinate to or at least independent of the sign. It is against this broad cultural backcloth that Japan has long been able to project information more directly, more graphically, more powerfully and more profusely in its cities than has the West. Hence for Roland Barthes (1982), it was (and remains) the 'Empire of Signs'.

Buildings as Signboards and Vertical Streets

With the advent of Modern architecture, it was not uncommon to encounter a circulation stack (stairs and lifts) standing self-consciously as a prominent element of the building. It was one of those functional elements which could be easily expressed as a form in its own right (Gropius, Kahn, etc). In an extreme case it may even stand assertively independent of the main building with bridge links. In many Late-Modern designs, lifts and stairs have been joined by a host of other services on the building's exterior in even more conspicuous ways – as exemplified in Paris's Pompidou Centre and Lloyds of London Headquarters. Multiple slender piles or tubes have been stacked by or suspended from the main structure to be made more eye-catching by way of transparency, bright colour or other means.

In Japan, you may walk through virtually any city area where there are high buildings and encounter a distinct home-grown and unrelated variation on this theme. Such buildings may be commercial or residential or often both. Further, it is a building-type that has been around for a long time – at least since the 1960s. The main floor areas of the building are stacked up over the rear part of the plot. On each floor, there may be several establishments (bars, boutiques, offices or whatever) each with its own entrance onto a common area. Between the units and the street line will be the means of reaching them together with other services. Alternatively, there

3.40 *Signs about the Gateway to a Narrow Nagaya Lane. Numerous signs surround the entrance to inform passers-by of the people and services within. (Source: Shitamachi Museum; illustration from, 'Ukiyo doko' by Samba Shikitei)*

3.40

may be only a single establishment on each floor in which case the stacks of units and stairways/services may not be much different in size – both tall and pencil thin. There is, however, one big difference between these and the Late-Modern 'high architecture'. Stairs and services are joined by an unmistakable second element: signs to tell you what's going on in the building and how to get to there.

In other words, the building 'front' is much more than circulation: it is also information. The units in such a development may be very small indeed – as little as 20 or so square metres each. The building may rise through multiple storeys yet although this is not a Japanese tradition, the basic arrangement has otherwise a familiar ring. The earlier described *nagaya* units were small and reached by a small lane which was publicly

used and privately watched. At the entrance to the street, there were numerous signs advertising the services of the occupants within. Most services were shared. Each unit had its own entrance area (*genkan*) which opened directly to the outside and shoes were removed at this point. In today's buildings, there are distinct similarities, although upturned by the pressures urban economics and opportunity made possible by modern technology – building materials, lifts, neon and animated lighting.

In fact, the arrangement only duplicates what is still a common form at ground level, especially in bar areas today. (I have certainly been in some tiny bars in low ramshackle wooden buildings entered from narrow lanes – no more than 2 m wide – leading from the street to shared facilities, even in well-heeled pockets of Tokyo). In the

3.41 *Ichibankan (Architect: Minoru Takeyama 1968). The front circulation and service shaft towers over the narrow street as an enormous and powerful sign.*

3.42 *Ichibankan: Ground and Typical Above-ground Floor Plans. (Courtesy: Miroru Takeyama)*

3.41

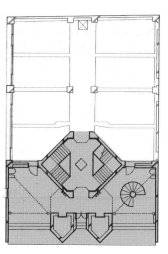

Ground Floor

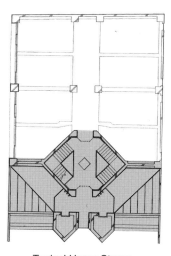

3.42

Typical Upper Storey

newer buildings, form may have undergone considerable transformation but essence certainly has not. In larger examples, the building is more like a pile of plots. In effect, the front zone is a vertical street which is both extension of the street below and of the building 'plots' behind. It is a hazy zone which is both alley and building edge, circulation and information.

3.43 *Ichibankan: Cut-away Axonometric Drawing. This shows clearly the 'sign and circulation' front, and the 'stack of plots' at the rear. (Courtesy: Miroru Takeyama)*

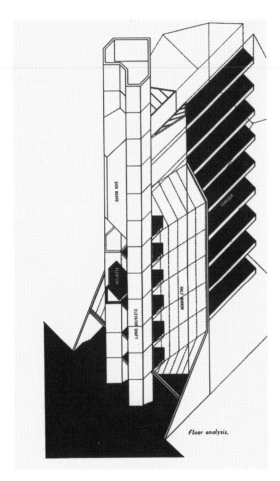

floor analysis.

3.43

For a significant building in the development of this genre we may look to a stack of bars in Shinjuku's Kabukicho district. 'Ichibankan' (or building one) rose during 1968 to be completed early the following year and brought Minoru Takeyama to prominence as an architect. At that time, East Shinjuku was a heartland of protest and porn and occupied a special place in the radical, intellectual and underworld cultures of the nation. The streets were thus seedy and savagely competitive places where assault from signs and speakers was at its most frenzied and furious.

The challenge was at least twofold. It was to standout in a section of the city saturated with signs yet, having joined the mob, to also retain self-respect. At that time, the city was not excessively high-rise and, in spite of the presence of the Metabolist school, Japan very much looked to the West for its multi-storey models of building. Thus to ignore that and transform the known horizontal into the vertical and so retain some continuity with the local past may not have been at all obvious.

Takeyama's 'Ichibankan' was an admirable response. Behind is the stack of plots with bars, numbering approximately fifty through eight square floors (except, that is, where the front stair well cuts a small triangle into the square). At the front is a soaring shaft of circulation which juts out menacingly above the street edge. This consists of two distinct parts, one solid (closest to the street) and one glazed (immediately behind). At both front and back, the solid bulges out at its upper levels, and is covered by loud stripes and smaller signboards: it reads like an enormous sign that has been shifted from the side of an American highway strip to be squeezed onto the side of this small (perhaps 8 m) Shinjuku Street. (It may be noted that this was three years before

3.44 *A Ginza Building with a 'Sign-and-Circulation Frontage'.*

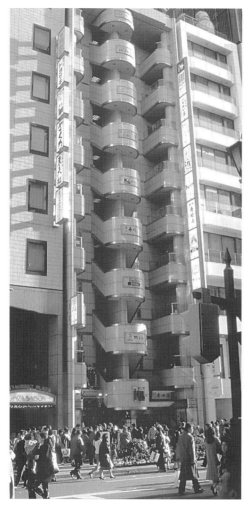

3.44

Venturi's iconoclastic celebration of Las Vegas signs.) At night the effect is only exaggerated as the glazed area lights up to emphasize the 'gap' between the striped solid and the rear stack of

'platform plots'. This is a classic front which is both sign and vertical street – or information and circulation – and, in various guises, is now to be seen all over Japan.

Streets, Sidewalks and Bridges

Streets without Sidewalks

When I step from my house in central Hobart or from my hotel in virtually any other Western downtown, I usually do so onto a pavement – or 'sidewalk' in America. In turn, the pavement ends and drops down by way of a kerb-and-gutter to the road and steps up again on the opposite side of the street in the same way. This is a typical Western street floor profile. Even narrow medieval streets were given pavements in most towns. Further, when these streets were first paved, it was their raised pathways along each side which were surfaced first – hence the term 'pavement' as distinct from the relatively rough and unimproved carriageway in the middle.

In Japan, wide or more commonly narrow, the standard street floor was flat – from one side to the other. When city streets were paved, it was not their edges that were favoured first for greatest improvement but rather their centres, where a band of paving maintained more solidly the grade of the edges.

Flat floored streets remain common today. Some streets, it may be argued, are so narrow that there is simply no room for kerbs and vehicles: white lines on a flat surface prevail indicating

3.45 *Street Floors. The two illustrations show the flat floor and central paving which was common in Japan (right), and the raised pavements or sidewalks typical in the West (left).*

3.46 *Flat Floored Street with Guard-rail, Osaka. In this Osaka street, a guard-rail separates people and cars but the street remains flat. In fact, so common is the flat floored street, that examples are to be found in photographs throughout this work. (Note also the maps of the district attached to the building wall. As noted in a previous section, maps are a common sight and very necessary in Japan.)*

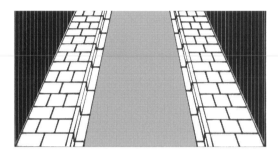
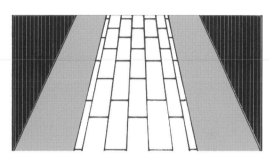

3.45

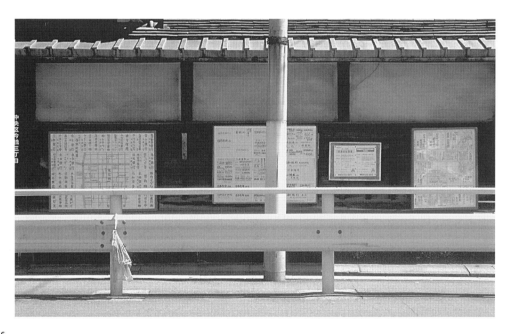

3.46

nominal areas to people and cars as the only way of accommodating both in a confined space. However, it is not uncommon to find wider streets which are also flat and uninterrupted. Sometimes a guard-rail or broken plinth will separate the area for pedestrians from that for cars. The flat street is, however, the Japanese tradition.

Where there are raised pavements, their paving patterns are generally less consistent than in the West. Patterns are as likely to be generated by

101

3.47 *A Patch of Local Sidewalk Paving, Nagasaki. Special paving associated with a particular colonnade in central Nagasaki. This kind of pavement improvement can be very limited in extent and initiated by very local interests. The domain is semi-private and semi-public and resources and initiatives resulting in such improvements commonly involve shopkeepers and local government.*

3.47

the interests of flanking properties or as extensions out from adjoining arcades with seeming disregard for continuity or consistency in the street as a whole. It would be easy to dismiss this as rampant capitalism with commercial interests exercising their private muscle to invade that which, in Western planning terminology is described as the 'public domain' (i.e. the public street as distinct from the private plot). Certainly in Australian cities, I am aware of developers who have sought to extend their (private) plaza's paving out over the (public) pavement to the edge of the roadway and so interrupt the sidewalk paving. I am also aware that this has been resisted

by some local authorities on the grounds that this would disrupt the continuity of the street, a strong element of which is the pattern (and usually linear continuity) of the paving.

However, the idea of a building extending into the street area for sales or for a special (for instance festival) occasion is not at all alien in Japan. It is, indeed, more common than not. The idea of paving patterns and other items of urban detail (lighting, railings, seats, etc.) being generated by or linked to individual or group interests along the street is also more acceptable. It may be the shopkeepers of a particular *machi* (or more localized group) who band together to improve only short stretches of streets (or cross-streets or street block) and this accords with the notion of the city as patchwork.

All of this is not to infer that the raised sidewalk is absent or even rare in Japan. On the contrary, it is today a very familiar sight, especially on wider commercial streets. Visitors who do not step beyond big city tourist spots might even take it to be the norm. It is, however, an imported (Western) practice dating from the Meiji era. Significantly, the famous 'Bricktown' transformation of the Ginza (a consciously Western development following an 1872 fire) was probably the first extensive area of streets in a Japanese city with raised pavements. Nevertheless, to this day, the flat floored street remains widespread and is to be found both in old city areas and in some newer ones where narrowness is not a constraining factor.

3.48 *Narrow Street with Raised Pavements, Lincoln, England. Even a narrow historic street such as this one has raised pavements on both sides. Their distinctive lines reinforce visually the street form as a defined linear space.*

3.49 *Shop Display invades the Street, Tokyo. Goods and signs spill out from the building onto the street edge: a zone shared by street and building.*

3.50 *Sidewalk Cafe, Hobart, Australia. On this historic frontage in Salamanca Place, Hobart, the tables and chairs are distinctly outside the building and in the space: i.e. beyond the wall and on the (public) street.*

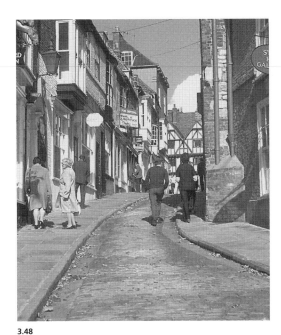

3.48

3.49

3.50

Visually, the raised sidewalk has contributed greatly to the shaping of the Western street as a continuous space. By paralleling the side walls, the step-up to each side pavement gives visual emphasis to the street as a formed linear space – and, indeed, to the pavement as an equally linear sub-space.

In Japan, the side areas are less conspicuous. When paving occurred centrally, this gave emphasis to the street as route. The side areas remain more susceptible to invasion both by traffic from the centre route and by activity and information from the flanking buildings. Thus, the structure of the Japanese street has been rather more inde-

terminate than in the West. It has occurred as the necessary interval to allow both for movement and connection between private plots and for the extension of flanking buildings by way of activity and information. In the West, even where private activity has invaded the street (as, for instance, with the street cafe) the spatial experience is generally one of being in front of the building and as part of the street ('to see and be seen' in the public domain) rather than of occupying a (private) extension to a building. In the case of the earlier-mentioned *machiya*, the nature of the building edge (the ground level floor which is under the roof but preceding the step up to the raised floor and true interior) further obscures the line between building and street. In other words, the Western arrangement, although changing, is again something more fixed and finite with less capacity for transformation.

Sidewalks as Streets

My text so far has given such emphasis to the narrowness of Japanese streets that readers without first-hand experience of the country may be wondering if there is such a species as the wide street. In fact, all Japanese cities have streets which are distinctly narrow and those which are similarly wide. The former are numerous and part of a vast grid or, more likely, labyrinth (depending upon the particular city or quarter) of small lanes, old and new. Most connect but dead-ends are not uncommon.

The wide streets are relatively few, widely spaced and frequently dual carriageway. In some places (e.g. Nagasaki, Kumomoto, Matsuyama, Okayama), they may carry tramlines at their centres. The wide streets are invariably the results of twentieth century road widening schemes where, in may cases, whole street blocks have been demolished to accommodate the new roads or they may have emerged in the wake of damage from earthquake, fire or war. And surprisingly often, they result from the filling of old waterways or reclamation of shorelines (river estuaries

and sea). I shall refer to these wide streets as 'big roads'. Whatever the process and wherever the city, it is usual for a new and coarser grain of big roads to have been superimposed upon an older and finer grained text. Moreover, the relationship between the two grains is a fascinating one.

The small streets are generally flat-floored and narrow (4 to 10 m wide) as illustrated in the last section. They are always home to pedestrians and bicycles, and used also by motor cycles and local motor vehicles as well. The narrowest and steepest streets are not used by vehicles.

The big roads usually include wider carriageways for vehicles plus generous sidewalks. However, sidewalks are only superficially like Western pavements. In reality, they are a continuation of that labyrinth of small lanes that extends over the rest of the city. They may not carry cars but, in addition to people, they do carry bicycles and are also frequented by small motorbikes (although whether this is legal I am unsure). The sidewalks are mostly raised although sometimes they remain at the same level as the roadway but separated from it by pipe-rail fence, plinth and/or clipped hedge. Power poles and/or trees may also punctuate the line between carriageway and sidewalk. The roadside edge of the sidewalk will probably accommodate bicycle and motorcycle parking, bus shelters, entrances to subways and a host of other urban paraphernalia. Signs and displays from flanking businesses and other sources may occupy both sides of a pavement.

3.51 *Typical Flat Floored Small Street. These are shared by people and local vehicles.*

3.52 *Typical 'Big Road' with Broad Carriageways and Sidewalks in Nagoya. (Photograph: Fumihiko Iwano)*

3.51

3.52

3.53 *Looking Down on a 'Sidewalk Street'.*

These three photographs are taken opposite Nagasaki Station and in very close proximity to each other. The first (3.53) looks down onto a 'sidewalk street' flanking a 'big road' (in fact, Route 202 just visible on the right). It is taken from a bridge leading from the station over Route 202. The second (3.54) is a street-level view of the same place. In both pictures it is possible to detect a left-hand turn into a small street (without sidewalks).

3.53

While the pedestrian may not be able to shut out the noise from the vehicles, the sense of separation and independence from the road can be substantial. Conversely, the sense of connection from the sidewalk to the small lanes running through the adjacent blocks is strong. What is more, in the Japanese city system, the sides of these big roads are likely to bear different names being parts of different *machi*. Likewise, each may display different paving patterns and design themes, generated often by the initiative of shopkeepers in the particular *machi*. They are, in a very real sense, 'Sidewalk Streets'.

The independence of each sidewalk flanking a wide carriageway is never more evident than where one side is covered by an arcade-like structure but the other is not. It has been quite common in Japan for groups of shopkeepers to band together and cooperate with local authorities to provide covered ways along their frontages. Where these are built along narrow streets, they span the whole street and there are hundreds of such places across the nation. However, sidewalk covers standing between shops and carriageway are also common and the structures employed in these places are not

The third (3.55) is the view along that small street, i.e. a 'street without sidewalks'. In fact, the sidewalk-street and street-without-sidewalks bear much of the same feeling and are part of the same system of small streets. They are quite distinct from the main route or 'big road'. This sense of continuity (of small streets) and severance (from the big road) is reinforced by name (they are part of the same machi) and street paving.

3.54 *Looking Along the Same Sidewalk Street.*

3.55 *Turning the Corner into a Street without Sidewalks.*

3.54

3.55

essentially different to those over small streets. They are usually freestanding with columns on both sides. They are normally of the same scale: two storeys high and incorporate similar infrastructure such as power lines and lighting. (More explanation of these phenomena appear in the next section on arcades and colonnades and some readers may wish to read that now.)

Such structures provide quite a contrast to Western street-side covers which are generally an integral part of the flanking building (such as the European colonnade) or an outgrowth from it (such as the Australian lean-to verandah or projecting canopy). The Western covers are also integral parts of the total street space and, hierarchically, form sub-spaces.

In short, the Japanese sidewalk covers replicate

the form and the spirit of their arcade counterparts which cover complete streets. This only reinforces the notion of the sidewalk as an extension of the system of small streets. In other words, the sidewalk as a small street and the great carriageway which, side-by-side, make up the big roads are, to a large extent, dislocated from each other. In the West, the pavement or sidewalk is invariably conceived as an integral component of the formal assemblage of parts which make the street space as a whole, no matter how broad. This is the Western urban design tradition: further, smaller and larger streets are part of a unified network of formal spaces. This occurs even in Paris, where Hausmann sliced through a city of relatively small streets with grand boulevards yet connected the two in a

3.56 *View from a 'Soft-yolk' Small Street to a Stilted Expressway above a Big Road, Akasaka, Tokyo.*

3.56

visually integrated manner. In Japan, the systems of big roads and narrow streets (including sidewalk streets) coexist but are strangely separate.

This dislocation between sidewalk street and big road is, in fact, not unlike that between ground level streets and the elevated freeways which snake through most big Japanese cities. Indeed the views along some of the small 'soft yolk' streets now close on multi-deck expressways which rise on steel and concrete stalks and stilts above established big roads. These structures can seem ominously large relative to the lines of lower foreground buildings along

the 'soft yolk' streets. To most Westerners, it is a rather offensive view and such a reaction is only reinforced by the tangle of decorative, functional and informative street elements such as lights, wires and signs which filter the 'view'.

Upstairs, drivers speed or crawl (depending on the time of day) quite oblivious to the city below, glimpsing from the topmost level (the expressways may be double or even triple-decker) only the city's taller towers. Where sound baffles give rise to a distinctively 'tube-like' passage across the city, drivers are quite unaware of the rest of the city. As in an underground train, where there are no visual clues to depth, here there are none to altitude. Indeed, I have had the dubious delight at the end of a Tokyo holiday weekend of watching drivers pay steep tolls for the privilege of watching their mini televisions from behind their wheels while hovering in standstill conditions on the expressways oblivious to the world below. There, at ground level, passage through the city proceeded smoothly – as I discovered when my taxi driver had the wit to forget his hefty toll and descend from the upper level.

Such scenes occur not through lack of sensibility but rather a different one which attributes greater independence to each element of the urban environment. The juxtaposition of stilted freeways over the big ground-level roads as well as over historic places (for example, over the nation's historic Nihonbashi) and scenic rivers is simply more obvious than that of the sidewalk street by big road. Both are, however, part of a

3.57 *Historic Nihonbashi (Bridge) in the Shadow of the Shuto Expressway, Tokyo. Such scenes are not restricted to the capital but are common everywhere. (Courtesy: Tokyo Metropolitan Government)*

3.58 *Nottingham's Council House Arcade. It is an integral part of the design of the building and the kind of form to which it is difficult to add or take anything away.*

3.57

3.58

way of thinking about space which sees elements of different scales (or even similar scales for that matter) as independent and relative equals, and one that is prepared to build a city by way of superimposition rather than visual integration. This is a point of considerable practical and aesthetic importance.

The Ways of Arcades

Arcades

At the centre of my boyhood city is a very big square – some two hectares in extent. Though the landscape that we see today is only seventy years old, the basic form of the space goes back over centuries. In 1927, Nottingham moved its market from the Market Place and rebuilt both the square (now known as Old Market Square) and its town hall (known as the Council House) at the head of the space. The 'new' square has a

central sunken axis leading up to an imposing ionic Council House front topped by a massive Wrennaissance dome (which landed in Nottingham from the Greenwich Naval College via London's Old Bailey courthouse). The landmark dome houses the city clock with a chime that rivals Big Ben. The whole design, building and square, has shades of English Baroque, America's City Beautiful and Milan's Galleria Vittorio Emanuele rolled into one.

3.59 *Nottingham's Old Market Square and Council House. The head of the arcade lies under the Council House dome and on the extended centre line of the square. In other words it is part of a civic concept which extends beyond the building. (Photograph: Steve Whitely)*

3.59

The Council House (the name itself echoes its City Beautiful connections) occupies the entire city block at the head of the square. When opened in 1928, it included civic, judicial, administrative and commercial functions. Shops remain on the ground floor behind the civic showpiece front. They enjoy double frontages –both to the surrounding streets and to an internal arcade. For behind the grand facade and under the dome is a T-plan arcade with an entrance from each of the other three sides. Topping the arcade is a barrel-vaulted glazed roof which, although an integral part of the whole design, is subservient to the classically detailed walls. The walls are the space-makers and the spaces climax under the dome where there is a pendentive form complete with frescoes.

In other words, the arcade, while a strong entity within itself, is also an integral part of the building as a whole *and* part of a composition that extends well beyond the building. The arcade's main axis is a continuation of the central axis of the square beyond the facade. Further, its focal point under the dome signified (certainly at the time of building) *the* centre of the entire city.

In this way, Nottingham's Council House arcade is a caricature of Western arcade design. Many may not be part of quite such an extensive design idea. Most are, however, designed as part of a concept which is inclusive, from the outset, of flanking shops and other built elements. The roofs of these arcades are integral to but subservient to their space-making decorative walls. They are normally glazed (a substitute for sky) and elegant respecters of those detailed building elements, such as cornices and pilasters, which have assisted since ancient times to give spaces definition and order. Flanking walls, roof and detailed building elements combine to make a total spatial composition. In other words, they are conceived at one time as complete entities which are difficult to change in an additive fashion.

In Japan, a shopping arcade of some description is to be found in just about every self-respecting town. The significance of the shopping arcade to urban Japan is not unlike the main street mall was to the Australian or American town twenty or so years ago. It was the *sine qua non* of municipal progress and commercial prosperity. Superficially, the most developed Japanese arcades bear resemblance to Western arcades –

3.60 *An Arcade in Nara City. The entrance projects out into the street, emphasizing its independence as a structure. The arcade is lined by buildings which are themselves independent structures.*

3.61 *An Arcade in Shimabara, Nagasaki Prefecture. At this point, the arcade 'marches' uninterruptedly across two streets and a river. It also widens in the form of a glazed coloured dome at the river's bridging point.*

3.60

3.61

with a semicircular roof and regular vertical elements on each side. However, only a little further consideration will reveal what a very different structure and idea it really is.

To start with, it is the structure of the Japanese arcade which is visually dominant as an entity within itself and this is quite independent of flanking buildings. The Japanese arcade is neither a building nor an enclosed spatial entity in the Western sense: it is rather a covered route. The

rhythm of the arcade comes not from the repetitive elements of the flanking walls but from the regular pairs of columns which are the structure of the arcade itself. In place of the regular line of the flanking walls are an *ad hoc* collection of voids (walk-in open fronts), more conventional shop fronts, and great arrays of signs and display. Lights and signs are suspended and otherwise attached to the arcade structure rather than projected out from the walls (as in the West) to

3.62 *Japanese and Western Arcades. In the former, roof and supporting columns are the dominating route-making elements: the structure is likely to be flexible (e.g. retractable roof) and the flanking buildings are independent and therefore changeable. In the West, the walls are the dominating space-making elements: the roof is a substitute sky and all are part of a fixed and total form.*

 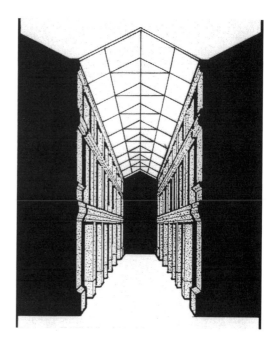

3.62

further assert 'the arcade' as an independent structure and covered route. In some instances, the arcade structure will project out well beyond the line of the buildings at its street entrance to give added emphasis to its separateness. And in the same vein, arcades will commonly march without interruption across little and even large streets to give final confirmation of their autonomy.

Flanking buildings and arcade stand independently of each other. Accordingly, the shopper can stop along the route and glimpse slits of light between many of the buildings along the way. One may even find an occasional big hole in the side where new development is underway.

Very occasionally, there may be a building with an ornate facade: here, the arcade is unlikely to make design concessions to the building's special characteristics but cut callously across its composition. It seems no exaggeration to liken the covered route to a station platform which offers protected access to the carriages (in this case, to the shops) parked temporarily along the sides. If the roof is part open (many have retractable roofs) and part translucent (which is a common recipe), then the wires, catwalks and other elements of the superstructure may be glimpsed in their nakedness or as sharp shadows of utility.

The contrast between the utility and the formality of the respective Japanese and Western arcades is a direct extension of that between the street forms of the two cultures. This is perhaps to be expected since the Japanese arcade is usually a structure that is superimposed over an existing street: it has a similar ambiguous relationship with its surroundings as does the street. Some even accommodate vehicular traffic. As such, even the most sophisticated Japanese arcades (and some are technologically very sophisticated) are not the aesthetic delights of their Western counterparts but they are extremely practical – flexible and comfortable. They are indoor-outdoor. They allow buildings to sprout and fall along each side. And they offer welcome protection from prolonged rains, hot sun and, to an extent, winter cold.

The arcade concept in Japan is thus that of a covered way and so reinforces the contrasting notions of street-as-route and street-as-formed-space. Its parentage is to be found in another elemental typology from the Japanese city, 'the Shopping Street'. If an enquiry is made into the background of most arcades, the chances are that it replaced a Shopping Street. It is important therefore to introduce the shopping street, albeit very briefly. Also, I should not complete this section without reference to the *torii*-delineated route to a Shinto Shrine. For whenever I pass through a Japanese arcade, I am always reminded of both the experience of both shopping street and the *torii* route.

Shopping Streets

For every arcade that exists in Japan, there are at least several shopping streets. These are not merely streets with shops along them but streets with particular features. The first and most common indicator is the entrance defined by two upright posts and one or more straight or curved connecting elements which will probably bear a name and decoration. Some entrance gates are very bright and colourful but all, in form, are a commercial variation on the *torii* theme. This latter point is given further weight by the use of such gates to announce that a shopping street is imminent if not in sight – like the memorable dragon gate, in Nagasaki, which signifies the route to Chinatown.

Sometimes, as on the route to a Shinto shrine, there is a whole sequence of these free-standing 'gates'. More likely, the rhythm established by the entrance uprights will be continued by pairs of posts that support fancy lights, banners or little gate like projections (as in the *kanji* character, 'mon' meaning gate). Special paving and other urban details may be added to give the particular stretch of street even further identity of its own. Above and about the columns are the inevitable tangles of wires although these fade surprisingly quickly from one's consciousness. (After only a short while in Japan, these seem as natural and inevitable as the tough and ubiquitous spider webs that link power poles and trees over Japanese country lanes.)

Behind the column pairs, there are the shops,

3.63 *Shopping Street and Arcade. Beyond this arcade in Nara, the gate to a shopping street is visible across the road ahead. In fact, the two are part of the city's net of 'small streets' and the road one of its 'big roads'.*

3.63

many of which open their fronts (metal roller shutters are increasingly common) to allow their displays to extend outwards and occupy that transition zone between the shops and route in which the columns also stand. Shopping streets may be long (certainly several hundred metres) but they are rarely wide: the common widths would be from 5 to 10 metres. Vehicular access is often restricted but rarely banned altogether. Always however, the rhythm of the flanking columns gives a strong sense of route independent of the buildings. It is a proven typology to which a roof may be added to equal 'arcade'. Indeed, they will sometimes continue the line of an arcade.

Colonnades

There are many examples of colonnades along Western city streets. Perhaps the best known of all are in the Italian city of Bologna. Here, the colonnade on each side of the street echo each other's form. They are an integral part of the design of the buildings and the street. Consistent colonnade form may even be repeated around whole street blocks, as in the original centre of Canberra. Around that earlier mentioned Nottingham square (and beyond in some directions), there are also colonnades. The buildings span several centuries from old and ornate to bland and modern. All however incorporate colonnades which are both an integral part of the individual building designs and collectively part of a concept which extends cover around the edge of a big city space.

Other forms of street edge cover are common in Australian cities. These are the verandah and sidewalk canopy. The verandah is the older of the two types and is effectively a lean-to structure, with the roof spanning between building wall and a row of verandah columns. The later canopy is usually projected from the wall of the building (and a bi-product of traffic engineers who did not want verandah posts close to the road edge). The important point is, however, that in both instances the structures involved are very much outgrowths from the building and the resulting covered spaces are experienced as sub-spaces within the total space of the street.

As earlier indicated, Japan also has covers over some of its sidewalks but they are markedly

3.64 *Colonnade Italian-style: Bologna.*
(Photograph: Richard Blythe)

3.65 *Verandah Australian-style: Adelaide.*
Although the two are very different, both
colonnade (as a part of the building) and verandah
(as an extension to it) are integral to the design
concept of both building (as outdoor cover) and
street (as subspace) compositions.

3.64

3.65

different from those of the West. These covered
ways commonly replicate in form the Japanese
arcade. That is, there are columns on both
sides of the walkway with a roof, often curved,
spanning between the two. It is thus not a true
colonnade (a walkway behind columns under the
edge of the building and open to one side) or anything like the verandah (effectively a lean-to). It is
again a freestanding covered route with, in all
likelihood, banners hanging from the columns on
both sides or centrally from the structure above.
Either way the colonnade has its own centre line
– like an arcade. The signs partly obscure the
building fronts as they do the views of the wider
street including the sidewalk on the opposite
side. The shops stand independently as they do
along the arcades: any one may be demolished
and replaced in isolation.

Where colonnades occur on both sides of a
street then, likely as not, these will be different in
design. Sometimes, a sidewalk colonnade will
connect with a small street arcade and the two
will share the same design language – perhaps
within same *machi* or *chome*? In other words,
the sidewalk colonnade, as with the street arcade
stands strongly in its own right as a covered
route.

115

3.66 *'Colonnade' Japanese-style: Nagasaki. In fact, it is little different from a Japanese arcade: the colonnade's structure is usually symmetrical and stands independently but between building and road rather than building and building.*

3.66

This similarity of the structure of a colonnade over a sidewalk and an arcade over a small street only reinforces an earlier point: namely, the similarity of big road sidewalks and small streets and the high measure of visual independence enjoyed by the sidewalks from the wide carriageways alongside and road as a whole. The similarities of cover treatment gives further emphasis to the notion of small streets and big road sidewalks as part of one system of routes which is relatively independent of another system consisting of the big road carriageways. Hence my analogy with the old cities of waterways where sidewalk streets and side streets provide one system of small streets while the carriageways of the big roads supersede waterways.

Bridges

One may ride, walk or go by boat to any quarter of the town; for it is not only divided by two rivers, but it is also intersected by numbers of canals crossed by queer little bridges curved like a well-bent bow.

Lafcadio Hearn, 1894 (Glimpses of Unfamiliar Japan,
p. 161)

Taken together, Japan's four main islands are roughly 2000 kilometres long but on average only 200 kilometres wide. In addition, the coast is highly indented. Japan has therefore a very long coastline. At the same time, its land is mostly (70 per cent) mountainous and few people live in these parts. It is also very wet with numerous rivers and streams. Most cities of any size grew up by water – most by some combination of coast, river and marsh. As a consequence, shore, rivers, streams, canals and moats (about defensive sites) became very common elements of the Japanese urban landscape. Further, these various waterways were often connected to provide an extensive system of waterways for both transport and recreation. Wheeled vehicles played a very minor role in Japan's cities until well into the Meiji period when the country made the conscious effort to modernize in Western mode. Both Tokyo and Osaka are good examples of such cities.

Extensive infilling of the canals, moats and rivers as well as reclamation of swamps and shorelines has occurred since the Meiji period which makes it very difficult for today's observer

3.67 *Kintaikyo Bridge at Iwakuni. The five arches of this bridge make it unusual. However it is perhaps the one place in Japan today where one can still stand on a high timber bridge and enjoy a view over town buildings: one view from the bridge is over buildings to a steeply-wooded hillside immediately beyond.*

to appreciate just how watery most of Japan's cities once were. Although if we read today's city maps, we quickly discover that many places which are now quite dry were once extremely wet. Place-names incorporating the terms *hashi* or *bashi* (bridge), *jima* or *shima* (island), and *kawa* or *gawa* (river) are frequently spotted where none appears today. In other words, these once watery places have been wiped from their city's topography. Indeed, one does not have to venture far from Tokyo Station to discover dry places with water-under-the-bridge names: for instance, Kyobashi, Sukiyabashi and Shimbashi.

As outlined earlier in this chapter, a fine grained combination of *yashiki*, *machiya*, *nagaya* and streets once made up the built-up districts of Japanese cities: these were separated by water and joined by numerous bridges. While some bridges were flat or at least flattish, many were steeply arched to achieve considerable height. Thus, in cities of low wooden buildings (essentially one and two storeys), the bridges could offer sweeping views out. And since so many towns were by both water and hills, views could be had out over the grey-brown buildings to the green or other colours (depending upon season) of the agricultural terraces and forested slopes (where there were temples and shrines), beyond. Further, at ground level, open areas would often occur around bridges – sometimes by order as fire breaks. Thus, in a dense and extensive built-up city, the bridge and its environs offered some sense of spaciousness.

3.67

Bridges and their surroundings were indeed Very Important Places. They were nodal points in the city. What is more, they could be just as nodal whether they rose towards the middle or the periphery of a city's amoeboid-like mass of variable density. The environs of some bridges were commercially orientated while about others, often towards the periphery, they may be more geared to the pleasure side of life (though in a money-making sense, no less commercial).

117

3.68 *Nihon-bashi. The most famous and perhaps busiest bridge in the whole of Edo Japan still gave an experience of openness and view out in a setting that was far from monumental. (Source: Shiraishi, 1993; original in Edo meisho Zue)*

3.68

In Edo, the prime example of the former type was Nihonbashi and of the latter, Ryogokubashi.

One is left in no doubt about the importance of these and other bridges after only a casual perusal of any screen painting or series of Edo period or early Meiji prints, especially *meisho zue* (tourist scenes and landmarks) of a Japanese town. Drawing upon such works, Professor Jinnai has given us some vivid impressions of Edo's bridges and their surroundings.

Of Nihonbashi, he refers to thick foot traffic, intense market activity and the view of the bustle from the bridge. He also refers to its social function for public notices and for the public exposure of criminals with places reserved for each on the west and east sides respectively of the southern (i.e. Ginza) end (Jinnai, 1995, p. 78). Of course, in European cities the same public functions occurred in their (enclosed) central squares and in the shadow of their (monumental)

3.69 *The Public Bulletin Board or Kosatsu at Nihon-bashi. The board (as pictured in an 1876 publication) is just visible in the top left of the previous figure (3.68). (Source: Griffis, 1876)*

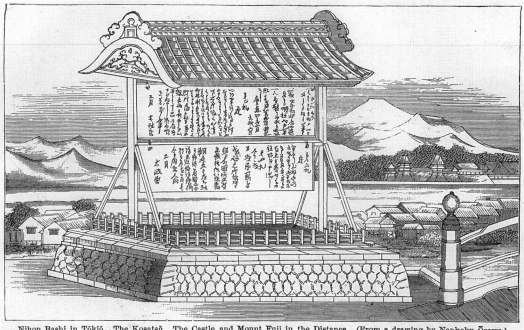

Nihon Bashi in Tōkiō. The Kosatsŭ. The Castle and Mount Fuji in the Distance. (From a drawing by Nankoku Ōzawa.)

3.69

institutional buildings. (See figure 1.6 for a diagrammatic comparison of the bridge and square.) At Nihonbashi, the scene could not have been more different. There were no monumental institutional buildings. The centrepiece was in fact a utility, the bridge. The view was more 'open, over and out' than 'closed, restricted and contained'. The bridge environs were at best loosely defined with a clear centre object (the bridge) but no obvious boundary – rather a field of influence.

The structure for public notices is itself worthy of comment. It was a roofed structure (superficially reminiscent of a lych-gate or well roof in the West) in a small raised fenced area which was something of a cross between a mini plot and plinth. This very important object was the town bulletin board. Its raised free-standing nature again makes a telling contrast with the West where town notice boards were attached to the walls of important buildings (the boundary walls to public spaces) or, indeed,

3.70 *Ryogoku-bashi. This large bridge over the Sumidagawa (river) and its open environs provided a peripheral festivity and pleasure centre. This picture shows the early summer firework display. (Source: Shiraishi, 1993; original in Edo Meishi Zue)*

3.70

proclaimed theatrically (in England by the town crier) against the backdrop of enclosed and monumental solidity.

Illustrations of Ryogokubashi seem to outnumber even those of Nihonbashi – no doubt due to its association with pleasure and festivity and to its sheer size and strategic position. The bridge provided the eastern entrance to Edo. About its ends, ground was, by order of the authorities, to be kept free as firebreaks only to

be occupied by people and temporary structures serving as teahouses, restaurants and abodes for storytelling, puppet theatre, erotic shows and other entertainments. Beneath, the river teemed with craft offering pleasure in the summer months on the relative cool of the water. Again there was no clear edge but the focus was unmistakably the bridge, hump-backed and over 200 metres long. The hump rose high over both river and the squat city buildings beyond. Also,

3.71 *Fireworks on the Sumidagawa Today.*
The traditional display of fireworks to mark the
beginning of summer was revived a few years
ago – in the vicinity of Ryogoku-bashi.
(Courtesy: Tokyo Metropolitan Government)

3.71

its sweeping vistas took in Japan's most revered mountain, known affectionately as Fujisan.

Various artists captured the force and fervour of the activity on the bridge and on both land and water about it: they also portrayed the strength and scale of the bridge itself (sometimes by way of a fragment), together with more distant views of the squat city buildings and occasionally the cone of Fuji. At Ryogoku on the Sumida sensational displays of fireworks on the twenty-

eighth days of the fifth and eighth months marked the beginning and the end of the summer river season: these occasions were too celebrated in prints.

The bridge was nevertheless the focal constant in an open centre of temporary components (tents, stalls and boats) which together supported a vast array of signs, lanterns, people and activities that made Ryogokubashi the colourful and magnetic place that it was. Taking a term from contemporary planning, it was very much a peripheral centre.

However, Nihonbashi and Ryogokubashi were but two of many bridges that served as the focal points of Edo's central places in a city of many centres. Other bridge centres, which also caught the artists' eyes, included Nakabashi, Kyobashi, Suidobashi, Sukiyabashi and Shimbashi to name but a few. Further, these centres offered less a sense of enclosure than one of spaciousness which might extend far beyond their immediate environs.

While a massive fortified compound stood at Edo's centre, it was for most people an empty centre with the activity centres distributed through the surrounding Edo spiral. There is an Hiroshige bird's-eye view of Edo which is much symbolic of this pattern and quality. The only cloud over the city hovers above the middle of the picture to obscure much of the Imperial compound which has the effect of emphasizing the compound's void-like presence while directing the eye to the relatively tiny Nihonbashi (to the

3.72 *The Pattern of Hiroshige's Bird's Eye View of Edo. This abstraction of Hiroshige's print shows only the coastline and river, the extent of the city (dark shade), the distant Mount Fuji and the sites of the city's famous places (each represented by an upright rectangle (in fact, a banner-like marking on the original). The 'emptiness' of the castle area at the centre is reinforced by a substantial covering of cloud. Beyond is the distant Fujisan whose dislocation from the city is also emphasized by cloud. What is surprising is the even spread of famous places over the full extent of the city. In fact, many of the famous places are bridges including Nihon-bashi marked by the larger rectangle in the middle foreground.*

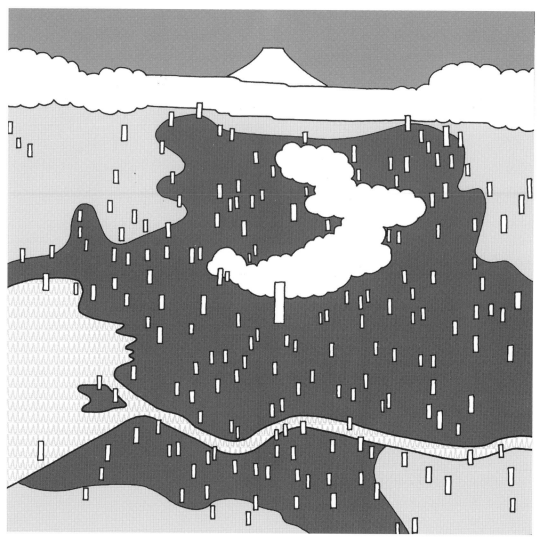

3.72

fore within the city) and to the mass of distant Fujisan (behind the city).

It should not surprise therefore that in the Meiji period and later moves towards 'modern-

3.73 *From Waterway to Big Road and Subway: the Nagaborigawa, Osaka. The maps show the river in the late seventeenth century (left) and the same place now (right): in today's city, it is site for both 'big road' (the Nagabori-dori) and subway. However, while the water has disappeared, three subway stations still bear the names of bridges: Nagabori-bashi (A), Shinsai-bashi (B) and Yotsu-* *bashi (C). (Source: Adapted from Jokamachi Kochizu Sampo 4: Osaka-Kinki (1) no Jokamachi)*

ization' (and Western-style 'enlightenment'), the bridge environs, became focal points for change. It was around those places that the tallest and most solid buildings with decorated fronts and feature corners (sometimes even towers) tended to appear first. Again, Professor Jinnai has shown how Tokyo's bridge areas became the early recipients of such buildings: examples included the First National Bank (1872) at Kaiunbashi and the Central Post Office and Central Post and Telegraph Office (1874 and 1892 respectively) at Edobashi; the Yomiuri Shimbun (newspaper) Office at Kyobashi (1908): at Nihonbashi, there was the Murai Bank (1910), Imperial Hemp Spinning Company Building (1911) and Nomura Building (1929) and the transformation of the bridge itself in 1910 to its present form (Jinnai, 1995).

Where waterways and bridges were primary elements in a Japanese city, it was the waterways that provided the widest arteries; and along these the more significant nodes occurred around the more important bridges. The waterways were however crossed by scores of lesser bridges – in status though not always in size. An 1687 map of Osaka shows some ninety bridges crossing the city's main waterways. Where the rivers and canals formed T-junctions or crossings, the bridges often spanned the watery gaps across all three or four openings to connect the city's streets. Compared to most of the waterways, the streets were narrow. They crossed the city in a more or less grid-like pattern and

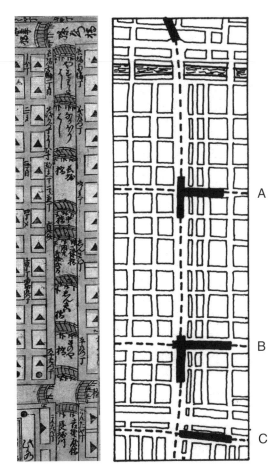

3.73

included streets immediately alongside the banks of most river and canal sides. In other words, there was a system of big scale and widely spaced waterways and a finer net of small scale streets. The bridges were the points at which the two crossed.

3.74 *From Old Bridge to Modern Node: Sotobori (moat), and Sukiya-bashi, Tokyo. Sukiya-bashi was once the bridge between castle (later, government area) and commercial quarter. Today, the waterway has long gone, having given way to the 'big road' (Sotobori-dori), stilted expressway and* subway; *yet the old bridge site remains as a centre of gravity with three department stores (on sites 1 and 2), the Sony Building (3) and a cinema complex within its immediate field. A small police box (4) is very close to that centre of gravity. (Source: Based on 1884 and 1986 maps of Tokyo)*

Twentieth century transportation has of course placed new transport pressures upon cities. Railways, trams and motor vehicles, have all exerted their demands for more space to which the old Japanese street systems were ill-equipped to respond. Extensive demolition has occurred in all cities for street-widening purposes. But in the water cities, prime candidates for the new vehicle routes were the old waterways. Extensive engineering programmes turned countless waterways into *odori* (big streets or avenues) with wide carriageways and generous sidewalks. (In addition, there may sometimes be tram-routes at their centres or subways beneath.) Thus, to continue an earlier thread, it should come as no surprise that we find the *odori* sidewalks more like Japanese small streets than Western pavements. In a very real sense, many sidewalk streets replaced canal-side streets to become, in effect, more part of a general system of 'streets without sidewalks': as roadways replaced waterways to become part of the system of big roads.

For the pedestrian in today's city, the primary experience is that of walking on 'small streets without sidewalks' *and* 'sidewalk streets'. When walking in a city where water was once prevalent, the chances of following an old waterside street are quite high when flanking an *odori* route. Further, many of the nodal centres that one encounters in such a city are likely to be the old crossing points of waterways and streets, i.e. the old bridging points. Today, they are the crossing points of big roads and small streets,

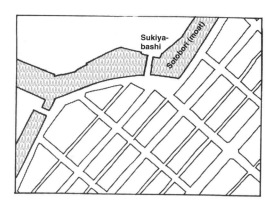

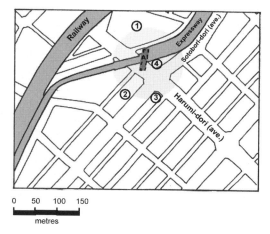

0   50   100   150

metres

3.74

including sidewalk streets. They are also the foci for higher buildings and it is usually easy in these places to obtain an elevated cafe seat or equivalent vantage point to look down over the crossing. From above, today's ground plane is dominated by two colours: black and white. These are the massive and multiple zebra stripes

3.75 *Looking North-west across the Intersection of Sotobori-dori (Outer Moat Avenue) and Harumi-dori. This photograph, taken in 1989, shows the crossing of the two 'big roads' and the elevated Shuto Expressway. Sukiya-bashi Hankyu Department Store is on the extreme left and a playful police box (architect: Yamashita) on the extreme right: the latter stands just to the fore of the former (Sukiya-bashi) bridge.*

3.75

which provide the crosswalk paths for people who wish to get from one side of each roadway to the other. Thus, when I look out over such crossings today, they tend to rise and arch themselves in my mind's eye.

The meeting of the two big roads, Sotobori Dori and Harumi Dori, in central Tokyo is a crossing that springs immediately to mind. It occurs right next to the site of the old Sukiyabashi (bridge) and Gate which together once provided both the connection and barrier between the quarters of artisans and aristocrats. Gathered about it today are Yurakucho Mullion (a multi-use retail, cinema and cultural centre), the Sony Building (a commercial exhibition and restaurant centre) and two large department stores. At the centre of gravity sits the eye of authority in the form of the playful-looking Ginza Sukiyabashi police box by the architect, Kazumasa Yamashita: this must, incidentally, bear the same scale relationship to the node as a whole as did the bulletin board (and voice of

3.76 *Looking South-east over the Crossing of Sotobori-dori and Harumi-dori in 1966. This view is in the opposite direction to that shown in figure 3.75 and shows better the spaciousness of the 'big road' crossing. The Sony Building on the extreme right (architect: Ashihara) was at the time, one of Tokyo's new glamour buildings. (Courtesy: Tokyo Metropolitan Government)*

3.76

authority) to the old Nihonbashi. Sotobori Dori even retains the name of the old canal (in fact moat) and the node includes at its centre the place where the waterway turned to be crossed by the old bridge.

It may not offer the sweeping views once associated with the old bridge centres but it is spacious and dynamic (with people, activity and information): however, although totally transformed, the node remains closer in spirit, and even form, to the bridge-related past than to any

Western notion of formed space. In other words, it conforms, in its own right, to one of the great archetypal Japanese urban forms and one that, in principle, is repeated now across Japan in many urban places that may not have the same watery past.

Although smaller (past and present) than Tokyo, Osaka may provide even better examples of the same phenomenon. This energetic commercial centre is also a metropolis whose twentieth century systems of arteries (big roads,

3.77 *Central Bridge, Hisaya Odori, Nagoya.*
This modern pedestrian bridge, although over a
highway, displays some of the classic curves of the
traditional water-spanning structures. (Photograph:
Fumihiko Iwano)

3.77

railways, subways and expressways) and nodal points are very much patterned by its former waterways and bridges. The previous meeting points of streets and water, namely the bridges, remain as today's nodal points. It is largely their names that bear the memory of a city of water. In the subterranean vicinity of a one kilometre stretch of Nagabori Dori (it too has the watery name of Long Moat Avenue), there are three subway stations. These all continue to bear the names of bridges which have long disappeared from the city's topography: Yotsu Bashi, Shinsai Bashi and Nagabori Bashi. Such was the power of the bridge (see figure 3.73).

Sometimes today, these road crossings are also bridged albeit with rather more angular structures than was the case in timber times. Nevertheless, there is at least one city that may offer a real glimpse of a modern concrete counterpart of the old water-spanning structures. In central Nagoya, there is a large but elegant arched bridge which offers safe passage to people over the busy six-lane Sakura-dori as well as space around it in the form of a broad band of park (really a super-sized median strip) which is part of the city's Hisaya Odori.

127

Heavy and Horizontal, Peripheral but Central

The city (Matsue) proper is as level as a table, but is bounded on two sides by low demilunes of charming hills shadowed with evergreen foliage and crowned with temples or shrines.

Lafcadio Hearn, 1894 (Glimpses of Unfamiliar Japan, p. 161)

Japanese streets are rather monotonous because they have no public buildings, except police stations.

Douglas Sladen, 1903 (Queer Things About Japan, p. 46)

It (Tokyo) is a monotonously gray city, closely packed for the most part, practically cellarless. and hugging the earth – length and breadth in abundance, but lacking a noticeable third dimension.

Alfred M. Hitchcock, 1917 (Over Japan Way, p. 36)

Japanese towns depend much on mood and atmosphere. They do not have the kind of monumental magnificence that takes the mind by storm in European cities; there is nothing even remotely resembling the Parthenon or St. Peter's.

George Woodcock, 1966 (Asia Gods and Cities, p. 296)

Europe has a long history of monumental architecture and urban design. Buildings have been endowed with monumental qualities in various ways, including scale (especially height), symmetry, elaborate decoration, frontality, axiality and placement or, at least, some combination of these. Especially significant has been their placement in relation to each other and to other elements in the urban landscape: streets, squares, circles, axes, vistas, gateways, etc. which may themselves possess some of the same qualities. Thus, the sense of monumentality that pertains to a particular object will stem partly from the pattern of connection or relationship between it and other things. As such, monumental qualities may be bestowed on something quite small – for instance, a statue or fountain – by virtue of its placement in relation to other spatial and built forms. Camillo Sitte, regarded by some as the father of modern town planning, wrote an extensive volume, *Der Stadtbau* on the principles of such relationships in 1889 and many books on related themes have emerged ever since – from Hegemann and Peets' *Civic Art* 1922, through Ed Bacon's *Design of Cities* 1967 and Rob Krier's *Urban Space* 1979 to Cliff Moughtin's *Urban Design: Street and Square* 1992, to name but four. All comb through the history of Western form to tell their stories and extract their principles.

My present country is not one associated with formality or monumentality in any field, including city building. Australian cities are still in their infancy by European and Japanese standards: even the most seasoned have witnessed barely two centuries of development. Yet even in Australia, substantial examples of monumental urban design are to be found in most cities. The capital, Canberra (initial plan by Walter Burley Griffin) has an extensive network of monumental

3.78 *Urban Monumentality in Australia's Capital. The Parliamentary Axis in Canberra may not have emerged quite as Walter Burley Griffin envisaged it in his 1912 plan; however, the alignment and scale of the axis remain.*

3.79 *Urban Monumentality in South Australia's Capital. The symmetrical and hierarchical plan of streets and squares that make up Adelaide's 'square mile' is itself monumental. Further, Col. William Light's Plan of 1836 remains substantially intact.*

3.78

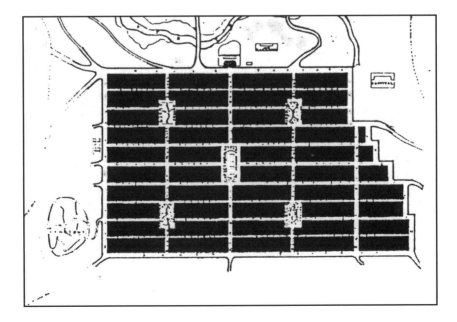

3.79

axes and geometries graced by grand buildings and other features: foremost of these is the main Parliamentary axis which traverses nearly 4 kilo-metres to include the new and old Parliament Houses, the Australian War Memorial and Anzac Parade. Further, it is part of a much larger composition known as the National Triangle: the three axes which define this area march over the city's landscape over a combined distance of 8 kilometres. In Melbourne, one can stand at a tramstop in spacious Swanston Street to the north of the city's heart and see, to the south, the grey bulk of the State's War Memorial loom over the street's axial extension some 3 kilometres away: at right angles to this, one can proceed along Bourke Street to the monumental face of the Victorian State Parliament. In Adelaide, the plan with its symmetrical hierarchy of streets and squares is itself a masterpiece of monumentality (although, it may be argued, subsequent building has failed to live up to its potential).

Sydney's outstanding physical qualities may stem rather from its harbour setting than any man-made plan but its justly famous Opera House is, nevertheless, in a form and location that together exploit the site to the advantage of both building and city. If a building can be both informal and monumental as well as occupy a monumental site in an informal landscape, then Sydney Opera House is it. Its unique form occu-pies centre stage in a magnificent landscape and gives a focal point to a very wide sweep of a big city. All of these examples involve the design of buildings both as entities in themselves and as parts of larger urban landscapes in ways that are designed to enhance the visual qualities of both.

Yet, as urban latecomers, Australian city forms pale on a scale of monumentality to most big European cities: Paris, Rome, Vienna, St Peters-burg or even London or Washington. In these and most Western cities (it is largely a matter of degree) monuments are placed in formal relation-ships with each other over extensive areas. In other words, buildings as objects have not been conceived in isolation but in terms of a broader visual strategy and pattern of connection. In a very real sense, the elements are placed and designed to help bind a city together into some larger cohesive whole: in the process, they give to a place a good measure of what Kevin Lynch described as 'identity' and 'legibility' (Lynch, 1960).

Monumentality in the West is not restricted to large cities or those with extensive formal geometries. Towers, strong facades and enclosed spaces have long combined to give a visual focus and powerful sense of centre to small towns of quite irregular form. Here, I refer yet again to Newark on Trent, where the Market Place is a great but far from 'square' civic and social space with a classical Town Hall at its head. Immediately behind the buildings flanking the opposite end of the square is the splendid spire of the Church of St. Mary Magdalene soaring to the imposing height of 77 metres. This is the classic enclosed space and vertical object duo

3.80 *Monumentality and Centrality in an English Market Town. The enclosed space of the Market Place gives to Newark on Trent a central and dominant focus. In particular, the Town Hall (A) and parish church (B) offer respectively classical and soaring monumentality.*

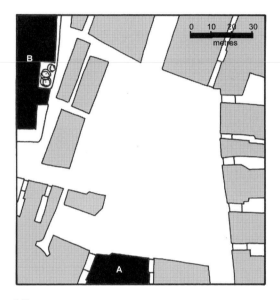

3.80

which gives that powerful sense of centre and monumentality to so many European towns. Similar principles are even more forcefully at work in justly more famous centres such as Bruges, Delft and Sienna. Such relationships have been central to the Western idea of the city for centuries.

For most of Japan's urban history, however, such notions have been an anathema. Buildings were lower with 'centres' (plural) less obvious and less central. Until only a hundred years ago, most buildings in urban Japan were almost uniformly one and two storeys. In Japan's ancient capital, Kyoto, the transformation from a single to a two storey city took place between the sixteenth and seventeenth centuries. Yamasaki

notes from pictorial evidence of the city that two-storey town houses were not generally built until the end of the Muromachi period (third quarter of the sixteenth century). He also observed that by the end of the following century streets were flanked almost exclusively by two-storey buildings (Yamasaki, 1994, pp. 47 and 48), but no higher. Further, this did not much change until after the Second World War. Certainly, a gaze over a screen painting or print of any Edo-period town will most likely reveal a remarkably uniform roofline, and this especially applies to the warrior and commoner-cum-commercial districts. Further, it is hard to recognize a single or dominant centre.

If a building of real height is to be seen, it is almost certainly a castle. A temple or shrine might also appear as a higher structure but if so, more as a bump in the roof-line than a sharp vertical object – in fact, as a higher single storey. Most large temples and shrines were, however, offset from the towns with their presence muted by trees and terrain. In the main living and working districts, a few store houses might push up above the general roofline but only marginally. There may also be temporary roof-top signs and, in the later Edo period, there would almost certainly be some fire watch-towers. Nevertheless, in most instances, the pre-modern Japanese skyline would have appeared remarkably flat and uniform to the Western eye. Where objects did protrude, these tended to be fewer and lower than in the West, in unlike

3.81 *A Tokyo Roofscape in the Meiji Period. Low and flat. (Source: Morse, 1972)*

3.81

locations (tending in Japan towards or beyond the periphery) and essentially of a different kind (either heavy and downward-thrusting or spindly and see-through in form).

First and foremost was the fortress. But here, it should be emphasized that not all towns had castles – only those where a *daimyo* had his headquarters. From the early seventeenth century, one castle for each province was the Tokugawa policy which greatly restricted their numbers. (Of 250 *daimyo* in the country as a whole, over half were entitled to a castle seat.) Thus even substantial cities like Nagasaki, which grew comparatively late (from the late sixteenth century) as a trading port, may not have had one: Nagasaki was governed by the central shogunate. Also, not all castles were the towering structures of picture postcard fame like Himeji or Kumamoto. Some were more like a big house and rather squat on a fortified base: for instance the House of Matsuura at Hirado.

Where high, however, they could be ominously dominant in the landscape. A typical plan was for the castle to occupy a central position yet maintain a peculiar physical remoteness from the main town, their central sites being surrounded by extensive fortifications and warrior (*buke-yashiki*) residences beyond which lay the denser settlement of the merchants and artisans plus temple quarters. Beyond this, there may have developed an *ad hoc* patchwork of warrior, commoner and religious areas, rice paddies and woodland. Edo itself showed this pattern.

This is significant because the areas of densest settlement and most intensive activity rarely occupied the geographical centre: on the contrary, they were commonly toward the periphery and in some cases were more of a sinuous edge than a consolidated blob. It follows that the richest activity mixes were towards the edges. Further, there were no grand or axial approaches to the centre. In fact, the areas within the walls

3.82 *Castle Town Patterns. Although there were several types, the top figure shows the main underlying concept for a town: the castle is at the centre surrounded by a moat and (low density) warrior residences and, in turn, (higher density) merchants and artisans quarters: temples (centres in their own right) are at the edges and often on* higher ground. As a consequence, the densest areas are peripheral as are the many gathering places. The lower plan shows a variation on the same theme: in effect, a wedge is taken from the model and applied to a headland site.

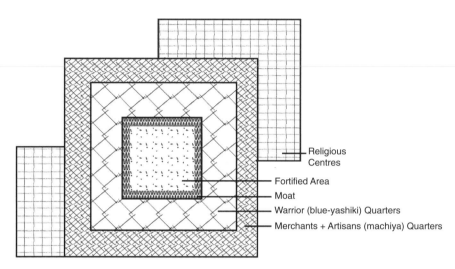

— Religious
    Centres

— Fortified Area
— Moat
— Warrior (blue-yashiki) Quarters
— Merchants + Artisans (machiya) Quarters

3.82

and moats were irregularly planned to fox an enemy's approach: and, for similar reasons, the districts beyond were also laid down with un-expected turns and dead-ends. In this sense, the town was a dispensable extension of the fortress itself.

In such cases, the geographical centre was highly ambiguous for it was both a physical land-mark and political stronghold yet, in a very real sense, an 'empty' centre. Indeed, for the common majority in most towns, both castle and skirting samurai quarters were very much out-of-bounds. In the earlier mentioned town of Iwakuni, for instance, the commoner and warrior quarters were actually divided by a wide river but con-nected by the famous Kintaikyo (bridge): samurai could cross the bridge but commoners with

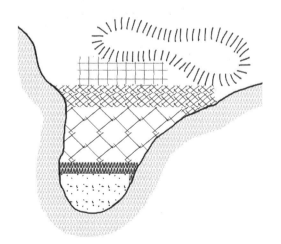

business in their quarters had to cross by the riskier means of a small boat.

The other buildings in old Japanese towns which achieved greater height than your typical

3.83 *The Castle Town of Sasayama, Hyogo Prefecture. It shows the castle with warrior quarters (buke-yashiki), merchant quarters (machiya) and temple areas in more or less concentric rings about it. (Source: Adapted from Toshi Design Kenkyutai)*

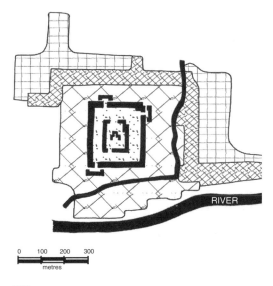

RIVER

0   100   200   300
metres

3.83

one and two-storey *machiya* were religious. Larger temples and shrines associated with most towns, tended to be on or even beyond the periphery. In these locations, they would commonly stand in leafy surrounds with their roofs only partly visible amongst trees. The lower slopes of hills provided the common sites where natural contours and colours tended visually to smother their scale and form.

However, where temples occurred on the flat and within the denser built up areas, they too could remain peculiarly inconspicuous. Typically, temple walls have passed largely unseen behind the boundary walls of their grounds: thus the experience within the town would have been more that of a walled area than of a high object.

The most visible part of the building, as in samurai houses, was the roof, and this was seen as a heavier and more extensive mass than surrounding roofs which were no less weighty and spreading at their own scale. In other words, it was more expansive and higher than its surroundings but not essentially different. The overwhelming impression was that of a spreading mass pressing down over an extensive but unseen area and this impression is to be felt today in fragments of most Japanese cities. In no way did temples and shrines rise to dominate like a European church, town hall or palace.

In the West, so many monumental urban structures have thrust symbolically upwards. The spire has pointed to the heavens. The column moved skywards to culminate in statue and silhouette. Finials, bartizans and other devices gave vertical extension to towers. Even without towers and spires, whole buildings were still capable of exhilarating upward-reaching movement, perhaps the best examples being the skeletal and finely buttressed structures of French Gothic cathedrals. And inside and out alike, domes made spirits soar. In other words the Western eye has so often been drawn to some culminating central or axial end point, and upwards.

Japanese composition has, on the other hand, largely ignored the vertical. It has directed the gaze to hover in the horizontal or spread outwards and earthwards. For instance, heavy roofs and wide eaves provide strongly horizontal lines and appear almost in suspension above their sites

3.84 *Temples as Bumps in the Skyline. They may be higher than their surroundings but not essentially different. (Source: Morse, 1972)*

3.85 *Heavy Roofs and Deep Shadows. Temples and shrines are commonly seen on wooded slopes at the edge of town where shadows reinforce their heavy horizontal lines.*

3.83

3.85

(like the suspended roofs over the ring in the modern sumo hall). Alternatively, the break in many roofs to a gentler angle and extended eaves gives a distinct feeling of downward, outward spread. Further, these visual impressions can be double-dosed where there are two tiers with one

135

precincts tending to be the more extensive and regular). Relationships with the wider city, however, were much more tenuous, if at all. Certainly in Edo, larger shrines and temples were typically found in one of two places: on a hill or by water, and sometimes both. Hence, the tendency was to be geographically peripheral to the main built-up areas.

If 'in town', a temple compound would most likely be defined by a perimeter wall with an axis connecting a gateway to the central door of the main building (See, for instance, in the plan of Kyoto's Higashihonganji temple complex in figure 2.36.) With a perimeter hillside temple (by far the most common), the main axis of the compound may or may not be extended out to touch some part of the main built-up area. In the case of a shrine, a connecting route (or routes for there may be more than one) was usually marked by one or more *torii*. This may or may not be straight and often rather steep. Further, any axial arrangement within a compound would not, extend beyond the rear. In other words, axial connections between built elements were generally confined to within religious compounds: only occasionally was there frontal extension and then of limited extent.

These edge phenomena were, in a very real sense, peripheral centres. Within and about them, were large open areas which were the scenes of major events in the national and local calendars: at New Year and other festivals. The compounds and their environs were both parks, market places

and urban pleasure-grounds – offering opportunities for activities such as blossom-viewing and kite-flying, as well as for trading, theatre, eating and erotic delights. Many equivalent functions were to be found in and about central squares and streets in European towns. At the same time, the Japanese religious compounds encompassed the largest of the city's structures to display a measure of axial frontality. Their urban presence was, nevertheless, usually foiled by a combination of their walled perimeters and/or wooded locations, as well as the tight and narrow nature of the town streets themselves. The most likely memory of the distant view was of the massive downward thrusting roof midst trees and this may well have been best gained from a high bridge or hill, for between the buildings and walls of the narrow city streets, views were restricted.

There were a few examples of urban streets where the vista ended not on a man-made object but on a distant mountain and this is shown clearly in pictures from the Edo and Meiji eras such as Hiroshige's 'Suruga-cho' and the view along Sanbancho Dori in the 'Illustrated New Selection of Tokyo Landmarks (*Shinsen Tokyo meisho zue*) of 1897. For the eyes (but not legs) these streets lead to Mount Fuji. Jinnai refers to work by Kirishiki Shinjiro which suggests that some subdivisions might have been laid out purposely to allow such views. This would be consistent with the general Shinto attachment to nature and the particular reverence for Fuji. Nevertheless, if it was purposeful, then it should

3.88 *A Street with 'Borrowed' Mountain. The street is, however, dislocated from the sacred Fuji by a 'void' of landscape and particularly cloud. (Print: Hiroshige's 'Suruga-cho')*

3.88

3.89 *Skyline and Fire Tower. In this street scene in Konya-machi, Yamato-Koriyama, Nara Prefecture, only the fire tower breaks the skyline – as in an Edo period scene except that metal has replaced timber and pushed up slightly higher.*

3.89

also be emphasized that the focal object is clearly not part of the city but disconnected from it, with the intervening landscape (often shrouded in cloud) a void – hence the visual but not actual connection The approach is not unlike that in Japanese landscape design which employs 'borrowed scenery' but in an urban context.

In the main living and working areas of old Japanese towns, the object which rose permanently above the general roofline was a slender open-framed structure topped by a small look-out. This was sometimes roofed or, in its more basic form, little more than a watch ladder and platform. In most instances, they were both spindly and just high enough to do the job and give an across-the-roof-top view, although in Edo, while still timber and open-framed, they could rise higher. The fire-watch towers provided the front-line warning system in a city's attempt to protect itself against its number one enemy – conflagration.

The second structure which sometimes rose above the general roof height, was the *kura* or store house. However, so slight was the difference that it was conspicuous more on account of its plain plastered walls than its height. Nevertheless, these store houses sometimes rose through two storeys in a single-storey environment or even three storeys in a two storey environment. In 1688, a book appeared of the title, *Nihon Eitaigura* (The Eternal Storehouse of Japan) in which the writer, Ihara Saikaku, described the rich Kyoto merchants as those 'who had bails of rice at their door, a two-storey building and a three-storey storehouse' (quoted from Yamasaki, 1994, p. 49). The *kura*'s timber structure was contained within a thick fire-retardant plaster coating and it was here that family valuables and precious stores were kept. In effect, they were like great outdoor safes of an urban scale and again constructed against the nation's premier urban hazard – fire. Many still stand today, some of which have seen neighbouring dwellings razed. Like the fire-towers, they were not concentrated in one place but scattered over the city and of minor impact – certainly built as part of the utilitarian general text and not something special within it.

It may thus be said that Japan emerged into its Meiji period of modernization with low one and two storey cities and towns. The largest structures in those select towns with remaining castles were functional and physically central but peripheral to the lives of most townsmen. The next largest structures tended to be physically peripheral but central to the lives of the populous. Their roofs, more often than not, peeped ponderously over verdant edges rather than shadowed over the built-up middle. In the most peopled parts of the cities, the structures that raised their heads highest were scattered, modest and of practical necessity – spindly towers for spying smoke and private 'safety boxes' for excluding fires once raging. These were, however, either slender and see-through or minor bumps in the general roofscape.

Neither axes nor geometry established broad relationships between buildings across the city. Such relationships were generally confined by the walls of a religious complex or, at most, enjoyed limited frontal extension. A city street might very occasionally gain its orientation from a distant mountain. However, in all of these instances, lines are short, singular, self-contained or, in the case of the distant mountain, disconnected from the object.

Clarity of connection is not a quality that has been sought by the Japanese in their cities. In fact, evidence is to the contrary. Routes to shrines and temples are often circuitous and have much more to do with the experience of the journey than visual linkage. Often it is not a matter of the singular route but alternative paths even between the same starting and end points. In festivals, the experience of the activity is paramount and often independent of the setting – underscored by routes which are not fixed but variable.

All of this stands in such contrast to the Western experience. For instance, the Japanese tendency to central fortification and peripheral town was the inverse of Europe. In medieval Europe, the castle stood at a strategic edge to extend its defensive walls out like great arms to embrace and protect the town. Within the town, the fabric was more mixed and culminated in its own centre in which structures were taller, denser and more elaborate than on the periphery. Further, this latter centralized pattern was one that continued in later (i.e. from the Renaissance on) urban foundations which knew neither castle nor walls and was reinforced by classical notions of order. Also, it was continued in the rebuilding and extension of the older cities.

It is against this background that the Japanese started to look at Western urban design models and tried to absorb them, during the Meiji era. The results, reflect the difficulties in both conceptualizing and implementing them.

Particularly interesting are the many examples of Western-style government (administration, military, educational and health) buildings which date from this time. A common solution was the two-storey symmetrical front with a central portico and central roof-top tower facing towards the street. In spite of the principles employed, their impact upon the wider urban structure was slight, the reason being that they sat in generous gardens and their relationship to a larger order generally stretched no further than the plot – usually via a short central driveway which formed an axis between portico and gateway. Indeed, they were generally built in the spacious (*buke-yashiki*) garden properties of the former warrior classes and aristocrats. In other words, they were something of a cross between the familiar *buke-yashiki* plot and unfamiliar Western classical building. A further Japanese form that may have assisted the introduction and acceptance of this building type was, as Jinnai notes, the Buddhist temple compound with its 'similar nature of spatial arrangement' (Jinnai, 1995, p. 166): in the compound an axis also ran between the main gate and a main building with a symmetrical front. The Tokyo Medical School is representative of the type and its architect, Saburo Horikoshi, designed several such buildings.

The phenomenon was not, however, confined to government buildings or even to non-commercial buildings. At least two early Tokyo banks stood on plots behind walls and symmetrically behind gates. Both the First National and Mitsui Banks mixed freely elements of lordly castles (tiered forms), Western features (symmetry and detail) and *yashiki* characteristics (in space behind walls). Especially interesting is the Mitsui Bank: old illustrations show that the building (demolished long ago) introduced this mix of characteristics to an area of street-aligned *machiya*-type buildings, namely the famed Surugacho where

there existed the street view to Mount Fuji, referred to above.

Indeed, the use of the tower during the early Meiji period is quite revealing. Tower placements were made independently of their physical contexts and even independent of the building styles to which they are attached. An example is the Kojima Watch Store in Tokyo as depicted in a contemporary print. The building is like many of the period with its plastered fire-resistant walls, tiled roof and projecting cover over an open front. Interestingly, although occupying a corner site, there is no recognition of this in the general form of the building. In turn, the placement of the tower is entirely within the context of the building, and without acknowledgement of the wider urban form. Further, the classical tower, with its octagonal top over a cube with cornices, could have been sliced from some main street public building in provincial America and superimposed over the heavy ridge of a Japanese roof. It is a curious sight but, nevertheless, a not untypical eclectic pile from the period.

As one might expect, following a towerless tradition, the assimilation of such features in the process of Westernization was difficult. The taller structures which had existed in Japanese cities (castles, pagodas and fire-towers) generally stood independently (albeit often within a complex) rather than as outgrowths of buildings. Early rooftop towers were, I suspect, seen more as elements of information and promotion in the government and commercial buildings, respectively, than as

3.90 *Western Tower atop a Japanese Building. On the Kojima Watch Store, Tokyo, the tower as a feature on the building roof is somewhat incongruous and independent of the rest of the building – like many roof-top signs today. (Source: Adapted from Jinnai, 1995; original from Tokyo shoko hakuran e).*

3.90

elements of townscape. The clock was a necessity in the new time-conscious world of industrial and administrative organization. And in the commercial world, the roof-top advertisement (centrally placed on the individual building) was an already familiar urban sight: thus the tower became a novel variation on the theme.

Perhaps the boldest attempt at European grandeur during the latter part of the Meiji period was the Akasaka Detached Palace in Tokyo's Moto-Akasaka district. The palace was designed by Tokuma Katayama and built in 1909 as a lavish Baroque residence for the crown prince of the day. In fact, it proved too lavish for his restrained Japanese taste, and for that reason it was not much used for its intended purpose. Nevertheless, as a piece of architecture, it has been described as 'the largest structure and most outstanding achievement of the Meiji Era' (Bognar, 1995, p. 105) The two-storey spreading complex rests symmetrically on an axis running from the rear garden though the building, fore-court, inner gateway, garden and outer gateway. Further, this extends out into the city beyond for another 200 metres (perhaps 400 metres if you really stretch it) to peter out (rather than stop) in the vicinity of Yotsuya Station. It is, incidentally, the one place I know in Tokyo where an urban landscape has actually taken precedence over an expressway, the latter tunnelling under and out just beyond the garden walls on either side. Taken from the rear garden, the axis is 500 metres (perhaps 700 metres if really stretched) but, in the final analysis, it is yet another well-defined plot which sprouts a tenuous one-way axis to nowhere.

Half-a-century later, came Tokyo Tower which is of interest for not dissimilar reasons. If the Akasaka Detached Palace was an attempt to replicate eighteenth century Parisian grandeur in Meiji times, then Tokyo Tower was an equivalent endeavour to recreate a piece of urban experience from the nineteenth century French capital in the post-war Showa period. The tower (dating from 1958) has the essential form of its Parisian counterpart and outshines it in height by more than 30 metres: but its visual impact upon the Tokyo landscape is weak. While there is no doubt

3.91 *Akasaka Detached Palace. The symmetrical patch of the palace, although with grand intentions, projects an axis that peters out (rather than ends) before Yotsuya Station. It is, nevertheless, Tokyo's strongest example of European-style grand planning in Japan's early period of modernization. (Courtesy: Tokyo Metropolitan Government)*

3.92 *Tokyo Tower. This was a post-World War II attempt at imitating Paris: while taller than its French counterpart, it is devoid of any relationship to a strong plan and, consequently, its presence in the city is relatively weak. (Courtesy: Tokyo Metropolitan Government)*

3.91

3.92

that it may be seen from many parts of the city, it is undoubtedly best seen from other high buildings and elevated expressways. Its lack of relationship to an organized surface pattern together with its functional 'I'm a hazard' red and white banded paintwork (there are many utility towers wearing the same clothing) have negated its inherent potential as a visual anchor in the urban landscape. Instead, the tower tends to 'float' shiftingly over a general area rather than prescribe a point and lines within the city

structure. No matter what its scale or how sophisticated the individual building may be, the intent of monumental structures of Western descent cannot be fulfilled in the plot-based Japanese patchwork.

Lastly, since attention has been drawn to the low and horizontal lines of Japan's older city forms as well as the utilitarian nature of any exceptions, it is worth noting for just how long even sizeable Japanese cities remained low (and, for that matter, wooden). Whether Kyoto (which

3.93 *A Tall and Slender Carpark Rises Above Trees.*

3.94 *A Tall and Slender Carpark Rises Above Tiled Roofs. In Japan, breaking the skyline has rarely been for splendour but rather utility. Thus, these Nagasaki carparks continue a tradition.*

3.94

3.93

was spared wartime American incendiary bombing) or Nagasaki (a city substantially destroyed by the atomic bomb), photographs from the 1950s show extensive inner city scenes which are surprisingly low and uniform. There is a continuous two-storey spread of mostly tile roofs (over timber structures) which is only occasionally broken by higher modern prismatic forms: further, even these are not high (mostly three or four storeys) and dispersed. Significantly, amongst those structures which do break the sky-

line, utility is strongly apparent – in particular, fire-towers (by then in concrete and equipped with loud-speakers and sirens) and early telecommunications towers. An even more recent phenomenon which continues the vertical and utilitarian projection within (and above) a lower and more human fabric is the high-rise 'slim-line' carpark in areas of lower residential and commercial buildings. The idea of a parking station as a solid but slender square shaft rising high over humble (sometimes) timber-framed houses is the kind of scene which offends most Western sensibilities. Such a result stems from a culture that has mainly reserved the potential for experiencing vertigo in the city to monumental objects in visually strategic places.

Two Recent Tokyo Buildings

During the boom years of the 1980s, the Tokyo Metropolitan Government embarked upon four massive building projects of which I shall comment on two: New Tokyo City Hall and Edo-Tokyo Museum. By any stretch of the imagination, both are big buildings. The first occupies an L-shaped site taking in three large street blocks in the high rise western part of Shinjuku. The second is on a site almost 300 m in length on the northern side of Ryogoku Station and end-on to Kokugikan, the national home of sumo. These two building forms are of special interest given the preceding discussion.

The Tokyo Metropolitan Government headquarters is the design of Kenzo Tange and Associates and rises to the dizzying height of 243 m making it Japan's second tallest building. On the pivotal part of the site, at the bend in the L, stands the tallest part known blandly as Tower One and includes the Governor's offices. In appearance, even this part reads as two towers, one on either side of a lower section with a central entrance. Everything about the composition emphasizes height. To this extent, it can only be compared with the great works of Western Gothic, especially the twin-towered west fronts of cathedrals such as Wells or Amiens. It is undoubtedly a composition of soaring verticality.

To the fore of this on the east side of the street block (i.e. closest to Shinjuku Station) is the comparatively low Assembly Building containing the ceremonial front and housing an elliptical Assembly Hall at its top centre. At the front on the outside, this building is rectilinear but behind, it extends out two massive arms about a semi-circular plaza to embrace and contain the soaring 'cathedral' on the street block behind: in other words, the two arms extend over the intervening street which in turn bridges the plaza. To describe the plaza as 'grand' is understatement. You can put an Olympic sprint track easily within it and the colonnade about it is over ten times the height of the average Japanese. Combine this with its palatial Spanish white pearl and Swedish mahogany granite finish and it compares with the grandest of European Baroque.

There is also a lower stepped tower, Tower Two, on the third street block rising to a mere 163 m and connected to Tower One by two bridges. The whole thing is an urban-political complex of gardens, plazas, formal assembly halls and rooms, conference centres, galleries, studios, gymnasia, restaurants, observatory, library, not to mention the offices themselves. Although centred upon a massive plaza, the base of the development is in fact a complex configuration that includes street, sub-street (including the plaza) and above-street levels connecting with various surrounding elements (streets, buildings, gardens, underground walkways, etc).

Edo Tokyo Museum has a very different function and also a very different form. However, in neither case is function the primary determinant of form and it is the contrasting conceptual ideas

3.95 *New Tokyo City Hall and the West Shinjuku Street Grid. The City Hall complex straddles three large street blocks and includes a plaza of enormous scale. The plaza is crossed by an elevated road which, in turn, is bridged by the building's giant colonnade. Thus, two systems superimpose at a grand scale. (Source: Adapted from a plan in Ashihara, 1994)*

3.96 *New Tokyo City Hall, Nishi-Shinjuku, Tokyo (Architect: Kenzo Tange Associates, 1991). A view from beneath the giant colonnade which wraps around the enormous central plaza to the soaring twin shafts of Tower One. (Photograph: Miki Okamoto)*

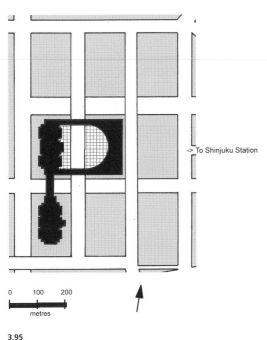

-> To Shinjuku Station

0   100   200
metres

3.95

3.96

which are of interest. While the New Tokyo City Hall shows effectively three front facades (one to the station side of each street block), the Edo-Tokyo Museum has none. The Museum stands on a raised platform base, above which there are four colossal legs supporting a massive 'roof' – rather like a tortoise standing on a flat rock with its head retracted but legs fully extended. The base contains an auditorium, the foyer, an exhibition hall and several ancillary functions. The 'roof' houses the main Edo-Tokyo exhibit, storage and some lesser functions. The whole

rises to a height of over 70 m. Between the roof and platform base is a vast open area, itself 16 m high. The roof hovers ponderously over this (plaza) base and, rather than taking the limelight itself, directs the gaze down onto the platform 'site'. Under the roof, the eye is taken to the primary red of a futuristic escalator which connects foyer (below) to plaza to exhibition space

3.97 *Edo-Tokyo Museum. The building is massive but not monumental in placement or form.* *(Courtesy: Tokyo Metropolitan Government)*

3.97

(above). The building, in spite of its enormous bulk, is peculiarly contained. Its hovering bulk is seen yet ignored until close by – almost until taking the steps and rising to its platform plaza. This is all the more surprising given the relatively small scale and taller-than-wide proportions of most near-by buildings: although, I might add, some similar qualities (platform plot and widely spreading roof-form) are exhibited by the squarer but lower Kokugikan next door.

Both buildings might be criticized for their inhuman scale. However, from the standpoint of some kind of Japanese monumentality, there is no doubt that Kikutake's megastructure is closer to the country's past.

In spite of Tange's rhetoric about the recti-linear lattice tradition and its influence upon the Metropolitan Government Centre's surface composition, the building is overwhelmingly of European inclinations, soaring to Gothic heights

3.98 *Beneath the 'Roof' of the Edo-Tokyo Museum. The horizontal lines of the underside bear down heavily to shadow the elevated 'plot'.*

3.98

and bristling with Baroque bravado. The Centre is of a scale and composition that seeks a wider grand order in the city to be itself successful as a piece of urban design and that simply does not exist in Tokyo. In fact, Shinjuku is becoming increasingly thick with towers and observation decks and merely as a landmark the Government Centre's visibility is being whittled down, especially from the station side to which it puts its face. In the end, it will exert a monumental presence essentially to its own plaza but even that is compromised by the street that runs over half of it. (Although these qualities might be seen as faintly Japanese in that the road is superimposed over the plaza and the building's monumental qualities tend to be drawn back to within the site.) But even that is being over-generous for this was not how the building was conceived and it must be judged ultimately as a dubiously placed hybrid of Western ideas.

Kikutake's museum, on the other hand, has a monumentalism that bears down on the plot. It shadows powerfully its own ground. It occupies a strategic position in the city, not far from Ryogokubashi and next to Ryogoku Station and the Kokugikan (Sumo Hall). There are, however, no grand axes with which to connect nor vistas to close. From where the building is seen in the wider city, it appears bigger and bulkier than its neighbours but it does not reach outwards and is visually self-contained. In this building, Kikutake created a monumental plot and overshadowed it with a monumental hulk of a roof. The space between might one day be peopled by activity much as temple and shrine grounds were themselves peopled with sellers, performers and people out for pleasure. This Museum is, after all, like the temple and shrine, both a centre of culture and leisure.

Chapter 4

Strands of Culture

Shinto and City Landscapes

It is now clear that, in Japan, whether we are looking over the pages of the child's first magazine, along the very adult streets of the seedier side of Shinjuku or across the glamorous glitz of Ginza, the important can take its place with the inconsequential, the large with the little, and the famous alongside the anonymous with some measure of visual equality. Similarly, gliding over the urban landscape on stilted train track, monorail or highway, there are many areas of cheek-by jowl factories, 'farm' fields, *pachinko* parlours, civic centres, ramshackle timber houses, smart new apartment blocks, and other (to a Westerner) seemingly incongruous neighbours. In this muddled man-made landscape, signs can rise on poles from agricultural plots like trees to shadow a ground cover of vegetables, fruit, flowers or even rice.

In this way, the Japanese urban landscape can be an extraordinary decentralized mix of activities, objects and signs. There can be an enormous variety of plots (shape and size) which, in turn, can support a mind-boggling array of objects and information (size, shape and intensity of messages and light). And there are multiple but unclear centres. Thus, much of it is a collage-like scene which offers little clarity of pattern, form or line. Which brings me to Japan's oldest religion for this seemingly bizarre commercial mix of our times has some conceptual consistency with the Shinto landscape – ancient and modern.

Long before Buddhism arrived in Japan from China via Korea in the middle of the sixth century, Japan's religion was Shinto. Little known overseas, Shinto has never been discarded by the Japanese and today is everywhere apparent in their landscapes. Shinto shrines are a ubiquitous sight. They are to be found in every corner of the city and country, including most family homes, and frequently co-exist with Buddhist temples.

Shinto means 'the way of the Gods' with emphasis very much on the plural for it is a polytheistic and pantheistic belief. In Shinto, spirits or *kami* dwell in almost every living and non-living aspect of nature: the sun and the moon; rivers and mountains; wind and thunder; fertility and production, trees and rocks, islands and waterfalls, some animals and even human-beings, for all beings are potentially *kami*.

As a consequence spirits are associated with things vast and universal, small and local, and both tangible and abstract. In this way, the Shinto landscape consists of countless specialist deities represented by places of worship (i.e. shrines or dwellings for *kami*) which may themselves be natural objects, small single buildings or large building complexes or indeed small do-it-yourself constructions (literally from the local hardware store) on the wall (or post) of a humble household.

They are revered and worshipped to varying degrees according to the different priorities of their various followers. There is no real hierarchy

4.1 *A Shrine alongside Street-side Drink Dispensers, Nara City. The shrine is an ubiquitous sight in Japan.*

4.1

and certainly no absolute creator or deity as in the Christian West. Dr. Sokyo Ono (the first Japanese author of a comprehensive book on Shinto to reach the English-speaking world) wrote that his countrymen 'do not have a clear idea regarding kami. They are aware of kami intuitively at the depth of their consciousness and communicate with kami directly without having formed the kami-idea conceptually or theologically.' It is thus substantially non-intellectual and without sacred scriptures, that are common in many other religions. It makes no clear distinction between good and evil, material and spiritual, or people and *kami*. Further, writes Ono, 'In Shinto, there is no absolute deity that is

the creator and ruler of all. The creative function of the world is realized through the harmonious co-operation of the kami in the performance of their respective missions' (Ono, 1984, p. 8).

Thus, Shinto is a collection of beliefs that manifests itself over the landscape in a profuse but uneven scatter of diverse natural and man-made forms at many scales and with various degrees of definition. There is no single dominant form or place but rather an *ad hoc* harmony arising from some kind of trusted but chance co-operation between the many contributing *kami* housed heterogeneously in their wide array of abodes. In other words, it is a non-hierarchical, decentralized and fragmented landscape; and

153

4.2 *A Shrine with an Ancient Tree in a Carpark.*
Shimabara, Nagasaki Prefecture.

4.2

intellectually, there is no framework for organizing it into a conceptual whole.

Urban and rural landscapes alike may literally be littered with shrines. One may encounter a protective fence about a sacred tree or stone; a kennel-sized shelter at the foot of an expressway column or in the corner of a petrol service station; something more of garden shed proportions squeezed between vending machines or in the beautiful surrounds of a Buddhist temple

(for instance protecting its comparatively giant neighbour from fire in an act of David and Goliath proportions as at Nara's famous Todaiji), as a part of a large complex of buildings on a wooded hillside or wherever. A small shrine may cover less than a square metre while a large area covering hundreds of hectares may be regarded as home to a *kami* (e.g. Kirishima, Kyushu).

Approaches to shrines are also varied. Excepting very small shrines, the common signifier is, of

4.3 *'A Wayside Shrine in Modern (Meiji) Japan.'*
(Source: Griffis, 1876)

Shintō Wayside Shrine in Modern Japan.

4.3

course, the freestanding gate (or *torii*) which may be of a scale that can straddle a wide motor road (for instance, the Heian Shrine in Kyoto) or relatively small giving just enough space for just two people to pass. They may be straight, curved or cornered, single or multiple, bunched up or widely spaced. Shrines may be found singly or in groups with no consistent orientation.

Thus, the function of each part of the Shinto landscape (each shrine) can be very independent and its form, scale, arrangement and setting unpredictable, idiosyncratic and very localized.

All this, of course, is the antithesis of the centralized, hierarchical, absolute and metaphysical Christian position. Over the Christian world, there presides a supreme and single all-pervasive God. Ordinary men are made in the image of that singular spirit to carry out his (masculine) will. In the scriptures, God made the earth for man's domination and sustenance. Man, in turn, made and arranged his monuments to God on earth in a strictly hierarchical and dominating manner. In England, a town could, by definition, only bear city status if it had a cathedral. To this day, cathedrals and churches such as York, Lincoln, Delft and Bruges stand to such soaring heights over their surroundings that they seem to wear their towns and villages like skirts about them as well as dominating the countryside for miles about. Further, planning authorities, with strong citizen support, devise regulations to ensure that this domination is not lost.

Unlike the Christian God which resides in heaven and inspired these symbolic towers and spires, Shinto spirits are mostly of the earth (entering the ground via rocks, trees or man-made objects). There has been little aspiration in the Shinto world to reach for the skies or, indeed, to dominate the earth. Significantly, the only high and slender structures to be seen in any number in pre-Modern urban Japan were, as has already been discussed, products of utility erected with some form of protection in mind: these were castles to withstand military attack and watchtowers to guard from fire. The pagoda was an exception but uncommon in its tall form and product of Japan's other and later imported faith: Buddhism.

155

Buddhism and Built-form

Buddhism takes a prominent place in most built environment histories of Japan with Buddhist temples such as Kyoto's Kiyomizu-dera or Kencho-ji at Kamakura featuring prominently. Also included are the early Japanese capitals which were modelled on the ancient cities of Buddhist China (Nara and Kyoto are best known since these have survived as substantial cities). Nevertheless, the characteristics of almost all Japanese cities, and certainly those given emphasis here, seem to have little connection with the formalities of either the temples or cities of Chinese lineage. They do however, in a rather more abstract way, have strong relationship with certain ideas and beliefs which are central to the Buddhist faith.

Unlike Shinto, Buddhism was brought to Japan from outside. Eleven centuries after its foundation in India, Buddhism reached Japan in the sixth century via China and Korea. Thereafter, it did not displace Shinto but came to coexist with it. Further, this was not a side-by-side toleration of one by the other, for both Shinto and Buddhism together became part of the lives of virtually every Japanese. Buddhist temples were established beside Shinto shrines to encourage their kami to aspire to Buddhahood while shrine *kami* became the guardians of many temples.

At the heart of Buddhism is a concept of nothingness and of life as a series of temporary existences. While Christians set themselves on the idea of salvation and eternal life in a domain watched over by an omnipotent and omnipresent God, the Buddhists' goal is a condition in which worldly desire, intellectual concept and consciousness give way to some sort of empty tranquillity. This is the condition generally known as Nirvana, and sometimes the Great Void.

Similarly, salvation and eternal life hold promise of something fixed and absolute for the Christian while all that exists for the Buddhist is temporary and transitory. 'Everything in this world', writes Bognar, 'is only the temporary coexistence of its composing elements and subject, therefore, to decomposition' (Bognar, 1985, p. 27). Within such a belief, attempts to cling to things which are fixed and permanent are in fact to oppose the natural cycle of change.

The impermanence of all things was expressed by the original Buddha: 'All things arise and pass away'. Life is a constant cycle of birth, death and rebirth or growth, decay and re-growth. Further, in the Buddhist mind, there are rarely simple binary opposites, for instance living and dead, good and evil, material and spiritual, but 'in-between' or 'and-both' conditions in which Western opposites co-exist. The 'dead' remain very much alive with their spirits neither banished to another world nor feared in this one and destined to reappear in some living material or earthly form.

Against this backcloth, Fritjof Capra concludes that 'we (in the Christian West) divide the world into individual and separate things and thus attempt to confine the fluid forms of reality into fixed categories created by the mind' (Capra, 1975, p. 107). For the Buddhist, this can only be a root of frustration: thus the fixtures of Christian belief (and the whole line of Western metaphysical thought) are intrinsically negative. The escape is by way of deep meditation aimed at Nirvana in which the division between the self and all else is dissipated and the individual is indistinguishable from the wider universe. By this process, the Buddhist becomes at one with the world: thus the ultimate achievement (Buddhahood) is a kind of nothingness or void. Moreover, this possibility is not reserved for a select (and righteous) few, for all human beings are deemed to carry within them the potential for this ultimate condition.

Three points seem especially pertinent here. The first is that the world of which human beings are an integral part is seen as being in constant change. This is the normal or natural condition and to resist change can only lead to frustration. Thus, notions of static permanency in everyday life carry no great value. In the same vein, the idea of the perfect object cannot be for if change is constant then the possibility (and, indeed, desirability) for improvement is also ever present.

The second is that within the constant cycle of change, opposite states are not exclusive of each other but are accepted as necessarily co-existing.

Third is that all human-beings are capable of Buddhahood for which past virtues are not a precondition of achievement. Thus like Shinto, there is something intrinsically grass-roots, non-hierarchical and democratic about it.

Japan's cities have long traditions of temporariness: that is, of temporary fabric. In Europe, there are millions of old buildings that have seen their hundredth birthdays and tens if not hundreds of thousands which have seen the Renaissance come and go. This is all the more remarkable given that the region was the cradle of industrial change and has been at the focus of two world wars as well as having experienced massive population and economic growth over the last century. But in Japan, very few buildings reach back over centuries and of those that do, most are parts of religious complexes and castles. What is more, it is surprising how many of these are reconstructions. Old city buildings are rare. The settlement of Imai-cho (near Nara), with a high proportion of its buildings dating from the Edo to Taisho periods, is unique. In most cities, buildings dating from even before the Second World War are uncommon. However, while the country suffered enormous damage during that war, regular and large-scale destruction has been a hallmark of Japanese urban living for centuries.

The country at large is subject to regular typhoons, volcanic activity and earthquakes. Historically, timber buildings have not only been at the general mercy of these phenomena but also of fires both in the wake of nature's disturbances and man's negligence. There is hardly a city in Japan which cannot recall near obliteration at

4.4 *Buried Houses following Volcanic Eruption in 1996: Mount Unzen, Nagasaki Prefecture. Buddhism's emphasis on temporariness has been reinforced in Japan by the repeated destruction of buildings from earthquakes, volcanoes and typhoons and associated fires. Like life itself, buildings have not been expected to last.*

4.4

some point in its recorded history or at least the repeated destruction of whole districts. (In this sense, Tokyo's experience of substantial destruction in 1657, 1668, 1682, 1772, 1855, 1872 and 1923 from earthquake and/or fire is not unusual.)

Against this background, traditional Japanese buildings were conceived as something destructible, replaceable and even movable. Destructible by men that is, for breaks had to be made in the face of fire. The 'very structure (of the house) enables it to be rapidly demolished in the path of a conflagration' wrote Morse. 'Mats, screen-partitions, and even the board ceilings can be quickly packed up and carried away. The roof is rapidly denuded of its tiles and boards, and the skeleton framework left makes but slow fuel for the flames' (Morse, 1972, pp. 12–13).

Natural and man-made disasters aside, the climate over most of the country is hardly conducive to building longevity, especially in timber. It is persistently hot and very humid over part of the year and similarly cold and damp at another. Further, building maintenance has not been a Japanese strong point and there seems to have been a measure of collaboration with the elements to foster gentle decay and periodic re-generation. Thirty or so years was a ripe age for a city building. Permanency lay in the plot with the building a temporary resident certain to succumb, like human mortals, to the processes of time – decay and regeneration.

This attitude has not changed. Natural disasters have not ceased but another phenomenon reinforces the short-life tradition. That is the speed of technological change. The rapidity with which today's information and service technology develops is as natural a progression to the Buddhist mind as summer following spring. The building as a comfortable prop for human life (rather than a visual object) needs to incorporate that change and it is better to rebuild than repair and refurbish. The well-detailed (and technologically innovative) building destined to deteriorate sooner than later is thus entirely consistent with Buddhist thought as well as an extension of the Japanese building tradition.

Short-life Japanese buildings are explained too often in simple economic terms ignoring the fact that economic circumstances and actions are themselves conditioned by culture. Shinto attachment to nature and timber, and Buddhist belief in the temporary together with the natural

hostilities of the Japanese archipelago have combined to promote an attitude to urban building which lies in sharp contrast to that of the West.

In a very real sense, the vulnerability (or weakness to the Western mind) of Japanese buildings may be seen as their strength and success. For Daniel Boorstin, it was a case of 'conquest by surrender' or triumph by submission, which he suggests is general to Japanese life. (Boorstin, 1993, p. 138) He makes the analogy with judo in which one does not oppose an opponent's strength but rather turns it to one's own advantage. The national sport of Sumo shows similar inclinations especially when contrasted with Western boxing which is brutally belligerent. Thus, in boxing, it is necessary to have weight categories to even up the match. Not so in Sumo in which weight is both advantage (stability) and disadvantage (agility), as recent years' championships have tended to show. Western man, through his buildings and cities (both of which, I might add, can be stunning in scale and monumentality), conquered climate, landscape and ultimately time with acts of strength and subjection. Further, he has struggled to maintain that domination through repair and improvement. Meanwhile, the Japanese through their buildings were collaborators with all three: they touched lightly on the land, admitted the elements and succumbed to time. Strength lay in submission.

Lastly, as we learned from the previous section, the Shinto landscape is scattered, uneven and far from centralized. Also, its spirits are very much part of the day-to-day world with earth-bound (rather than heavenly) spirits as house guests and neighbours. In Buddhism too, the distinction between the human and spiritual worlds is not great in that the potential to attain higher spiritual states lies within all living men. The processes can occur anywhere and at any time, and are not exclusionary. This can only serve to reinforce a scattered decentralized view of a world in which the potential to transform is everywhere. If the physical world bears resemblance to the spiritual (and the two are inextricably linked in belief) then each unit in the landscape has some inherent right and capacity to transformation.

Co-existence and Superimposition

Japanese Society is a kind of conglomerate, in which borrowings from many places at many times are fossilized and united by the cement of Japanese tradition.
George Woodcock, 1966 (Asia, Gods and Cities, p. 280)

The history of the West has tended to be sequentially exclusive. In other words, one intellectual movement has displaced another; one style or fashion has been followed by another. For the present Post-Modern generation, this may not be quite so apparent for one characteristic by which we like to give ourselves (sequential) identity is to differentiate our age from previous ones by its pluralism – that is, the co-existence of beliefs, movements and styles.

This bears contrast with Japan where new practices and beliefs have been less inclined to supplant old ones. It is a point which may already be apparent from the preceding text, if only from the discussion of Shinto and Buddhism. Following its arrival, Buddhism did not oust Shinto. While the history of the two has not been entirely trouble-free, it has not resulted in a divided co-existence – 'Shinto or Buddhism' but rather 'Shinto and Buddhism'. Even today, most Japanese would visit both shrine (Shinto) and temple (Buddhist) which exist both separately and together. Indeed, many Japanese do not find it at all inconsistent to embrace aspects of Shinto, Buddhist and Christian practices as parts of their wedding celebrations.

Returning to yet another element of Japanese life raised earlier in this work, when phonetic writing systems were invented in Japan, they did not spell an end to the pictographic *kanji*. They were combined to make a richer and a more flexible whole. *Romaji* (that is, the use of the Western alphabet) is in the process of joining the other three in much the same way. All are taught concurrently to children. All appear alongside each other or interspersed as a matter of course in the newspapers, on the streets, etc.

Even in today's consciously eclectic West, historical costume does not make common matter-of-fact appearances on the streets of our cities. Certainly, there are no standard high street shops specializing in traditional attire. To the extent, that past styles may appear, it is generated

4.5 *Continuity of the Old and Co-existence with the New: Dress. Kimono and contemporary dress remain a common sight on city streets.*

4.5

by media and industry and aimed at the fashion-conscious young. This happens in Japan as well, perhaps even more vigorously. But also in Japan, the age-old kimono remains steadily alive and well alongside modern fashions. Kimonos are worn on many occasions throughout the year and, to an extent, in a more day-to-day manner. Kimono shops are a common high street phenomenon as are kimono sections of department stores. In the regional daily newspapers, one is as likely to encounter a pull-out advertising supple-

ment on kimono as promoting Burberry blazers or Dior dresses.

Thus, to maintain the theme but return more closely to built-form, the traditional home itself is composed of coexisting parts from house types of different times. There are the earth (i.e. ground level and hard), wooden, and *tatami* floor sections clearly distinguished and dating from early, middle and later eras respectively. None were discarded. Each was added. Moreover, traditional houses (modified according to modern building

4.6 *Continuity of the Old, Co-existence with the New – Houses. Modern and traditional style houses standing side-by-side. This is a common scene in which the 'old' building may well be newer than the 'modern' one.*

4.6

regulations) still rise in the suburbs with their ponderously heavy roofs above high garden walls. They sit between so-called Western-style houses which are altogether lighter and often more exposed. Nevertheless, even behind the Western-style exterior wrappings, there would be few dwellings which would not include distinct native and exotic parts. There may be anything from one room to half the house where life on the *tatami* floor continues alongside a more elevated life on furniture with legs – thus continuing the side-by-side tradition.

In the city, stilted expressways stride over historic waterways and big street carriageways which in turn stretch-out alongside separate human-scaled sidewalk streets: these are yet other dimensions of this inclination to juxtapose or superimpose something new without change to the existing. Arcades, independent of their flanking buildings, stand without interruption across intersecting streets, some of which may be considerably wider than themselves. Practically, this is an additive process of separate working parts. Aesthetically, the result is one of visual superimposition and coexistence with scant attempt at integration.

4.7 *Continuity of the Old, Co-existence with the New – the House. These two images are from the same advertisement and show the kinds of Western-style and traditional Japanese style components that are offered in the same building. (Source: Leaflet from Euros Home, Nagasaki branch)*

4.7

Text and Town (or Chapter 2 Revisited)

The written or printed page, the traditional building, the city and the city map were chapter 2 topics. This arose from the fact we commonly refer to the 'legibility' or 'readability' of all four: since each has visual, spatial and formal dimensions, each must be seen as a kind of sign system. In each, some quite fundamental differences were observed between Japanese and Western approaches. More significantly, the differences bore strong similarities across the topics.

In Japanese writing, each character has an *areal* base and an invisible centre of gravity. Since each bears meaning and is, to some degree iconic, it has a good measure of *independence*. Further, characters may be readily understood if they appear in any one of several directions. Their number is potentially infinite and they co-exist readily with other symbols. In other words, they are quite *flexible*.

The letters of Western alphabets, however, show none of these qualities. Our letters are abstract symbols without meaning and depend upon precise *linear* spacing to achieve it. Further, they are complete within themselves (finite in number) and can only be readily understood if written in a horizontal left-to-right format. Thus, in these terms at least, they are rather *inflexible*.

In Japanese traditional building, the key element has been the floor (an *area*) which is, in turn, composed of rectangular *tatami* (more areas). The floor (singular) is raised and continuous and is the single most important element in defining the private 'inside' from beyond.

The standard areal (modular) unit allows for extension in any direction. Space (singular) is aesthetically neutral and can accommodate varied activity. There is thus an inherent *flexibility* which includes a capacity for multi-directional and (conceptually at least) infinite growth.

The key Western element is, however, the wall which is *linear*, and it is wall-to-wall dimension upon which measurement is based. Walls are, of necessity, multiple as they are dependent upon other walls to give inside definition. Symmetrical and linear hierarchical plans with purpose-built spaces have tended to result in inherent *inflexibilities* and even finite qualities.

In the Japanese city, the basic units of reference and organization have likewise been *areal* – the *machi* or *cho*, *chome* and plot. Further, plots have been numbered irregularly over the area of the *machi*. The collective pattern of the city is thus a kind of *patchwork*. Each plot is endowed with a good measure of autonomy and the wider city has a certain *flexibility* (arising from the relative independence of the parts).

In the Western city, however, the basic units of reference and organization are *linear*, namely streets. Identification of buildings is sequential along each street. Thus, collectively, the city is a *network* of formed linear spaces. Further, this sequential arrangement reflects a formal idea which demands a certain consistency of physical expression. Sites and buildings are street-orientated which brings with it, a certain interdependence and *inflexibility*.

The most fundamental difference between the two 'ways of seeing' in these fields appears to be that the Japanese is based on *area* while the Western is on *line*, and it is from here that other differences tend to flow: namely the relative independence and flexibility exhibited by the parts in the Japanese systems.

The Western ways only echo a more general characteristic that has been at the heart of Western thought since Antiquity – namely, linear sequential logic rather than something more lateral, intuitive or seemingly inconsistent or muddled. In the latter, the strength (and weakness) is not in making sequential connection but rather in making connections between scattered and seemingly disparate points, if making them at all. It is, to use a term which has surfaced in this work, a kind of 'patchwork' thinking.

For the moment, however, I shall return to the city. Each bounded plot or patch in a Japanese city has an invisible centre (*oku*) and a measure of autonomy arising from a higher level of disconnection from its surroundings. Thus in Japan a high level of introversion and autonomy is accepted for each site. There are, relatively speaking, not the same (linear) demands for harmonious visual continuities along 'public' frontages and mannered overtures to neighbouring buildings that might be expected in the West. Without sequence and connection, there is no strength of line – rather dispersed points or patches, each of which is surrounded (usually densely in Japan) and yet peculiarly isolated. This gives opportunity to 'glide', 'twist' or indeed 'jump' in any direction within or even beyond (including under and over) the plot, if it seems desirable to do so. And if it is a question of 'jump', the intervening points or patches might as well be void.

Although also consistent in their points of contrast, I have left maps until last for good reason. Maps are unique in that they combine text and graphics in their representation of the spatial phenomenon which is the subject of this work – the city. They use characters or letters. They can show *machi*, streets, plots, buildings or other topographical features. Further they may show any or all of these in a variety of ways: for instance, from single or multiple viewpoints. They offer, therefore, the potential for both synthesis and summary.

On Japanese maps, we saw writing used vertically and horizontally and, orientated through 360 degrees. Buildings and their plots were fragmented to show their different parts by multiple means and direction. This is in contrast to their European counterparts which have attempted to observe in singular ways and from single viewpoints both the city and the map. We noted the named plots and anonymous streets of Japan which is the reverse of Europe where the dominant feature is the hierarchy of named streets. We also saw empty plots which subsumed their buildings as distinct from European buildings which possessed their sites. We observed that both city buildings and the intervening spaces

(streets, squares, courts, etc) were interchangeable as 'figure' in Europe but not so in Japan. Further, we saw the results of a greater Japanese readiness to abstract, distort and transform the city onto plan, sometimes reducing it to a *kanji*-like diagram with patchwork fragments and anonymous connecting routes whose distortions may reflect time, the experience of travel or something else.

Rarely, past or present, has there been a consistent indication of surface or street form in Japan (at least until official maps of the modern age which were modelled on the West's). They have emphasized land over building, plot over street, street as indeterminate route over formed space, fragmented over continuous (or whole) places and time-space over topography

City and Country, Public and Private

In the English-speaking West, the terms 'city' and 'country' bear powerful connotations that have long stood in opposition to each other. This is underpinned by such notions as God having made the country but man the town. One is seen to represent some kind of heavenly purity while the other is viewed as being too much tainted by man's darker side to bear anything other than shades of hell. Indeed, the great Modernist attempts to place their ideal 'cities' in gardens or intersperse them with farmland fall within an anti-city outlook. While the proposed new city forms varied enormously from Le Corbusier's vertical garden city (La Ville Radieuse) through Howard's Garden City (each house to a garden) to Wright's stretched out Broadacre City, their advocates were generally damning of the forms and evils (the two being very much synonymous) of the existing cities. Certainly these three very influential gentlemen all wished not only to surround new buildings with verdant growth in new cities but also to demolish and replace the evil forms of the existing ones.

The Japanese experience is again very different. In his 'Tokyo Anthology', Paul Waley is at pains to stress that the Japanese language has no equivalent words for 'city' and 'country' and there is no strong idea that sets the two kinds of places in some sort of binary opposition (Waley, 1992, p. 183). He points to the word *inaka* which has more to do with rural isolation and ignorance, but this is hardly a positive or even romantic image of the rural scene, rather a negative product of space and time. In searching for some vaguely related notion he was able to note only the home place or *furusato* as a notion holding some positive out-of-the-city association for urban Japanese – for most do continue to retain some link with and affection for their 'home' place. This is, however, more a personal point of reference of family or home surroundings (which may be much more than a village) than a general concept of countryside.

For the Japanese, the city has not so much been in opposition to the country but rather an outgrowth of it. When, for instance, novelist Tanizaki comments upon the excessively bright and garish influences of Western technology on the more subdued and refined Japanese aesthetic, this was in no way related to city ways or intertwined with anti-city sentiments: he lamented the loss of certain aesthetic qualities irrespective of place. For centuries, midst the green 'edges' of Japanese cities, the city people have founded and found their urban centres of worship, pleasure and commerce. The grandest Japanese vista of recent centuries is probably that between (city) street and (rural) mountain. Removed as the mountain was from the immediate street and city, it was brought visually into the city in the manner that Japanese gardens 'borrowed' scenery from (sometimes far) beyond their perimeter walls and hedges. In a variation on the theme, *yashiki* gardens have miniaturized rural landscapes and, through the art of bonsai, even (country) forests have been squeezed into (city) *nagaya* pots. Further, the city has been built with knowledge of its vulnerability to natural forces.

It is this backcloth that no doubt allows architects to see and place nature in the city in the most un-Western of ways. For instance, Itsuko Hasegawa is inclined to imitate nature with landscapes of metallic trees, mountains and even planets – as in her Shonandai Culture Centre. While the Modern era in the West is littered with ideal models for green and complete cities which are intrinsically hostile to existing urban forms, the grand complete design has not featured in

Japan. Significantly, the grandest idea for the city was an organic model: namely, that of the Metabolist group in the 1960s. This focused on the construction of a relatively permanent megastructure-cum-infrastructure of services (skeleton and arteries) onto which shorter life buildings (akin to cells) could be grafted and from which they might be cut (growth, decay and replacement). This group's members included such figures as Tange, Kurokawa and Isozaki – all of whom became very significant architects of international standing. The relationship of their work with nature is not, however, a literal embrace of nature (the green city or natural materials) but rather by analogy: the city as an organism. And, unlike most grand Western models, theirs was to extend and coexist with the existing city rather than replace (i.e. succeed) it.

Just as Waley suggests that there are no equivalent Japanese words which pit the idea of 'city' against that of 'country', another writer, John David Morley, reports in a not dissimilar way on words which in the West separate the city itself into two distinct domains: 'public' and 'private' (Morley, 1986). In the West, 'public' is a powerful term. If something is 'public' it is generally accessible and available to the community as a whole. Hence, in the city, the public domain encompasses all those places to which the entire community has both access and for which it has responsibility. By contrast, that which is private is possessed by an individual or group and is not generally open to the public.

It is within this context that architecture is referred to as the most public of the visual arts. Painters, for instance, prepare works that are hung generally away from the day-to-day public gaze. It is accepted therefore that artists may (and perhaps should) be more individualistic and indulgent than their architectural counterparts. Though works of architecture may stand on private land, they are nevertheless inflicted on the public gaze. Like it or not, they influence the appearance and quality of public places. This is part of the reason why public authorities sometimes make considerable demands upon private development by way of controls which are underpinned primarily by aesthetic considerations. These are put forward in the public interest.

The Japanese, writes Morley, have had no real equivalent for 'public'. Hence, they imported the word 'public' – pronounced 'paburikku' in Japan. He therefore draws our attention to the nearest native approximation of the 'public-private' duo which is uchi-soto. Uchi in fact refers to the family, clan or group: soto means outside. Thus soto is all that which is outside of the uchi. As such, it is a negative idea or, in Morley's words, 'a non-concept' (Morley, 1986, p. 123). In effect, it refers to that which is left-over after the positive has been identified. If it is possible to transfer the notion to space and interpret this in Western terms, then that which is beyond the domain of the uchi comprises space which is both 'other private' plus 'public' and together conferred with lesser status. This would certainly seem to correlate with several observations on the nature of space made elsewhere in this work: for instance, the perceived strength of the individual plot, the utilitarian nature of public spaces, as well as public space as a domain for temporary invasion and annexation. At the same time, however, the areas of the city (e.g. *chome*) form another kind of insider group beyond which is another outside. While these latter suggestions may show a measure of ambiguity (the street may be 'outside' of the plot but inside of the *uchi*), it is no more so than is common to most aspects of Japanese life. In fact, what we have are layers of (positive) insides and (conceptually empty) outsides.

Chapter 5

Learning from the Japanese City

Learning from the Japanese City

The Japanese language and culture have a certain flexibility in them. In the field of philosophy it is believed, in European languages and thought, that at the centre of things resides God . . . So there exists such a centre at some point, by which everything is controlled. In other words, the whole can be universal . . .

A place (in Japan) is originally defined as an empty place into which anything may be brought. The way of integration is not that the centre holds everything together, but rather only that there exists coordination at some point but with nothing inside it.

Yujiro Nakamura, 1984 (Process Architecture, 49, pp. 62–63)

Its [Tokyo's] incomprehensible complexity (each object/event is autonomous, separated from the next by earthquake laws, by scale, by type and by the time-delay of a fax transmission).

Its apparent absence of hierarchy (conditions of downtown, quiet residential, neon zone, artificial landscape, movement corridors, and so, are folded together, like movie cuts or hologram plates where each fragment contains the whole image).

Its overall melancholic greyness (punctuated by neon galaxies and revealing on close inspection an array of infinitely subtle and variable hues).

This ordered chaos is today's urban frontier: the sedimentary consequence of media/electronic technology, an endless humming cloud.

Peter Wilson, 1996 (The Idea of the City, p. 102)

Fifty years ago, the dominant metaphor for the city amongst designers and planners was the machine. The house according to the gospel of St. Corb was a machine for living in: similarly, the city was a series of functions (classifications of activities and traffic flows), each to be accommodated in its own purpose-designed element. By 1960, however, this had started to change and over subsequent years, cities came to be conceived more in terms of their meanings than functions. The 'text' metaphor was on the ascendancy at the expense of that of the 'machine'. The city came to be seen as an expression of and, like language itself, inextricably bound to the wider culture. In the process, 'professionals turned to literary criticism in an effort to interpret the city and culture as literary critics do a text' (Ellin, 1996, p.253). Since that time, terms once reserved almost exclusively for the written text such as 'legibility', 'punctuation', 'syntax', 'grammar', 'reading', 'discourse', 'narrative' and even 'language' itself have permeated urban and design literature. 'The city', wrote Rolande Barthes, is a discourse and this discourse is truly a language' (Barthes, 1975, p. 92, quoted in Harvey, 1989, p.67). In fact, cities, buildings and landscapes joined with other dimensions of visual culture such as paintings, prints, magazines, maps, clothes and ritual (Barthes wrote about most of them) as texts to be read.

Certainly, in writing about the Japanese city, I have strayed repeatedly into these other dimensions. Sometimes, it is because they have presented a way of seeing the city: for instance, maps as images of the city. At other times, it is because I have observed phenomena in other areas which seem to parallel those in the city, thus shedding light on the city itself: for instance, the areal basis of the *kanji* characters or the everyday occurrence of collage in the print media.

Of all the images that I have shown in this latter group, perhaps the most telling are the cover pages of the children's magazines shown in chapter 2 (see figures 2.9 and 2.10). On the Japanese cover, drawings, photographs and multiple texts of many colours are scattered and superimposed in frenzied and patchy arrays across the entire surface resulting in a truly fragmented, decentralized and incomplete collage. On the other hand, the Western cover shows an altogether simpler and more ordered composition of elements about a dominant centre.

The Japanese image, as earlier observed, is far more conducive to repeat viewing with an expectation of fresh discovery with each perusal. Also, it is possible to take away significant patches without destroying the whole for it is more an accumulation of only loosely connected parts than a totality of interdependent ones. By contrast, the Western image is gleaned quickly. More important, it is much more susceptible to major damage in the face of minor surgery. Similar things may be said of typical Japanese and Western cities.

Indeed, most Japanese cities give the distinct impression of an accumulation of parts where the severing of bits would be far from catastrophic for the image as a whole. This makes Kisho

Kurokawa's reference to a biological metaphor of 'rhizome' and 'tree' for the two kinds of city – Japanese and Western – an appropriate one (Kurokawa, 1994, p. 64). A rhizome is an interwoven complex of heterogeneous parts which is centre-less yet dynamic and forever changing. It is a cluster of connected yet autonomous parts which is vigorous and can extend in any direction (according to conditions and need). Structurally, it is the antithesis of a tree structure. With the latter, there are roots which successively branch like the boughs, branches and twigs aboveground. If a major artery is cut then all of the sub-branches will wither and die. Moreover, the possibilities for connection between the radiating lines are non-existent. And it goes without saying that a branch (a more peripheral element) does not grow a trunk (a central one). In other words, it is a linear hierarchy. If, on the other hand, one severs an element from a rhizome both the main body and cut part are likely to thrive – and potentially in all directions. There is no hierarchy, vertically or horizontally, and there are possibilities for connection from any part to another. The two models represent extremes in the plant world of hierarchy and non-hierarchy and may, by analogy, reflect extremes in cities too.

Kurokawa, in making the analogy, was drawing on the work of Gilles Deleuze and Felix Guattari who were theorizing in the area of semiotics. Martin Pearce and Maggie Toy use the same source with reference to architectural education

5.1 *Rhizome and Tree. While the diagrams may not look exactly like a rhizome and tree, they do represent certain principles embodied in the two forms which resulted in their use as a biological metaphor for two kinds of city. The former is a* *cluster of connected yet autonomous parts: collectively or independently, they have the capacity for multi-directional expansion. The latter is a structure of hierarchically dependent branches where extension is primarily in one direction.*

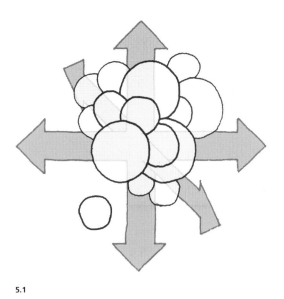

5.1

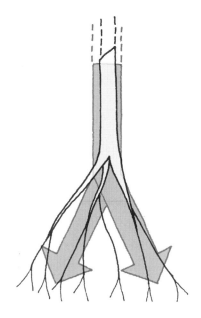

and summarize the Deleuze/Guattari position as proposing 'a condition where the tap root of ideology has been aborted in favour of the shifting layers and boundless interconnectivities of the rhizome' (Pearce and Toy, 1995, p. 7).

There is another kind of image to which I would also like to draw attention because it too speaks loudly of a Japanese way of seeing. It is the kind of print which, in depicting a particular place, shows only part (sometimes a very small bit indeed) of a near object and only a glimpse of the wider scene beyond. For the great print artist, Hiroshige, the use of such fragments were, I suspect, as 'natural' as sitting cross-legged on *tatami*. A great many of the artist's subjects in his 'Meisho Edo Hyakkei' (One Hundred Famous

Places of Edo) series employ fragments to infer whole places in the Edo landscape. Part of a leg plus the hands of a ferryman and the end of a rope-steadied scull provide the frame for a small tree-shrouded grey-brown portion of a middle-distance shrine complex to evoke 'Haneda Ferry and Benten Shrine'. Only a short length of a single bridge rail midst pilgrims' lofted crest-bearing towels and banners suggest 'Kanasugibashi'.

Similarly, beyond a sliver of a fish bucket, part of a single bridge post and a metre or so of three gently curving rails (one deliberately and disturbingly incomplete), there is a distant glimpse of one end of another bridge to rouse a sense of the place about 'Nihonbashi and Edobashi'. Sometimes, fragments of near objects

5.2 *Hiroshige's 'Nihonbashi and Edobashi'. In the foreground, only a small fragment of Nihonbashi is to be seen (not even a whole part of one element of the bridge) and in the distance a glimpse of the north end of Edobashi is shown. (Hiroshige, Meisho Edo Hyakkei)*

5.2

5.3 *Hiroshige's 'Kanasugibashi'. Here, the bridge, from which the print takes its name can barely be seen. The dominant elements in the picture are the signs of a religious sect (the Nichiren) indicating a pilgrimage – probably heading for thirteen more kilometres to the Honmonji Temple, Ikegami. It is Henry D. Smith's speculation that Hiroshige even captures in the single image both the setting out and return of the pilgrims for he observes that the fluttering of materials infers movement in one direction while the positions of umbrellas, drums and drumsticks suggest the opposite (Smith, 1986a). In other words, different times co-exist while place is dominated by fragments, activity, signs and above all, ambiguity. (Hiroshige, Meisho Edo Hyakkei)*

5.3

will cut completely across (vertically and/or horizontally) to dissect the broader landscape and together depict a particular place-event such as the pole and banner which bisect a flat wet landscape and distant procession in his 'Sumiyoshi Festival at Tsukudajima'. Such techniques negate the power of the frame to result in compositions which are antithetical to the Western frame surrounding something that is relatively complete. For the Japanese, emphasis is so often on parts at the expense of wholes. Incompleteness is the 'natural' order.

In other words, to disconnect and focus on one or more fragments is part of the Japanese way. Alex Kerr refers (via the architect, Sei Takeyama) to the ability 'to narrow their focus', to shut out the universe and concentrate on one small thing. In the same breath, he refers to a lecture he gave in Kameoka in which he spoke of a local mountainous landscape dominated by sixty-plus power pylons: these massive objects had passed quite unseen to every member of the audience (Kerr, 1996, p. 50). For a Japanese, the beauty of the blossom upon a cherry tree remains intact and cause for concentration, no matter what monstrosities it may have to squeeze between for its survival. Wholes, in the Western sense do seem to pass unseen. Bigger pictures are far-from-complete or, at least far-from-continuous collections of parts.

In this same vein, there has been scant attempt to see cities as wholes in Japan and this is quite different from the West. This is not to suggest that the West has been successful in its holistic endeavours or indeed that it is necessarily advantageous. Nor is it to suggest that the complexities and diffuse boundaries of today's cities may not defy overall legibility and comprehension. It is, however, that ideas of completeness and the ordered bounded whole have long been prominent in Western urban design ideas and ideals. From the many Renaissance ideas for geometric and physically bounded ideal cities through Ebeneezer Howard's abstract structure for a self-contained garden city (1898) to Christopher Alexander's recent more process-based notion of 'wholeness' in his *New Theory of Urban Design* (1987), the concept of urban wholes with clear and legible structures and hierarchies of centres has been central. Further, such ideals and approaches cannot be divorced from a culture rooted in a religion whose belief is highly centralized and hierarchical and in a tradition of intellectual enquiry which is essentially linear and rational. This is the backcloth to Western approaches to urban intervention.

Japan, on the other hand, shares neither this past nor our patterns of city form. Key words and phrases which have surfaced through these pages in my attempt to capture some of the essences of Japanese cities (especially when set against their counterparts in the West) include:

patchwork (against network);
horizontal (more than vertical);
piecemeal (versus integrated);

decentralized (rather than centralized);

shifting and cloud-like order (rather than fixed and clock-like);

temporary (versus permanent or even eternal);

flexible (more than fixed);

content (against physical context);

and vague (as opposed to clear) boundaries between object (building or city) and surroundings.

Certainly, the legacy of Japan's urban history is very different from the West's in terms of those elements and phenomena which have taken precedence in the making of the urban experience. Again, reflecting back over this work, it is not difficult to link some of the more tangible aspects of form – past and present – to the more abstract 'essences' as outlined above.

There is, for instance, the primacy of land plot and *machi* over building and street – patchwork and network.

The floating floor was preferred to the foundation wall – temporary and permanent.

The spreading ground-peering roof precedented over the sky-aspiring dome, spire or tower – horizontal and vertical.

Temporary and changeable space (singular) was more common than formed and fixed spaces (plural) – flexible and fixed.

In the broader sweep of the city, signs, services and activities have prevailed as place-makers *vis à vis* buildings – content and context.

And functional or activity nodes about particular objects have provided multiple centres rather than one or two formal spaces offering a more centralized experience (particularly bridges and their environs rather than a formed square or plaza) – decentralization and hierarchy.

Further, in the making of these qualities and characteristics, the underpinning values and attitudes which have guided the approaches to urban design seem, consciously or otherwise, to have favoured:

areal (over linear and sequential) organization;

fragmentation (over integration);

disconnection (over connection);

transformation and metamorphosis (over the static or unchangeable);

autonomy (over interdependence) of parts;

attention to details and to fragments before wholes (more than wholes before parts);

the flexible and indefinite (over the fixed and finite); and

superimposition and co-existence of unlike parts (over compromise and integration).

Of course, such broad-ranging contrasts between built patterns and forms are neither absolute nor exhaustive. Taken one by one, they are interesting but perhaps of limited consequence. But together, they do reinforce each other to make two sets of tendencies which pull potently in rather different directions – perhaps East and West. Further, the dissimilarities assume even more significance when it is realized they are not the product of recent times but can, for the most part, be traced far back as thick threads though time.

In today's world of instant information and rapid international exchange, differences between the cities and cultures of the two realms are, to some extent, diminishing. Comparative inquiry, one may think is less relevant in what may be seen as an inevitable (and partly unconscious) slide into some variation on Kurokawa's 'intercultural' theme (Kurokawa, 1991). It is, however, precisely this position which makes better understanding of the experiences and images of the Japanese city both more relevant and necessary. At a practical level, Western architects are increasingly receiving commissions to design in Japan and vice versa: here, enhanced understanding of traditions and differences can only assist. At another and more fundamental level, there are sensibilities and attitudes which are only now emerging in the West that bear comparison to the long-standing nature of Japanese intervention. Thus the contrasting Japanese experiences should give us further insights into our own (Western) urban conditions, their strengths and limitations.

These newer sensibilities and attitudes involve approaches whose techniques are more disposed to fragmentation, fracture, decentering, scattering, layering, superimposition and collage. In other words, they echo some of the often long-standing Japanese ways highlighted through this text. Likewise, they shy away from the notion of the perfect and consistent whole (so strong

in Western rationalism) which is seen as difficult, if not impossible, and indeed irrelevant in today's chaotic and fast-changing world. However, unlike the Japanese ways, those of the West follow largely in the wake of relatively recent (and essentially Western-generated) ideas and discoveries in science and philosophy such as chaos, complexity and catastrophe theories, non-linear science, fractal geometry and its self-similarity, and deconstruction.

Amongst the first large urban proposals to reflect these ideas and receive wide publicity were entries to Paris's Parc de la Villette competition in 1982, particularly those of Bernard Tschumi (the winner) and OMA (Office for Metropolitan Architecture, the runner-up). Both schemes employed a layering approach through the superimposition of relatively autonomous elements.

In the case of Tschumi, the imposed elements were threefold: lines (or channels of movement, axial, geometric and circuitous); points (fragments of building scattered at grid points over the entire site); and surfaces (geometric and irregular horizontal planes for extensive outdoor space-consuming activities). Uses for points and surfaces were part designated and part not.

For OMA, the elements were listed as five: narrow banded areas of landscape suited to different activities; small elements scattered on an irregular grid and referred to suggestively as 'confetti'; circulation routes; large elements, both inherited and new; and connections with the wider city.

5.4 *The Conceptual Layers of the OMA Entry in the Parc de la Villette Competition 1982. These were: (a) 'Strips' – to ensure that the 'clustering of any particular programmatic component is avoided'; (b) 'Confetti '- scattered small facilities; (c) 'Access and Circulation' – routes; (d) the Final Layer – created and found major elements; (e) 'Connections and Elaborations' – partly in the context of city elements beyond the site; and (f) the 'Summation' – the superimposition of all. (Source: OMA, International Architect, No. 1 1983, pp. 32 and 33)*

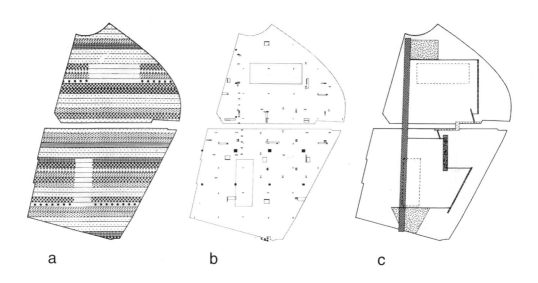

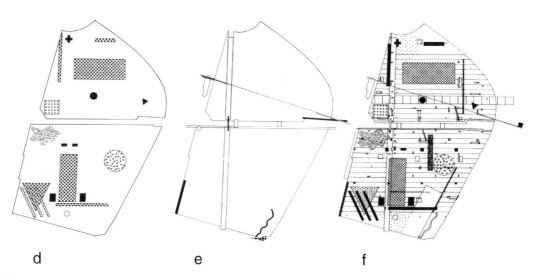

5.4

In fact, both schemes superimposed an array of surfaces, points and lines upon each other and, in turn, upon a site with two large and several smaller found objects (i.e. structures to be kept) and cut by a canal. While there was a measure of manipulation to generate an advantageous relationship between some parts, much was consciously left to chance. In other words, chance relationships of largely independent elements (near or distant, complementary or conflicting) were left to generate a decentered dynamic of unpredictable events with an inbuilt capacity for change. These are processes of tactical super-imposition to sustain diverse activity and create surprises. In fact, it was the second placed, OMA entry which offered the more complex scheme: the multiple thin bands of landscape/activity zones and the more numerous and irregular scattering of confetti would together have generated the greatest potential for creative interaction between the parts (the greatest length of interface, the most complex pattern of fields and the most intersections between all elements). As in any ecological system, it is these meeting points that usually offer the richest and most interesting experiences. And here is a clue to the success of the Japanese city, for its widely acknowledged vibrance stems particularly from the meeting or crossing points (often unusual juxtpostions) of multiple and diverse areas, points and lines (in rich three-dimensional above-and-below-ground superimpositions)

Since that competition, the sensibilities and values which underpinned those entries have evolved and gained considerable ground. It is a process that has exercised the attention of Charles Jencks in his *Architecture of the Jumping Universe* which is the first broad popular attempt to make some of the connections between the more recent design aesthetics of fragmentation, folding, superimposition and collage and the scientific backcloth of our age (the new sciences of complexity) which increasingly views the systems which make up our universe as chaotic, self-organizing, non-linear, self transform-ing, and unpredictably creative (Jencks, 1995). The condition of the universe is seen as a process which is always emergent, forever reaching new levels of self-organization and complexity. The city is one of the best examples of all and it is only now that Jane Jacobs's description of the city as 'a problem of organized complexity' is being fully appreciated (Jacobs, 1961, p. 24). This is very different from the previous era when scientists were preoccupied with the idea of a grand unifying theory applicable to all phenom-ena. Again, this was reflected in architecture and planning with universal theories of total form and linear concepts of environmental deter-minism, of which Jacobs was an early critic. Chaos theory is especially pertinent with its notions of both organized chaos (apparently ran-dom phenomena as organized disorder) and non-linearity (insignificant forces, by way of positive feedback, being magnified into enormously powerful ones). Fractals are important in that they introduce the notion of parts that repeat themselves at different scales with resemblance but not replication: in other words, there is self-similarity (but not sameness) between wholes and parts as well as between parts of the same scale.

Further, the intrinsic uncertainty and attention to parts which characterize the new scientific backcloth are echoed in philosophy and linguistics. These posit that all knowledge is relative and fallible, and the quest for ultimate truth and totalizing reason, which is at the heart of the Western intellectual tradition, is no more than 'a futile exercise in linguistic game-playing': it is both self-deceptive and ultimately destructive (Tarnas, 1981, p. 400). In this context, totalities are viewed as some kind of tyranny. Such sentiments are central to Post-Modernism which has been described by Ihab Hassan as 'an antinomian movement that assumes a vast unmaking in the Western mind . . . deconstruction, decentering, disappearance, dissemination, demystification, discontinuity, *difference*, dispersion, etc. Such terms . . . express an epistemological obsession with fragments or fractures . . .' (quoted in Tarnas, 1981 p.401).

Of all cities, Japan's offer experiences which mirror most the various dimensions of this contemporary cultural backcloth. Car parks are more likely to be pencil-thin sky-reaching points scattered like confetti across the city than bulky rationalized blobs at strategically located centres. Expressways, large roads and little streets are more like separate but co-existing systems, one superimposed upon the other, than a carefully integrated hierarchy. Roofs, at whatever levels, are as good as any ground as sites for any kind of building, even a revered shrine or temple. Buildings themselves – short and towering, small and bulky, timber and concrete – are intermingled over wide areas rather than channelled into obvious centres and hierarchical patterns. Units in multi-storey developments are colonized by varieties of activity in unexpected vertical mixes rather than in hierarchically layered single uses from retail upwards to residential. Streets are not just horizontal surface phenomena but also subterranean, suspended and bolt upright. Form and structure are swamped by information and animation which display themselves two and three dimensionally, horizontally and vertically, and at all levels. Buildings are transformed from shabby to stunning and vice versa at the touch of a switch. Structures depreciate and are refitted or replaced with amazing rapidity. *Machi*, *chome*, plot, floor (and often *tatami*) lie as areal components thus sharing some measure of self-similarity and difference at various scales. These phenomena and countless more, together present a cloud-like (and far-from-clockwork) image in constant flux – shifting, decentred, incomplete and forever reforming.

At another level, Japanese cities seem to combine Rowe's notion of the city as 'collage' (Rowe, 1978) with that of a centreless city where multiple centres are dispersed and even peripheral ('edge cities') with, if it is not too much of a contradiction, that of a cityless city condition. In the latter case city frontiers have been so dissipated and form has drifted so far from established associations with the word that we may be better off with a new term: Francoise Choay suggested 'post-urban' to better describe our late twentieth century condition and to free us from formal preconceptions about cities. (Choay, quoted in Ellin, 1996, p. 245) For many, including Manuel Castells, cityness has for some time been a condition involving a measure of integration into a global system that embraces advanced technology and communications, and global capital and culture (Castells, 1972, 1997). Thus cities become forever less tangible, less fixed and therefore less easily pinpointed by simple spatial coordinates.

Amongst advanced regions, Japan has some of the highest settlement densities. Nevertheless, these form some of the most centreless and collaged (urban) agglomerations with hazy and shifting boundaries – conditions which are conceptually reinforced by the culture itself which has not distinguished between town and country. All are part of and subject to the Gods' multiple and ill-defined powers and territories, some relating to abstract or tangible phenomena and some to physical place. Within such a cultural milieu, and in the context of the nation's economic success, it is natural that Japanese architects should be to the fore in the creation of buildings which both reflect and contribute to these conditions.

If, in their instability, cities are like clouds and wind is the force behind the latters' unstable motion then the idea of an urban structure that is a shimmering transmitter of the wind's performance is most apt. Toyo Ito sees architectural design as 'an act of generating vortexes in the currents of air, wind, light and sound' and aims 'at spaces of unstable states' (Ito, 1992, p. 22). Ito's Tower of the Winds in Yokohama is, at one level, the ultimate in utility – a cylindrical ventilation shaft above one of Japan's ubiquitous subterranean shopping centres. But it is also a large (over 20 m high) tell-tale night sign which sparkles and shines with ever-changing computer-controlled lights and streaks of neon according to the direction and force of the wind and other environmental phenomena. With no sharp differentiation between city and country, man-made and natural, this high-tech installation is a 'natural' extension of nature. Moreover, it is in that context that its nightly transformation and constant flux occur.

As discussed earlier, the attitude to tower buildings in the West is that they should not only stand tall but look even taller: the soaring tradition is a long one with various devices to emphasize verticality (spires, finials etc.). If they are high and 'arched', the hole is likely to define an axis or centrepoint (e.g. Paris's Arc de Triomphe or Grande Arche). Hiroshi Hara's twin tower building in his Shin-Umeda City project in Osaka is, however, somewhat different. The towers stand over 50 m apart and rise

5.5 *Tower of the Winds, Yokohama. (Architect: Toyo Ito, 1986) Computer-controlled lights over the surface of this cylindrical tower provide a high tech extension of nature: they flicker and streak according to the behaviour of the wind and other surrounding conditions. (Photograph: Miki Okamoto)*

5.5

through sleek rectilinear shafts (self-similar but without replication): they are, however, blunted at the top by a shared platform structure (square with a round mid-air void) and an assemblage of small structures. These cross over from one tower to the next to make the whole thing into an arch (at least in the sense of La Grande Arche which,

incidentally, is much lower – 110 m against 179 m). This platform and its array of smaller structures (the top is a pile of smaller elements) would seem more at home as a ground-hugging complex (perhaps crossing a river or motorway in as much as it is also a bridge) than hovering high over a city plaza, as in Osaka. Indeed, there are elements in the 'top' which are not unlike Hara's Yamato International Building in outer Tokyo which is often likened to an Italian hilltown (albeit a shiny high-tech one) and therefore close to the ground. As if to further dislocate the experience of the top (referred to as a 'mid-air garden' by Hara) from that of the shafts, a pair of escalator bridges slope steeply and splay precariously out across the centre void to connect tower and platform. And in the void of the arch below, free-standing shafts and bridges rise and cross to provide further transparent connection between ground, towers and horizontal top. The irregular surfaces of the top are of polished aluminium while those of the shafts are mostly mirror and transparent glass: this leaves the top to boldly catch the light while the shafts, ever-changing, reflect the sky, exaggerating the sense of a 'floating' top. And, of course, all is transformed at dusk.

Another Japanese architect whose buildings seem to embrace both native tradition and the spirit of the age is Itsuko Hasegawa. Perhaps her best known buildings to date are two cultural centres: the Shonandai Culture Centre (1990) and Sumida Culture Factory (1994). Both provide stunning high-tech landscapes (urban oases)

5.6 *Sky City, Shin Umeda City Osaka. (Architect: Hiroshi Hara, 1993) The top is like a high tech hill village which has been forced upwards on two shafts extruded from below.*

5.6

in tacky neighbourhoods of Tokyo's outer and middle rings respectively.

The Sumida complex houses a planetarium, assembly hall, meeting rooms, library, study rooms and offices: like the Shonandai Centre it is a new building type: a community communication and information centre. The Sumida Culture

Factory is set out in three sections about a central plaza on an irregular heptagonal block. One section is dominated by billowing incomplete elliptical shapes, one by a sphere and one by triangular sail-like forms. The three are connected by no fewer than nine bridges at various levels though the site is only 3,400 sq m. Bridges, walkways, lift shafts and stairwells are transparent or translucent. The main surfaces are either metal, perforated metal or glazed.

It is a place which is absolutely contemporary (form, materials and technology) yet replete with tradition. On this latter point, it has multiple centres. The translucent and perforated surfaces allow silhouettes and shadows to animate the place. The complex is in constant transformation both through the day (surfaces responding to the light) and from day to night (internal illumination). Its image is undoubtedly one of lightness and transience – so much so that it has been likened popularly to a circus tent on its temporary site (Tajima and Powell, 1997, p. 24). These qualities result in a development whose many parts are autonomous, often veiled and yet connected three-dimensionally. Similarly, the whole development is distinct from its surroundings but connected to it. Further, at upper levels, there is a sense of the independent structure on the elevated plot. Overall, the complex has qualities of both cloud and rhizome.

An influence upon Hasegawa was Kazuo Shinohara in whose office she worked for some time. Although Shinohara's early work used

5.7 *Sumida Culture Factory, Higashi-Mukojima, Tokyo. (Architect: Itsuko Hasegawa, 1994) Approaching from this side street (one of several similar approaches), a variety of elliptical and triangulated forms plus a sphere 'billow' and 'float' above the screened edge to offer a tent-like and transient image. The edge signals simultaneously both protection (autonomous oasis) and connection (permeable net). (Photograph: Miki Okamoto)*

5.7

traditional forms, he began around 1980 to respond to the jumble of the Japanese city as an inspirational source. At a forum on 'Learning from Tokyo' in 1993, Charles Jencks reported that Shinohara had been educated according to the Western urban design considerations of 'visibility, legibility and comprehensibility' but after thirty years of practice, became acquainted with theories of chaos and self-organization (Academy International Forum, 1994, p. 15). Further, he started to link the latter ideas with the apparent urban disorder of Japan and in the process started to produce buildings which reflect both: such as his Tokyo Institute of Technology Anniversary Hall (1987) which is a mix of restau-

rant, bar, exhibition and meeting spaces. The external image is one of a fractured half cylinder (rather like a bent and dismembered aircraft fuselage) crashing through a main mass which is itself irregular in its footprint and surfaces. It is also situated in an acute angle of TIT's site where it thrusts wedge-like into the wider city (where there are shops, dwellings and railway station) which only accentuates its presence. It is not a huge building (24 m high) but its chaotic composition and siting give it an overwhelming and ominous presence which serves somehow to accentuate the chaotic qualities of its surrounds and exemplify Shinohara's notion of 'beauty' arising from 'progressive anarchy'.

5.8 *Tokyo Institute of Technology Centennial Hall. (Architect: Kazuo Shinohara, 1987) It is inspired by the anarchic urban conditions about it.*

5.8

These architects may now rank amongst Japan's international stars. They are, nevertheless, only indicative of the tremendous range of Japanese work which, though diverse, continues to show a powerful spirit which is consistent with both many of the nation's traditions and our contemporary world. This is in the best sense, 'contextual'. In *Architecture of the Jumping*

Universe, Jencks does not devote a great deal of space to the work of Japanese architects but he does acknowledge it as being at 'one of the forefronts' showing projects by both Hasegawa and Ito as well as by Arata Isozaki and Kiko Mozuna. Consciously or otherwise, all reflect the 'new sciences'. Of Hasegawa, he comments, interestingly, that 'she is now actively engaged in exploring the science of fractals, Fuzzy Logic and chaos' which presumably means that previously she was not (Jencks, 1995, p. 136). If he is right about her late exploration, then her work was already deep in the 'new science' camp without conscious pursuit of the theory. It is the Japanese condition.

In general, Japan's designers are far more inclined to embrace collage, rupture, lightness, transformation, disconnection (or at least loose connection), the indefinite, the cloud-like, the coexistence of unlikely parts, etc. than their Western counterparts. They are more at ease with these conditions. They have less need to resort to theory and theorizing. In short, it is more a part of their cultural and urban background. Even Fumihiko Maki, who from his experience bears more marks of the West, Modernism and a theoretical approach than most Japanese professionals, has produced a masterpiece of collage in the front zone of his now ageing (13 years old) Spiral Building on Tokyo's Aoyama Boulevard – a bustling stretch of an urban big road.

Maki is, of course, pre-eminent as a theorist and practitioner, and acutely aware of both past

5.9 *Spiral Building (or Wacoal Media Centre),*
Aoyama, Tokyo. (Architect: Fumihiko Maki, 1985)
The 'front' to Aoyama-dori gives a truly shifting
and cloud like impression in which the eye is drawn
to focus on sophisticated individual elements
without ever quite grasping the whole.

5.9

and present conditions in Japanese cities. He
is amongst the first to recognize that they bear
neither a clear relationship between centre and
periphery nor figure and ground, and that this is
far from new. He sees the city as a transitional
landscape in which buildings and their parts enjoy
a high level of autonomy. Overall, he describes the
city as 'collage-like' and generating an 'aesthetic
. . . that favours fluctuations, fluidity and lightness' (Maki, 1988, p. 8).

The Spiral Building is a thirteen level (nine
above ground) mixed use cultural centre and
showpiece building of the fashion and lingerie
company, Wacoal: inside, there are restaurants,
club, beauty salon, theatre, offices, video studios,
etc. and some very exciting spaces for moving
between and beyond these functional areas,
including a semi-circular atrium which rises
through four levels, an 'esplanade' and 'hanging
garden'.

The 'front' is not so much a facade as a slab
of space within which a great variety of two- and
three-dimensional elements are assembled to
interpenetrate, obscure, reveal, superimpose and
stand upon each other to give a truly shifting
and cloud-like overall impression. These include
a translucent screen (Japanese tradition), fluted
columns (Western antiquity), a pure cone and
free-standing wave wall (Modernism), frames,
columns, aluminium panels with sharp jagged
outlines, irregular window frames (some with a
logarithmic type spacing between the glazing
bars) and much more. Sometimes elements reveal
internal functions like the stepped floors showing
the rising esplanade; sometimes they deliberately
mask internal changes in function. All are
collaged into something that denies the eye the
satisfaction of grasping the whole but offers multiple visual delights in the fragments. And there
is absolutely nothing about it that is gimmicky.

When I first saw the building, I had just travelled from Fukuoka where I had seen a recently
completed building (in Seaside Momochi) by

186

5.10 *Apartment Building, Seaside Momochi,*
Fukuoka. (Architect: Stanley Tigerman, 1989)

5.10

the American architect, Stanley Tigerman. At the
time, I thought back immediately to make some
sort of comparison between Spiral and the
Momochi building – a six storey block of apartments. This is also an irregular pile of intersecting
parts: it involves the superimposition of lines,
planes and volumes and is said to be inspired by
the rectilinear nature of traditional Japanese
building. Though undoubtedly accomplished, the
result is nevertheless rather more predictable,
stolid and static than that of Maki. Like the

melange of *kanji* and other characters and images
on the cover of *Tanoshii Yochien* (see page 26),
Spiral offers a mix of strongly independent parts
which have individual strength and sometimes
direct meaning but together shift ambiguously
between harmony and conflict. Although irregular
as a whole, Tigerman's design is composed from
relatively few and more regular elements which
intersect in more repetitious ways. It is much
more difficult to envisage something being added
easily or taken away and is more the final object.
Maki's Spiral, on the other hand, is more fluid
and seems suspended in the process of becoming.

The Spiral Building (otherwise known as the
Wacoal Media Centre) is pertinent in other ways.
While its fragments are international in their
materials and often Modernist in their aesthetic,
the building is also extremely Japanese. For
instance, as a piece of urban design, it steps
down from the high hard (shell) side of Aoyama
Boulevard via a roof garden and atrium to the
lower softer (yolk) side of the interior of the
superblock. Though there are multiple centres
in the building, the stunning atrium space lies deep
inside (at the rear) and is reached by an indirect
route. Further, while the building whole may be
elusive (externally and internally) the details
are highly sophisticated and superbly crafted
– another Japanese traditional (and Maki)
characteristic. While there is little that is literal
in Spiral, its fragmented cloud-like qualities
envelope an incredible array of subtle responses
to context as city and culture.

Western designers, like it or not, carry with them the intellectual baggage of Greece, Christianity and the Renaissance. This is a rational, linear, sequential, etc tradition. Toying with the relevant new ideas in the sciences and humanities is an intellectual struggle – more blood, sweat and left brain work. As a result, much Western work (for instance, that of Peter Eisenman and Bernard Tschumi), no matter how immaculate in its own way, appears ultimately more forced, stilted and static, and more the result of intellectual formulae. Eisenman's N C Building in Tokyo is a case in point: in that building, toilets and lifts excepted, everything is distorted and fractured about a standard structure, to appear as many buildings might after the capital's next tectonic disturbance. My former colleague, Jian Fei Zhu reacted in not dissimilar ways when he placed Maki's Spiral Building alongside another Eisenman design, the Koizumi Building, also in Tokyo. He observed that the latter is a collision of volumes and only reflects a more general Western contemporary idiom of colliding volumes, planes and lines, whereas Maki's work 'is nowhere informed by such collisions'. For Zhu therefore, the Spiral Building 'engages an entirely different mentality' for although its 'plurality of forms are randomly scattered', they are also 'calm' and 'serene' and 'easily and freely co-existent'. This, he argues, shows a distinctly Eastern approach (Zhu, 1995, p. 116). For the Japanese, their cultural background is more compatible with collision, fracture, fragmentation, superimposition, etc and their work tends to be more natural, more fluid and more dynamic in working with these ideas.

The different cultural backcloths and traditional belief systems are crucial. Again Jencks makes reference, albeit tentatively, to these and their relationship with Modern science (Jencks, 1995, p. 130). It was, however, Fritzof Capra who, over two decades ago, brought so convincingly the profundity of that relationship to our attention in his already cited classic, *The Tao of Physics* – namely, the compatibility of the views of modern physicists and Eastern mystics. In particular, writes Capra, the latter's 'refined notions of space and time resulting from their mystical experiences appear in many ways to be similar to the notions of modern physics, as exemplified by the theory of relativity' (Capra, 1991, p. 164). Pertinent also to this work on form and space is that in the history of the West, geometry had an absolute status and, to the Greeks, was of divine origin; whereas in the East, it was used for practical purposes (e.g. measuring and making) but not to determine eternal truths (Capra, 1991, p. 163). Similarly, in Buddhism, and especially Japanese Zen, words were seen to be incapable of expressing ultimate truths (Capra, 1991, p. 122) whereas in the Christian West (Gospel according to St. John), the Word and God were inseparable: 'In the beginning, was the Word, and the Word was with God, and the word was God'. This raises the Western logocentric tradition upon which Zhu also makes comment and links with built-form. He refers specifically to 'the decline of Western Modernism and logocentricism' alongside 'the rise of Japan and East Asia's own cultural mentality' with its centuries old 'uniquely non-logocentric' qualities (Zhu, 1995, p. 115).

Put simply, there are dimensions of the new world views which, although Western-generated, bear closer comparison with Eastern (and especially Japan's) traditions than they do with the West's. Consequently, we find in Japanese cities a wider range of physical conditions and characteristics – some extremely long-standing – reflecting more closely the new views than in their Western counterparts. Similarly, we find embodied in the work of Japanese designers a range of attitudes and approaches which are also more in tune (though not always consciously so) with the new views than we do amongst their European and American peers. Indeed, the urban design and architectural traditions of the West seem to serve much as a handicap and hindrance to the kinds of change which might respond to the new views. In this new climate, Japan's cities take on a fresh significance.

As a final note, I should remind readers that the West has a record of ignoring (or worse, denigrating) the design characteristics and qualities of Japanese built forms until such times as these may be used in support of some 'new' theory, sensibility or model of its own. In the nineteenth century, Japanese gardens were a source of inspiration for the relatively 'new' Romantic inclinations in landscaping. Earlier this century, Modern architects turned their attention to traditional Japanese building when they realized it embodied design principles that they themselves were endeavouring to 'pioneer'. Now, it may be the city's turn and I am one of a small but growing band of designers and planners who are setting their sights in an Easterly direction.

Appendix

Early Japan

Yamato	350 to 710

Classical Japan

Nara	710 to 794
Heian	794 to 1185

Middle Ages

Kamakura	1185 to 1333
Muromachi	1334 to 1573

Pre-Modern Japan

Azuchi-Momoyama	1573 to 1603
Edo or Tokugawa	1603 to 1867

Modern Japan

Meiji	1867 to 1912
Taisho	1912 to 1926
Showa	1926 to 1989
Heisei	1989 and continuing

Bibliography

Academy International Forum (1994) Learning from Tokyo. *Architectural Design Profile*, No. 107. London: Academy Editions, pp 8–19.

Alexander, Christopher (1966) The City is not a Tree. *Design*, No. 206, pp. 46–55 (originally published in *Architectural Record*, 1965)

Alexander, Christopher (1987) *A New Theory of Urban Design*. New York: Oxford University Press.

Itsuko Hasegawa. Architectural Design Monograph No. 31, 1993. London: Academy Editions.

The Periphery. Architectural Design Profile No. 108, 1994, in *Architectural Design*, Vol. 64, No 3/4.

Ashihara, Yoshinobu (1983) *The Aesthetic Townscape*. Cambridge, Mass.: MIT Press (Originally published as *Machinami no bigaku*. Tokyo: Iwanami Shoten, 1979)

Ashihara, Yoshinobu (1987) Chaos and Order in the Japanese City. *Japan Echo*, Vol. XIV, pp. 64–68.

Ashihara, Yoshinobu (1989) *The Hidden Order: Tokyo through the Twentieth Century*. Tokyo: Kodansha International (Originally published as *Kakureta chitsujo*. Tokyo: Chuokoron-sha, 1986).

Ashihara, Yoshinobu (1994) *Tokyo no Bigaku: Konton to Chitsujo (Tokyo's Aesthetics: Chaos and Order)*. Tokyo: Iwanami Shinsho.

Bacon, Edmund N. (1967) *Design of Cities*. London: Thames and Hudson.

Barker, Felix, and Jackson, Peter (1990) *The History of London in Maps*. London: Barrie and Jenkins.

Barthes, Rolande (1975) *The Pleasure of the Text* (Translated by Richard Miller). New York: Hill and Wang.

Barthes, Rolande (1982) *Empire of Signs* (Translated by Richard Howard). New York: Hill and Wang.

Batty, Michael and Longley, Paul (1994) *Fractal Cities*. London: Academic Press.

Bentley, Ian, Alcock, Alan, Murrain, Paul, McGlynn, Sue and Smith, Graham (1985) *Responsive Environments*. London: The Architectural Press.

Bird, Isabella L. (1973) *Unbeaten Tracks in Japan*. Rutland, Vermont: Charles E Tuttle (Originally published New York, 1880)

Bognar, Botond (1985) *Contemporary Japanese Architecture*. New York: Van Nostrand Reinhold.

Bognar, Botond (1992a) Critical Intentions in Pluralistic Japanese Architecture. *Architectural Design*, Vol. 62, No. 3/4, pp. 72–96.

Bognar, Botond (1992b) Between Reality and Fiction. *Architectural Design*, Vol. 62, No. 9/10, pp. 9–21

Bognar, Botond (1992c) Anywhere in Japan. *Architectural Design*, Vol. 62, No. 11/12, pp. 70–72.

Bognar, Botond (1995) *The Japan Guide*. New York: Princeton Architectural Press.

Boorstin, Daniel J. (1993) *The Creators: A*

History of Heroes of the Imagination. New York: Vintage Books.

Broadbent, Geoffrey (1990) *Emerging Concepts in Urban Space Design.* London: Van Nostrand Reinhold.

Broadbent, Geoffrey (1992) Just Exactly What Is Going On, and Why? *Architectural Design*, Vol. 62, No 1/2, pp. 9–11.

Brolin, Brent (1980) *Architecture in Context.* New York: Van Nostrand Reinhold.

Capra, Fritjof (1991) *The Tao of Physics.* Boston: Shambhala (first published 1975).

Cartwright, T. J. (1991) Planning and Chaos Theory. *Journal of the American Planning Association*, Vol. 57, No. 1, pp. 44–56.

Castells, Manuel (1980) *The Urban Question: A Marxist Approach* (Translated by Alan Sheridan). Cambridge, Mass: The MIT Press (Originally published as *La Question Urbaine*, 1972).

Castells, Manuel (1997) An Inroduction to the Information Age. *City*, Vol. 7, May, pp. 6–16.

Castile, Rand (1986) Tokyo and the West, in Friedman, Mildred (ed.) *Tokyo: Form and Spirit.* Minneapolis: Walker Art Center/New York: Harry N. Abrams.

Cooper, Michael (ed.) (1965) *They Came to Japan: An Anthology of European Reports on Japan, 1543–1640.* Berkeley, Ca.: University of California Press.

Cooper, Michael (ed.) (1971) *The Southern Barbarians: The First Europeans in Japan.* Tokyo: Kodansha International.

Conder, Josiah (1964) *Landscape Gardening in Japan.* New York: Dover (Originally published 1893).

Cortazzi, Hugh (1990) *The Japanese Achievement.* London: Sidgwick and Jackson.

Cullen, Gordon (1961) *Townscape.* London: Architectural Press.

Davidson, Cynthia C. (ed.) (1996) *Anywise.* New York: Anyone Corporation / Cambridge, Mass: The MIT Press.

Edo-Tokyo Museum (1995) *Guide to Edo-Tokyo Museum.* Tokyo: Foundation Edo-Tokyo Historical Society.

Ellin, Nan (1996) *Postmodern Urbanism.* Oxford: Blackwell.

Farrell, Terry (1986) Villa Quattro. *Architectural Design*, Vol. 56, No. 10/11, pp. 49–53.

Fleming, John, Honour, Hugh and Pevsner, Nikolaus (1972) *The Penguin Dictionary of Architecture*, 2nd ed. Harmondsworth: Penguin.

Friedman, Mildred (ed.) *Tokyo: Form and Spirit.* Minneapolis: Walker Art Center / New York: Harry N. Abrams.

Garrioch, David (1994) House Names, Shop Signs, Social Organisation in Western European Cities, 1500–1900. *Urban History*, Vol. 21, Part 1, April, pp. 20–48.

Griffis, W. E. (1876) *The Mikado's Empire.* New York: Harper and Brothers.

Harvey, David (1989) *The Condition of Postmodernity.* Oxford: Basil Blackwell.

Hearn, Lafcadio (1976) *Glimpses of Unfamiliar*

Japan. Rutland, Vermont: Charles E Tuttle (Originally published 1894).

Hearn, Lafcadio (1984) *Writings from Japan.* Harmondsworth, England: Penguin (Originally published 1894).

Hegemann, Werner, and Peets, Elbert (1922) *The American Vitruvius: An Architect's Handbook of Civic Art.* New York: Architectural Book Publishing Company.

Hitchcock, Alfred M. (1917) *Over Japan Way.* New York: Henry Holt and Company.

Ishi'i, Kazuhiro (1982) Urban Beauty in Tokyo. *Japan Architect*, April, pp. 60–61.

Iso, Tatsuo (1996) Ichibankan – Nibankan. *Nikkei Architecture*, 12 February, pp. 107–111.

Itsuko Hasegawa: Selected and Current Works (1997) Mulgrave, Vic. Australia: Images Publishing Group.

Ito, Toyo (1992) Vortex and Current. *Architectural Design*, Vol. 62, No. 9/10, pp. 22–23.

Jackson, John B. (1991) The Past and Future Park, in Wrede, Stuart and Adams, William Howard (eds.) *Denatured Visions.* New York: Museum of Modern Art, pp. 129–134.

JA (*The Japan Architect*) (1991) Special Issue: 1991–93 Tokyo. No. 3.

Jacobs, Jane (1965) *The Death and Life of Great American Cities.* Harmonsworth, England: Penguin Books (Originally published 1961).

Japan: A Pictorial Interpretation. (1932) Tokyo: Asahi Shimbun Publishing Co.

Jeans, George (1992) *Writing: the Story of Alphabets and Scripts.* London: Thames and Hudson.

Jencks, Charles (1995) *The Architecture of the Jumping Universe.* London: Academy Editions.

Jencks, Charles (1990) *The New Moderns.* New York: Rizzoli.

Jinnai, Hidenobu (1987a) Ethnic Tokyo. *Process Architecture*, No. 72.

Jinnai, Hidenobu (1987b) Tokyo Then and Now: Keys to Japanese Urban Design. *Japan Echo*, Vol. XIV, pp. 20–29.

Jinnai, Hidenobu (1995) Tokyo: *A Spatial Anthropology* (Translated by Kimiko Nishimura). Berkeley: University of California Press (Originally published as *Tokyo no Kukan Jinruigaku*, 1985).

Kato, Akinori (1993) *Japanese Open Space as an Amenity.* Tokyo: Process Architecture.

Kawazoe, Noboru (1965) *Contemporary Architecture of Japan 1958–1984.* Tokyo: Kokusai Bunka Shinkokai.

Kerr, Alex (1996) *Lost Japan.* Melbourne: Lonely Planet.

Kinoshita, June, and Palevsky, Nicholas (1990) *Gateway to Japan.* Tokyo: Kodansha International.

Kobayashi, Katsuhiro (1994) Currents in Contemporary Japanese Architecture, in Meyhofer, Dirk (ed.) *Contemporary Japanese Architects.* Cologne: Taschen.

Koolhaas, Rem (1978) *Delirious New York.* London: Thames and Hudson.

Kreiner, Josef, Tadao, Umesao, Kasuya, Kazuki

and Shinzo, Ogi (1995) Edo-Tokyo as an Instrument of Civilization, in *Guide to Edo-Tokyo Museum*. Tokyo: Edo-Tokyo Museum, pp. 164–171.

Krier, Rob (1979) *Urban Space* (Translated by C. Czechowski and G. Black) New York: Rizzoli (Originally published 1975).

Kurokawa, Kisho (1990) Taking a Stand over Esperanto. **Architects Journal**, 19 September, pp. 42–47.

Kurokawa, Kisho (1991) *Intercultural Architecture*. Washington DC: The American Institute of Architects Press.

Kurokawa, Kisho (1994) *The Philosophy of Symbiosis*. London: Academy Editions.

Lindqvist, Cecilia (1991) *China: Empire of the Written Symbol*. London: Harvill.

Lynch, Kevin (1960) *The Image of the City*. Cambridge, Mass: MIT Press.

Maki, Fumihiko (1964) *Investigations in Collective Form*. St. Louis: The School of Architecture, Washington University.

Maki, Fumihiko (1979) Japanese City Spaces and the Concept of *oku*. *Japan Architect*, Vol. 54, No. 265, pp. 50–62.

Maki, Fumihiko (1988) City, Image and Materiality, in Salat, Serge (ed.) *Fumihiko Maki: An Aesthetic of Fragmentation*. New York: Rizzoli.

Masai, Yasuo, (ed.) (1986) *Atlas Tokyo: Edo/Tokyo through Maps*. Tokyo: Heibonsha.

Mengham, Rod (1993) *Language*. London: Fontana Press.

Meyhofer, Dirk (1994) *Contemporary Japanese Architects*. Cologne: Taschen.

Mitsuru, Maki (1994) *Nagasaki Omoide Sampo (A Stroll through Memories of Nagasaki)* Nagasaki: Shunkosha.

Montgomery, John (1992) Dressed to Kill Off Urban Culture. *Planning*, No. 989, p. 6.

Morley, John David (1986) *Pictures from the Water Trade*. London: Flamingo.

Morris, Jan (1986) Capital City: Kyoto 1957, in *Among the Cities*. London: Penguin.

Morris, Neal (1990) Kurokawa – Taking a stand over Esperanto. *Architects Journal*, September, pp. 42–47.

Morse, Edward S. (1972) *Japanese Homes and their Surroundings*. Rutland, Vermont: Charles E. Tuttle (Originally published Boston, 1886).

Moughtin, Cliff (1992) *Urban Design: Street and Square*. Oxford: Butterworth Architecture.

Nagasaki City (1989) *'89 Municipal Centennial Nagasaki* 100.

Nakamura, Yujiro *et al.* (1984) Tokyo as Mediocosm (Interview transcript). *Process Architecture* 49, pp. 12–15 and 62–72.

Narumi, K. (ed.) (1996) *Nihon no Toshi Kankyo Design '85–'95 (Japanese City and Environmental Design '85–'95)*. Kyoto: Gakugei Shuppansha.

Nitschke, Gunter (1966) 'Ma': The Japanese Sense of 'Place' in Old and New Architecture and Planning. *Architectural Design*, March, pp. 117–130.

Nitschke, Gunter (1994) The Manga City, in Ueda, Atsushi (ed.) *The Electric Geisha*. Tokyo: Kodansha International.

Nishi, Kazuo and Hozumi, Kazuo(1985) *What is Japanese Architecture?* Tokyo: Kodansha International (Originally published in Japanese in 1983).

Nishimura, Shigeo (1985) *E de Miru Nihon no Rekishi* (*Pictorial History of Japan*). Tokyo: Fukuinkan Shoten.

Nute, Kevin (1993) *Frank Lloyd Wright and Japan*. London: Chapman and Hall.

Office for Metropolitan Architecture (1983) La Villette Competition: Hypothesis and Demonstration. *International Architect*, No. 1, pp. 32–37.

Office for Metropolitan Architecture (1995) *Small, Medium, Large, Extra-Large*. Rotterdam: 010 Publishers.

Okabayashi, Takatoshi and Hayashi, Kazuma (eds.) (1995) *Old Photographs of Nagasaki*. Nagasaki: Nagasaki City Board of Education

Ono, Sokyo (1984) *Shinto: The Kami Way*. Rutland, Vermont: Charles E Tuttle.

Pearce, Martin and Toy, Maggie (eds.) (1995) Introduction, in *Educating Architects*. London: Academy Editions, pp. 7–9.

Pevsner, Nikolaus (1951) *The Buildings of England: Nottinghamshire*. Harmondsworth, England: Penguin.

Porter, Hal (1968) *The Actors: An Image of the New Japan*. Sydney: Angus and Robertson.

Popham, Peter (1985) *Tokyo: the City at the End of the World*. Tokyo: Kodansha International.

Process Architecture (1984) Tokyo Urban Language. No. 49.

Richards, J. M. (1969) Lessons from the Japanese Jungle. *The Listener*, 13 March, pp. 339–340 (Reproduced in Bell, Gwen and Tyrwhitt, Jaqueline (eds.) (1972) *Human Identity in the Urban Environment*. Harmondsworth, England: Penguin, pp. 590–594).

Richie, Donald (1991) *A Lateral View: Essays on Contemporary Japan*, revised edition. Tokyo: The Japan Times (First published 1987).

Rodrigues, Joao (1973) *This Island of Japon: Joao Rodriques' account of 16th-Century Japan* (Translated and edited by Michael Cooper). Tokyo: Kodansha International.

Rowe, Colin and Koetter, Fred (1978) *Collage City*. Cambridge, Mass: The MIT Press.

Royal Academy of Arts (1994) Academy International Forum: Learning from Tokyo, in *Japanese Architecture III. Architectural Design Profile*, No. 107, pp. 8–19.

Rudofsky, Bernard (1965) *The Kimono Mind*. New York: Prentice Hall.

Sadler, A. L. (1941) *A Short History of Japanese Architecture*. Sydney: Angus and Robertson.

Salat, Serge (1988) *Fumiko Maki: an Aesthetic of Fragmentation*. New York: Rizzolo 1988 (First published as *Fumihiko Maki: une poetique de la fragmentation*. Paris: Electa-France, 1987) .

Shelton, Barrie (1989) Book Review: *The Hidden*

Order – Tokyo through the Twentieth Century by Yoshinobu Ashihara. *Australian Planner*, September, pp. 22–23.

Shelton, Barrie (1992) Rethinking Our Images of the Japanese City. *Australian Planner*, September, pp. 14–18.

Shelton, Barrie (1997) Probing Japan's Patchwork Polis. *City*, Vol. 7, May, pp. 95–103.

Shiraishi, Tsutomu (ed.) (1993) *Edo Kiriezu to Tokyo Meisho-e*. Tokyo: Shogakukan.

Shitamachi Museum (undated) *Shitamachi Nagaya*. Tokyo: Board of Education, Taito Ward.

Sitte, Camillo (1995) *City Planning According to Artistic Principles* (Translated by G. R. and C. C .) in Collins, G. R. and Collins, C.C. *Camillo Sitte: the Birth of Modern City Planning*. New York: Rizzoli 1965 (Originally published as *Der Stadtbau*, 1889).

Sladen, Douglas (1903) *Queer Things about Japan*. London: Anthony Treherne and Company.

Sladen, Douglas and Lorimer, Norma (1905) *More Queer Things About Japan*. London: Anthony Treherne and Company.

Smith II, Henry D. (1986a) *Hiroshige: One Hundred Famous Views of Edo*. New York: George Braziller/The Brooklyn Museum.

Smith II, Henry D. (1986b) Sky and Water: the Deep Structures of Tokyo, in Friedman, Mildred (ed.) *Tokyo: Form and Spirit*. Minneapolis: Walker Art Center / New York: Harry N. Abrams.

Stewart, David B. (1994) GLOBALIZATION: Just Say No, *in Fumihiko Maki 1987–1992*. Tokyo: Kajima Institute, pp. 100–107.

Sudjic, Deyan (1989) Isozaki gets the Wagons in a Circle. *Blueprint*, July/August, p. 16.

Sudjic, Deyan (1992) *The 100 Mile City*. London: Andre Deutsch.

Taiyo Collection (1996) *Osaka Kinki no Joka Machi* (*Castle Towns in Osaka and Kinki*). Tokyo: Heibonsha.

Tajima, Noriyuki (1995) *Tokyo: A Guide to Recent Architecture*. London: Ellipsis.

Tajima, Noriyuki and Powell, Catherine (1997) *Tokyo: Labarynth City*. London: Ellipsis.

Tanizaki, Jun'ichiro (1984) *In Praise of Shadows*. Rutland, Vermont: Charles E Tuttle (Originally published as *In'ei Raisan in Keizai Orai*, December 1933 and January 1934 issues).

Tarnas, Richard (1981) *The Passion of the Western Mind*. New York: Ballantine Books.

Taut, Bruno (1937) *Houses and People of Japan*. Tokyo: The Sanseido Co. Ltd.

Thackera, John (1989) Pleasures of unease. *World Architecture*, Vol. 1, No.4, pp. 64–69.

Toshi Design Kenkyutai (1968) *Nihon no Toshi Kukan*. Tokyo: Shokokusha.

Trancik, Roger (1986) *Lost Space*. New York: Van Nostrand Reinhold.

Treib, Marc (1986) The Dichotomies of Dwelling: Edo /Tokyo, in Friedman, Mildred (ed.) *Tokyo: Form and Spirit*. Minneapolis: Walker Art Center / New York: Harry N. Abrams.

Treib, Marc (1993) Tokyo: Real and Imagined, in Yelavich, Susan (ed) *The Edge of the Millenium*. New York: Whitney Library of Design.

Tschumi, Bernard (1983) La Villette: An Urban Park for the 21C. *International Architect*, No. 1, pp. 27–31.

Ueda, Atsushi (1990) *The Inner Harmony of the Japanese House*. Tokyo: Kodansha International (Originally published as *Nihonjin to sumai*. Tokyo: Iwanami Shoten, 1974).

Ueda, Atsushi (ed.) (1994) *The Electric Geisha*. Tokyo: Kodansha International.

Venturi, R., Scott Brown, D. and Izenour, S. (1972) *Learning from Las Vegas*. Cambridge, Mass: The MIT Press.

Vago, Pierre (1992) Taking Fright in the Far East. *World Architecture*, No. 16, p. 81.

Waley, Paul (1992) *Fragments of a City: Tokyo Anthology*. Tokyo: The Japan Times.

Wilson, Peter (1996) Eurolandschaft, in Middleton, Robin (ed.) *The Idea of the City*. London: The Architectural Association.

Woodcock, George (1966) *Asia, Gods and Cities*. London: Faber.

Worthington, John (1991) Tokyo Visions. *Town and Country Planning*, May, pp. 146–147.

Wright, Frank Lloyd (1943) *An Autobiography*. New York: Duell, Sloan and Pearce (Originally published 1932).

Yagi, Koji (1992) *A Japanese Touch for Your Home*. Tokyo: Kodansha International.

Yamasaki, Masafumi (ed.) (1994) Kyoto: Its Cityscape, Traditions and Heritage. *Process Architecture* 116.

Yapp, Peter (1983) *The Travellers' Dictionary of Quotation*. London: Routledge & Kegan Paul.

Zhu, Jian Fei (undated) Between Post-Modernism and Buddhism: Kisho Kurokawa's Theory of Symbiosis. *Regenerating Cities*, pp. 44–49.

Zhu, Jian Fei (1995) Japan and the Convergence of Eastern and Post-Humanist Paradigms. *Artifice*, No. 2 (CD-ROM).

Index